Cooking
with Love and Paprika

by Joseph Pasternak

edited by Margo Rieman

COOKING
WITH LOVE
AND PAPRIKA

drawings by B. Gill Porta

PUBLISHED BY BERNARD GEIS ASSOCIATES

Distributed by Random House

I wish to express
my deepest thanks to
Elizabeth Sakall and Margo Rieman
for their
invaluable assistance
in the preparation
of this book.
J. P.

Joseph Pasternak Presents—

I'm now a motion picture producer in America, but I was born in Hungary, the land of glamorous women and gypsy violins, where stories grow tall and food is delicious and as wonderfully varied as the Hungarian imagination itself. In my native land and in other countries of the Continent where I have lived, loved, and cooked, I learned that the basic ingredient in good cooking *is* love—love of good food and love of the good people you cook for.

The spirit of this book and most of its dishes are continental, but the recipes have all been adapted for preparation in the kitchens of my adopted land, America.

I believe that good food makes for good living. And so it is with great pride and joy that I offer you this complete collection of my family's recipes, the recipes I have gathered during my travels all over the world, and the recipes of a wonderful woman who set the best table in Budapest, Elizabeth (Mrs. "Cuddles") Sakall. Many of these recipes are very old family treasures, and any recipe that can stand the test of three or four generations just has to be really and truly delicious.

One of my recipes, having stood the test of four generations, had to stand the test of the toughest critic I have ever had—the publisher of this book. Bernard Geis was skeptical about my ability in the kitchen, so I offered to cook him something he didn't like and then let him be the judge. "Goulash," he said. "I don't like goulash."

I borrowed Earl Wilson's kitchen, invited a bunch of people, and whipped up a batch of goulash. Well, Mr. Geis came, and I conquered. The proof is the printing—of this book!

Sincerely,
JOSEPH PASTERNAK

Contents

1

PARTIES
À LA
PASTERNAK

Helpful Hints, I Hope

There is one immediate, primary requisite to planning a party. You must want to! You must think of it as fun. If you don't, and must entertain anyway, take your guests to a restaurant for dinner. Only if *you* yourself are enjoying the party, will your guests enjoy it too. Of course, a party can be six people or sixty—that doesn't matter. If you are happy with the food you serve, and delighted to see your guests and to give them your hospitality, they will pick up the mood from you—and before you know it, you'll have a reputation as a wonderful hostess *and* as a wonderful cook!

Never, never, never apologize for a dish you offer. If it doesn't turn out well, don't serve it. Just skip it. If you start apologizing for a dish, your guests feel they have to reassure you and say they like it, and everybody knows everybody's lying anyway. When the food is good, compliments will come naturally.

Another good rule of hospitality, often overlooked, is never to insist that a guest eat a dish he has politely refused. He may be allergic to its ingredients, he may be on a diet, he may have psychological reasons. Let him eat what he does like in peace, and he'll think of you as a kind and considerate person forever.

"Duty" entertaining is a bore. And yet there are times when, for business or other reasons, we all must do it. Long ago, I worked out a solution to this problem. I invite the people I must invite, and then I invite a lot of my favorite people, too. I know I can trust these people to make a party "go." They can be counted on to help keep shy guests from feeling left out, and are, of themselves, amusing and entertaining. People like this create a contagious mood of fun, and they will guarantee your having a good time at your own party.

You don't have to be rich to entertain well. It's the spirit of the host, not the lavishness of the food and refreshments, that makes a good party. I'd rather come to your house for a plate of good spaghetti and a glass of wine—or even just a cup of coffee —and be welcomed with honest pleasure, than to go to an elaborate dinner that was obviously a chore for my host. Right in the

Bible it says, "Better a dinner of herbs where love is, than a stalled ox and hatred therewith," and I couldn't agree more. In fact, you can translate that "dinner of herbs" into a salad buffet for a hot summer evening, as I have often done, and offer the best of hospitality whether you're a budget watcher or a millionaire.

I suspect that, quite naturally, I entertain more often and on a larger scale than you do. But while I go all out on very special occasions, I *am* economical most of the time. I might invite some people home after the preview of my latest movie and serve them a supper consisting of a nice casserole, a salad, a light dessert, and coffee. This is a real feast, but it doesn't cost a fortune. You can invite your friends home after a movie and treat them to the same wonderful—and inexpensive—meal.

You can be even more informal and still have fun. During my first years in Hollywood I had a little cottage in Malibu. When friends dropped in, I'd put together a goulash like I used to make in Hungary. Nothing was ever planned about those gatherings, but the food and the friends were good, and so, now, are the memories.

These days, I still like to give impromptu parties. And my luncheons and midnight supper parties still take their cue from the days at Malibu. At these gatherings, I like to surprise my guests. In summer, the surprise dish could be a beautiful big salmon in aspic. In winter, it might be a tureen of steaming soup or platters of sizzling hot pizza. These dishes take some planning, of course, but I still get the same pleasure in giving my friends unexpected treats that I got from my unplanned gatherings. What's really important is creating a sense of spontaneous hospitality—whether the preparations have been spontaneous or not.

Now let's talk about dinner parties—first, some of the general rules I apply to all of them, and then some special hints about formal dinners and buffet parties.

PLANNING AND PREPARING THE DINNER PARTY

Planning and preparing is part of the fun of a party, but it requires a lot of thought and work. I have four tricks I use to simplify the job.

1. I plan the menu way ahead.
2. I do as much shopping as far ahead as possible.
3. I do much of the actual work a day, or even two days, ahead.
4. While I prepare the meal, I clean up as I go.

First, I plan the menu *carefully*. I don't include appetizers that require me to stay in the kitchen cooking them, and I don't include the kind of food that requires constant attention in the kitchen after the guests arrive.

Next, I check all my recipes (whether they're on paper or in my head), make up a complete shopping list, and go the rounds of my favorite food stores. I also make sure that I've got all the equipment I need, and that it's all in working order. Modern appliances are not just convenient—they're indispensable when you're working alone to prepare a big dinner. The housewares department of any large department store or "gourmet shop" will be stocked with electric hot trays, *réchauds*, chafing dishes, candle-warmers, handsome stove-to-table ware, and lots of other useful items.

If you are working without help in the kitchen, and most of us do, then anything you can do ahead of time will make your dinner that much easier. By making full use of your refrigerator and freezer, you can do a great deal of the work in advance.

The fourth trick of being a do-it-yourself host is to clean up as you go. I think the neater the kitchen, the better the dinner is likely to be. So, no matter how many people I'm cooking for, I clean up as I work. If I peel an onion, the peel goes into the garbage. If I crack eggs, out go the shells. I wash all the cooking utensils—and most important, the pots and pans—as I use them. A hot pot is easy to wash, since nothing has had a chance to set and stick in it, and it only takes a few seconds. If you follow my advice and clean up everything as you go, you'll have no mess when you least want it—after you're finished your dinner.

A warning, now, concerning guest helpers. If you are organized ahead of time, you won't need them, and if you aren't that well organized, they will only get in the way and distract you. Let them know, very politely of course, that it's *your* show and you want to do it yourself, without help.

I had a dreadful experience once with a determined helper. I was in Florida with a large group of stars, many of whom were friends of a Cuban millionaire (who shall be nameless, because he's really a nice guy and I don't want to embarrass him). He phoned and asked me to cook for a big party for all the stars, including Tony Martin and Cyd Charisse, Esther Williams, Van Johnson, and Jimmy Durante, who all know my cooking very well indeed. I was delighted to accept. But I soon discovered that my Cuban host wanted to stay in the kitchen and make suggestions. "Put a little beer in it, Joe," he said as I tasted the chicken *Paprikásh* and the veal *gulyás*. "Go on, put a little beer in it!" Somewhere he'd heard that you can cook with beer, and he was determined I should do so.

When I had the food all organized, I went upstairs to shower and change. And when I came down again, I automatically tasted the food, as I always do just before I'm ready to serve it. It was terrible! During my absence, Good Old Helper had poured about a dozen bottles of beer into my dishes and ruined them completely.

That day I probably made the fastest *lecsó* on record. It was a Sunday, and I had to rush out and wake up a delicatessen to sell me hot dogs, but half an hour after I'd thrown out my original meal I was serving a delicious dinner to my friends—and they never even knew of the catastrophe!

THE FORMAL DINNER

Millions of Americans, who return home from European vacations having learned the pleasures of dining "in the continental manner," find they enjoy the little extra formal touches that can make eating such a civilized pastime.

Preparing and serving a formal sit-down dinner single-handed requires a lot of advance planning and work. Of course, having a "couple" in the kitchen who are trained to help you and to serve your dinner is a tremendous aid. But you *can* go it alone successfully, especially with a small number of guests.

These rules of table etiquette have been worked out to make things easier for everybody—your guests *and* you. The list is not long, so you will remember it easily, and if you follow it your party will be a memorable one.

1. Use your best china, silver, linens, and crystal. (This is going to be a *formal* party.)

2. Arrange your table decorations low enough so that your guests can see over them, and never use heavily scented flowers. Their perfume might interfere with the aroma of your food.

3. If your china is flowered, place it so that the flowers line up in an even pattern. Never use colored or flowered linens with flowered china.

4. Knives, spoons, and glasses go to the right of the plate and forks to the left, with the silver for the first course on the outside, so that you work in toward the plate with each succeeding course.

5. If you want background music, keep the volume low so that it won't interfere with conversation. (Ever try to chat in a noisy restaurant?)

6. Plan your seating arrangement so that each person has congenial partners, and *direct* your guests to their places. The hostess is always given the main place, and to her right and left are seated the most important men guests; the host sits opposite her, with the most important lady guests on his right and left.

7. Never overcrowd your table. It's far better to have two tables, with the hostess at one and the host at the other, than to squeeze your guests around one table.

8. If you like candlelight, make sure the flames are above eye level. I like plenty of light on my table so my guests and I can see just how attractive the table and food look. (And pretty girls dressed for a party look even prettier when the lights help them sparkle!)

9. Allow at least half an hour for your guests to arrive and get acquainted over drinks and appetizers. Then serve your food. Any guest more than half an hour late for a dinner party is rude. Why penalize your well-mannered friends by serving them overdone food?

10. A cold first course, such as a chilled soup, may be placed on the table before the guests are seated. A hot first course is *always* served after seating, so that it can be eaten while it's hot.

11. Food is always served from the left and drinks from the right. In the days when there were lots of servants and two footmen behind each chair, this rule was evolved to keep them from

crashing into each other. The man on the right served the wine, into the glass that was placed on the right, leaving the other man free to serve the food.

12. Before dessert is served, the table is cleared of all plates, unused silver, salt and pepper servers, glasses, and used ashtrays. Then the dessert settings are placed before the guests, with the dessert spoon and fork on either side of the plate.

After-dinner coffee may be served in the living room or at the table, since many people like to sit and relax at the table after a good dinner. Liqueurs or cognac are served along with the coffee.

THE BUFFET DINNER

A buffet dinner is the perfect answer if you don't have the space to seat your guests at a table or the help to serve a formal meal properly. But a "come and get it" buffet requires just as much thought and planning as any other kind of dinner.

To begin with, you must arrange your buffet table as attractively as possible, so that the food will look inviting. Your arrangement must also be logical, so that there can be a progression, either around the table or from end to end. Equally important is what happens to your guests after they have filled their plates. It is absolutely essential that you *plan ahead* for places for your guests to sit and eat in comfort—and I don't mean on the floor!

I have been to parties where there was literally no place either to sit or to put a plate except the floor. Do I need to tell you what can happen to a beautiful white-carpeted room at a party like that? Those folding "TV" trays, if they're all you have space for, will at least give your friends a place to put a plate, a cup and saucer, and a glass—so they don't have to be jugglers in order to get a little nourishment.

As I endure ill-planned buffet parties, I often think what a pity it is that W. C. Fields never got around to working up a routine about this. I can see Bill now—bulbous nose gleaming with fury, little eyes screwed up in angry concentration—trying to balance a plate on one knee, a cup and saucer on the other, a glass of wine in one hand and a cigarette in the other, glaring at the knife and fork, trying to figure out how to *eat*. And it would take a juggler of his superb abilities to do it successfully, although many hostesses seem to expect it of their guests.

Now that I've given you my basic entertaining philosophy and party rules, let's get on with the show!

2

FAMOUS
FIRST
WORDS

Appetizers

The starring actor's first words in a movie are always crucial —they define his basic character. The audience must be vitally interested in the character from the beginning, so that first impression has to be a strong one. The effect of those first words is very often a good indication of whether or not you can expect the movie to be good.

Appetizers are your real "first words," and the same thing applies to them. Your first spoken words to your guests are important, too, in creating an atmosphere of warmth and hospitality. A delightful lady I knew when I first came to America had some trouble with the English language, and *her* famous first words to her guests were always, "Take, take, eat more than you want." This was fine with me, since her appetizers were always famous first words, too.

But you needn't urge your guests to "eat more than they want." You can greet them with your usual hospitality and then let the appetizers speak for themselves.

Your guests can tell a lot about the dinner to come by the appetizers you serve. Nobody's going to get very excited about a bowl of potato chips, but if you fix something interesting to dip the chips into, then your guests will start enjoying themselves right away. For the average dinner party, you need serve only two or three appetizers, but if they are delicious and different, you have set the mood—one of interested anticipation.

Canapés and Hors d'Oeuvres

Appetizers divide themselves into two categories. There are canapés, which are usually served in the living room, and hors d'oeuvres, which are usually served at the table, as a first course.

(In Europe, hors d'oeuvres are often served as a complete luncheon, their variety making a light and satisfying meal.) Here in America, however, we don't draw this fine line of distinction. Most of the appetizers in this chapter can be served as a first course. And, so long as it can be managed with one hand —and practically all of these can—an appetizer can be served in the living room.

Let's start with a discussion of caviar, the king of appetizers. The finest is fresh gray Beluga, made from the roe of Caspian sturgeon. The Russians share the Caspian Sea with the Iranians, and Iranian caviar is what I serve to my friends. (I don't think you have to have caviar to have a good meal. Myself, I like a little herring, a little liver pâté—but everybody to his own taste!)

Caviar is the most expensive food in the world; the very best costs at least thirty-six dollars a pound. So when you do serve it, you should serve it right, in the classic manner.

The first rule is that it must be served very, very cold, its dish nested in a bed of crushed ice. Metal, and especially silver, should never touch the caviar for more than a second. Serve it from a china or glass bowl and handle it with glass, wood, or ivory utensils.

It is traditional to have a side tray containing finely minced white and yolk of egg, finely minced onions, and lemon wedges. The egg is harmless, but I think it is a crime to spoil the delicate flavor of caviar with the pungent onion. A few drops of lemon juice from a quartered lemon will, however, point up that delicate flavor.

Finally, serve your caviar with *hot* toast spread with sweet butter. Then you will have the food of epicures, known and appreciated as far back as Roman days!

Red caviar, made from the roe of salmon, is not only much cheaper than the fine fresh gray caviar, but is far better than second-rate imitations of the real stuff.

There is one exception to the rule about not dressing up your caviar, and that is to serve it with *blinis*, tiny buckwheat pancakes, and cold whipped sour cream. This is a combination of flavors that sings like Mario Lanza sang! Well, maybe not so loudly. But just as beautifully.

CAVIAR AU BLINIS

SERVES 6–8

1 cake or 1 package active dry
   yeast
2 cups warm milk
2 cups sifted all-purpose flour
2 cups buckwheat flour
2 eggs, separated

4 tablespoons butter
¼ teaspoon salt
½ teaspoon sugar
sweet butter
caviar
1 pint sour cream

Soften the yeast in the warm milk. Stir in the sifted all-purpose flour, working until the mixture is smooth. Let it stand in a warm place for 2 to 3 hours. Then work in the buckwheat flour.

Beat the egg yolks with the butter, salt, and sugar. Add to the flour mixture, cover, and let stand for 3 hours. Beat the egg whites and add them to the batter. Let it sit for a few moments, then make your tiny pancakes without stirring the batter again. Blinis must be very thin and delicate, the batter the consistency of cream.

Fry the blinis one at a time in a round, 4-to-6-inch frying pan, greased lightly with melted butter or shortening. Drop in a soup spoonful of the batter and tip the pan with a swirling motion around and around, so that the batter is evenly spread and very thin. Cook over a medium to high flame, and turn with a spatula to lightly brown each side. Keep the blinis warm in a slow oven until ready to fill.

When you're ready to fill the blinis, brush each one with a little sweet butter, heap it with a teaspoon of good caviar, and on top, mound a big teaspoon of fresh sour cream, lightly whipped. The pancakes must be very hot and the caviar and sour cream very cold, and they must be served immediately.

This is a spectacular first course to serve—the batter ready ahead of time, the little pancakes cooked under admiring gazes, the whole served on a candle-lit table.

Great appetizers come in all varieties, from the simple to the elaborate. Here are some more of my favorites. They're especially good for living room serving, and they're all guest-tested. (I've even been told they taste better than caviar!) I think you'll agree that they are easy to prepare, festive enough for the gayest occasion, and most important of all, truly delicious.

FLAVORED BUTTERS
6–8 SANDWICHES, OR 2 DOZEN APPETIZERS

Canapés made of little rounds or fingers of bread or toast, and mounded with a savory topping, are always enormously popular at my parties. One of the secrets I use to make them so good is to spread flavored butters on the bread or toast under the topping. This makes the difference between the ordinary and the extraordinary, as you'll see when you try it.

Lemon Butter. ¼ pound butter, 2 tablespoons lemon juice, 1 tablespoon minced parsley.

Herb Butter. ¼ pound butter, 1 tablespoon *fines herbs* (if possible, use fresh herbs), 1 tiny onion, minced.

Watercress Butter. ½ cup butter, ½ cup minced watercress, 1 teaspoon lemon juice, 1 teaspoon onion juice.

Fish Butter. ¼ pound butter, 1 teaspoon anchovy paste, 1 teaspoon mustard.

Horse-radish Butter. ½ pound butter, 1 teaspoon horse-radish, 1 teaspoon lemon juice, a dash of sugar.

Have the butter at room temperature and work the seasonings into it. Then spread your bread and top with anchovies, sardines, ham slices, thin cheese strips, or cold meat loaf.

PICKLED EGGS
SERVES 6–12

12 eggs
2 cups vinegar
1 teaspoon ground ginger
½ teaspoon allspice

¼ teaspoon peppercorns
½ teaspoon salt
parsley for garnish

Boil the eggs for 20 minutes and peel them. (Here's a tip: if you crush the shells all over and peel them immediately under cold running water, the shells come off easily.)

Boil all the other ingredients slowly for 10 minutes. Pour the marinade over the eggs and let stand in the refrigerator for 1 or 2 days. As an appetizer, serve each one whole or in quarters on a lettuce leaf, sprinkled with fresh parsley. Pickled eggs are also delicious served as a garnish with roast pork or fowl.

MUSHROOMS WITH SOUR CREAM À LA BRILLAT-SAVARIN
SERVES 4-6

½ pound fresh mushrooms, sliced
2 tablespoons butter
1 small onion, minced
salt, cayenne pepper

⅔ cup beef bouillon
1 tablespoon flour
2 tablespoons water
1 cup sour cream

Brown the mushrooms carefully in 1 tablespoon of the butter. Brown the minced onion separately in the rest of the butter and season with salt and cayenne pepper. Warm the bouillon in a saucepan. Add the mushrooms and onion and cook gently until the mushrooms are tender. Stir in the flour mixed with the water. Lightly whip the sour cream, add it to the mushroom mixture, and simmer very, very gently for 5 or 6 minutes.

Serve as a hot dip for toast fingers, or spoon onto buttered English muffins or toast.

FRENCH ANCHOVY EGGS
SERVES 6

4 anchovies, drained
3 capers
2 small cloves garlic, minced
3 tablespoons oil

1 teaspoon vinegar
salt, pepper, cayenne pepper
6 hard-boiled eggs
lettuce and parsley for garnish

Add the anchovies and capers to the minced garlic and mash well together with a fork. Blend in the oil and vinegar and the spices to taste. Peel the eggs and quarter them. Serve on lettuce decorated with fresh parsley.

FRENCH TUNA
SERVES 4–6

1 can tuna, drained	mayonnaise
2 tablespoons soft butter	capers
1 teaspoon chopped dried herbs	parsley
(parsley, chives, tarragon, or	
thyme)	

Chop the tuna and mix with the butter and herbs. Shape into a small pyramid, cover with a thin layer of mayonnaise, and decorate with capers and sprigs of parsley. Serve with toast fingers.

KIPPERS

Trim kippered herring into neat strips. Wrap in bacon and broil until crisp, or wrap in thinly cut ham slices pinned with toothpicks. Serve on hot toast fingers that have been rubbed with garlic. Garnish with parsley.

BACON BISCUITS (*Tepertös Pogácsa*)
3 DOZEN

1 stick butter	½ teaspoon pepper
2 cups sifted flour	2 egg yolks
1 cake or 1 package active dry	½ cup sour cream
yeast softened in	1 pound bacon, fried crisp and
2 tablespoons water	crumbled
1 teaspoon baking powder	beaten egg
½ teaspoon salt	

Preheat the oven to 475°.

Cream the butter with the flour, yeast, baking powder, salt, pepper, egg yolks, and sour cream until smooth. Place the dough on a floured board. Knead it well, roll it out, and spread on it half the crumbled bacon. Fold the dough in half and roll it out again, then spread on the rest of the bacon. Now roll it to a 1-inch thickness.

Cut out the biscuits with a small biscuit or cookie cutter and make a criss-cross impression in each biscuit with a sharp knife. Place on a greased and floured baking sheet. Brush the tops with beaten egg and bake at 475° for 5 minutes. Lower the oven temperature to 375° and continue baking for 10–15 minutes, or until done.

CHEESE CAKES

1 DOZEN

1 stick butter
½ cup sifted flour
3 ounces grated Cheddar cheese

dash salt and cayenne pepper
beaten egg
paprika

Work the butter, cheese, and salt and pepper together with your hands. Chill the dough well, then roll very thin on a cool surface with a chilled rolling pin. Cut with a biscuit cutter. Place the biscuits on a buttered and floured baking sheet and brush with beaten egg. Sprinkle with paprika. Chill again for 15–30 minutes. Place in a pre-heated 425° oven and bake 5 minutes. Then decrease the heat to 375° and bake 15–20 minutes, until golden. Be careful that the cheese cakes don't dry out and become overcooked. Serve either warm or cold.

CHEESE SQUARES

1 DOZEN

½ pound cream cheese
2 green onions, minced
salt, cayenne pepper, paprika
¼ teaspoon anchovy paste
4–6 capers
3–4 stuffed olives, sliced
¼ teaspoon caraway seeds

¼ teaspoon mustard
5 drops Worcestershire sauce
12 squares rye or white bread, buttered and cut into 2-inch squares
additional stuffed olives for garnish

Mix all the ingredients together. Spread the mixture on the buttered bread squares. Garnish each square with a thin slice of stuffed olive.

TOASTED PRUNES IN BACON

1 DOZEN

12 large (jumbo) prunes   ½ slice bacon per prune
12 salted almonds or filberts

Soak the prunes, remove the pits, and replace with nuts. Roll a piece of bacon around each prune and pin with a toothpick. Broil or bake in a 425° oven until the bacon is crisp. Serve hot!

ANCHOVY TOAST

1 DOZEN

2 tablespoons butter   2 tablespoons anchovy paste
2 egg yolks   cayenne pepper
1 tablespoon dry sherry   12 hot buttered toast fingers

Melt the butter in a double boiler, add the egg yolks, and beat well with a fork. Add the rest of the ingredients, mixing well. Spread on the hot buttered toast fingers or double the quantity and serve hot as a dip.

CHEESE BALLS

1 DOZEN

1 3-ounce package cream   2 tablespoons ground, toasted
  cheese   hazelnuts (optional)
2 tablespoons minced capers   salt and pepper to taste
dash horse-radish   paprika (optional)

Blend all the ingredients. Wet your hands and shape the mixture into small balls. Roll in additional chopped hazelnuts or in paprika. Serve on toothpicks.

HUNGARIAN STUFFED EGGS (*Töltött Tojás*)
SERVES 8–12

12 eggs
3 tablespoons mayonnaise
2 tablespoons sour cream
1 tablespoon mustard
2 green onions (white part),
   minced

1 teaspoon Worcestershire
   sauce
cayenne pepper, salt, paprika

Hard-boil and shell the eggs. Halve them lengthwise. Slip the yolks out into a bowl and mash, setting the whites aside. Add the remaining ingredients and blend thoroughly. Fill the whites with this mixture, rounding it nicely and evenly. Sprinkle with paprika before serving.

PÂTÉ #1
SERVES 6–8

In France, almost every great restaurant (and little country inn) has its own recipe for a *pâté maison*, to be spread generously on crusty bread and used as an appetizer. Well, this and the next recipe are *my* two pâtés, a word that translates to "pastes" in English. The first one is delicate, subtle, and sophisticated—the second robust and hearty.

½ onion, minced
¼ green pepper, minced
1 pound chicken or goose livers
3–4 tablespoons butter or
   shortening
1 dinner roll or 2 slices
   white bread

milk
2 hard-boiled eggs, shelled
salt, pepper, cayenne pepper,
   paprika
1 teaspoon mustard
few drops Worcestershire
   sauce

Sauté the onion, green pepper, and livers in the butter, uncovered, until the livers are just barely cooked.

Soak the bread or roll in a little milk and press dry in a sieve. Put the bread and the contents of the frying pan through a food grinder twice, adding the eggs as you go. Add the seasonings and blend very well. Pack into a serving dish and refrigerate. Serve cold, with bread fingers.

PÂTÉ #2
SERVES 6-8

1 pound pork or veal liver, sliced	milk
1 large onion, minced	3–4 tablespoons butter or shortening
3 hard-boiled eggs, shelled	salt, pepper, cayenne pepper, paprika
4–5 slices white bread	

Sauté the liver and onion in an uncovered skillet until the liver is barely cooked.

Soak the bread in milk and press it dry in a sieve. Put the liver, onions, eggs, and bread through a food grinder twice. Add the seasonings, blend well, and pack the pâté in a mold. Refrigerate for a day, unmold, and slice very thin to serve with toast or bread fingers.

You can also present the pâté to your guests unsliced and garnished decoratively with slices of hard-boiled egg, olives, capers, or pimientos.

BLUE CHEESE BALLS
SERVES 6-8

2 ounces blue cheese	salt, cayenne pepper
½ pound cream cheese	2 tablespoons grated walnuts
1 teaspoon Worcestershire sauce	sour cream
¼ teaspoon minced garlic	additional grated walnuts or minced parsley
¼ teaspoon minced onion	

Mix all the ingredients together, adding enough sour cream to make a spreading consistency. Wet your hands and form the mixture into small balls, rolling them in additional grated walnuts or in minced parsley. Serve on toothpicks or with crackers or potato chips.

PIROSHKI
1½ DOZEN
ORIGINAL RUSSIAN PIROSHKI DOUGH

1½ cups sifted flour	6 tablespoons sour cream
1 teaspoon salt	beaten egg or milk
¼ cup butter	

Sift the flour and salt together. Cut the butter into the flour mixture with a pastry cutter or two knives until the mixture is in coarse lumps. Add just enough sour cream to hold the dough together. Roll out lightly on a floured board and fold into three or four layers. Chill for 1 hour or more. (This part of the preparation can be done the day before.)

Roll again, as thinly as possible. Cut small rounds with a cookie or biscuit cutter. Put a small spoonful of any of the following fillings on each round, fold over, and pinch the edges together. Brush with beaten egg or milk. Place on a greased baking sheet. Bake in a hot (425°) oven, for 15–20 minutes, or until golden brown. Serve hot.

FILLINGS FOR PIROSHKI

Traditionally, *piroshki* are served with cocktails (originally with vodka) and with Russian soups. And I have seen some very famous people (who had better *not* be named at this point) following a tray of them around the living room like starving Russian wolves after a *droshky* full of fine fat aristocrats! *Piroshki* can be made of almost anything, including leftover roasts or ham, and they can be frozen until just before serving time. What more can you ask of a truly delicious little morsel?

Grind the meat (fish, shellfish, turkey, chicken, ham, or liver) very fine. Sauté in butter with a little finely chopped onion. Season rather highly to taste, with salt, pepper, and Tabasco. Add a little sour cream to moisten.

Or: Moisten the finely ground meat with mayonnaise and add finely chopped pickles, capers, or your favorite relish, and season.

Or: Grind very finely 1 small head of cabbage and ½ small onion. Sauté in 3–4 tablespoons butter or shortening, add salt and black pepper to taste, and moisten with sour cream.

Or: Mince finely ½ pound mushrooms with a little onion and fresh parsley. Add salt and pepper to taste and sauté the mixture in butter. Moisten with sour cream.

Or: Hard-boil a few eggs. Peel, cool, and chop fine. Add capers, salt and pepper, and minced green onion and moisten with mayonnaise.

The main thing to remember about filling for *piroshki* is that it must be finely ground, highly seasoned, and creamed with mayonnaise or sour cream. The crust can be made of pie dough, or even puff paste, which makes superlative *piroshki*. But the *piroshki* must be served hot, no matter what the crust or the filling.

Piroshki can also be made as a regular-sized pie with a top and bottom crust. Prick the top with a fork and brush it twice with sour cream. Bake at 425° for 20–25 minutes and serve hot, cut in small wedges.

TINY PIZZAS

These handsome little individual pizzas are very easy to make and are always a smash success, even with beautiful young actresses who must watch their diets and their figures. They give me reproachful looks with their lovely eyes, but I know they don't mean it, because I see how happy they look when they think I'm not watching how many they eat.

I always make the pizzas in large quantities, so, I'm sorry to say, I can't give you exact measurements. The average can of frozen biscuits holds 8 or 10. You'll have to plan on how many of the little pizzas you want to make, buy as many cans as you'll need, and adjust the rest of the ingredients accordingly. Two for each guest is quite enough, if you have other appetizers as well, and three will make a very hearty appetizer before a light dinner.

canned biscuits	tomato paste
oil or melted butter	chili sauce
sliced tomato	cayenne pepper
salami	oregano
mushrooms	garlic
olives	grated Parmesan cheese
mozzarella, Jack, or	
Swiss cheese	

For your base, open a can of refrigerated biscuits. Flatten each with the palm of your hand and place on a baking sheet. Brush with oil or melted butter. Place on each one a slice of mozzarella, Jack, or Swiss cheese, a thin slice of tomato, a slice of salami, and sliced mushrooms and olives.

Make a topping by mixing tomato paste with chili sauce. Season with a dash of cayenne pepper, oregano, some minced garlic, and some grated Parmesan cheese. Spread this topping over the pizzas, and sprinkle with more grated Parmesan cheese.

Bake at 425° for 10 minutes and serve hot.

You can also use this same filling and topping on your favorite pie dough, rolled in a circle. But you must bake it at 400° for 25–30 minutes, or until golden brown. Serve in wedge-shaped pieces.

BACON PIE (*Dolder Zurich*)
SERVES 6–8

I'm not going to get into an argument about where this particular dish originated. The Swiss claim it and so do the French, who call it *Quiche Lorraine*. In Hungary, we made it, too, adding our own touch by using sour cream instead of milk. We called it *Dolder Zurich*. But no matter what you call it, it's sensational!

pie crust dough	½ teaspoon salt
1 pound bacon, fried and crumbled	½ teaspoon oregano
	¼ teaspoon white pepper
1 cup shredded Swiss cheese	cayenne pepper
3 eggs	mace
1 cup sour cream	minced parsley

Line a pie dish with your favorite dough. Spread on it the crumbled bacon and shredded Swiss cheese. Mix the eggs with the sour cream, season with salt, oregano, white pepper, a dash of cayenne pepper, and a dash of mace. Pour this mixture over the bacon and cheese. Sprinkle with a little minced parsley and bake at 400° for 5 minutes. Lower the oven temperature to 375° and continue baking for 25–30 minutes longer. Serve hot, sliced in narrow wedges.

WIENERS IN POTATO DOUGH
1½–2 DOZEN

It may seem odd to you that in this recipe I make a dough with two cups of flour to half a pound of potatoes and in the following recipe I make one with half the amount of flour to the same amount of potatoes. But the first dough is a heavier and more compact one that is good to wrap the little wieners in, and the second is much lighter and finer, good for making delicate doughnuts.

½ pound potatoes, boiled and mashed	salt and pepper
2 cups sifted flour	1 teaspoon baking powder
1 stick butter	18–24 tiny wieners
	1 egg, beaten

Note: Do not add milk or any seasonings to the mashed potatoes, and do not use any of the instant mashed potato products.

Knead together the potatoes, flour, butter, salt and pepper to taste, and baking powder to make a smooth dough. Let the dough sit for 30 minutes. Roll it out thin, fold it in half and then in half again, and roll thin once more. Fold again and let sit for another 30 minutes.

Roll thin once more and cut into 2-inch squares. Wrap each square around a tiny wiener and place on a greased baking sheet. Brush each with beaten egg and bake in a pre-heated oven for 20–25 minutes. Serve hot.

HAM AND POTATO DOUGHNUTS
1½–2 DOZEN

½ pound or 1 cup potatoes, boiled and mashed	about 1 cup minced ham
1 cup sifted flour	sour cream
2 egg yolks	beaten egg
salt, pepper	grated Parmesan cheese

Knead together very thoroughly the mashed potatoes, flour, egg yolks, and salt and pepper to taste. When very smooth, roll out very thin on a floured board. Cut into small circles with a cookie or biscuit cutter.

Moisten the minced ham with sour cream and season with salt and pepper. Spread the mixture on half the circles. Cover with the remaining circles and press together firmly. Place on a greased and floured baking sheet, brush with beaten egg, and sprinkle with grated Parmesan cheese. Bake in a 450° oven for 15–20 minutes, or until nice and golden. Serve hot.

CHEESE CANAPÉS

2 DOZEN

For the Dough:

2 cups sifted flour	dash salt
1 teaspoon baking powder	1 cup sour cream
¾ cup butter	

For the Topping:

3 egg yolks	1 cup sour cream
¼ cup butter	⅛ teaspoon garlic salt
3 tablespoons flour	1 cup grated Swiss cheese

Garnishes:

anchovies or sardines	shrimps
capers	sliced ham or sausages
sliced olives	sliced chicken

To make the dough, sift together the flour, baking powder, and salt, or mix them lightly with a spoon. Cut the ¾ cup butter into the dry ingredients. Add the 1 cup sour cream and mix to a smooth dough. Roll out the dough and place in a large oblong baking pan, which has been greased and floured. Bake at 425° for about 10 minutes.

While the pastry bakes, blend together the egg yolks, ¼ cup butter, 3 tablespoons flour, 1 cup sour cream, and garlic salt. Cook in a double boiler over low heat until smooth and thick. Add the grated Swiss cheese, blend well, and cool.

When the pastry is done, pour the filling over it evenly. Return to the oven and continue baking for another 10–15 minutes. Garnish with any or all of the garnishes, cut into small squares, and serve warm.

Dips and Spreads

Sometimes when I come home from the studio, friends drop in for cocktails unexpectedly. They never seem to mind if I take a few moments to go to the kitchen and make a dip or a spread to offer them with their drinks. Your friends won't complain, either, if you give them one of these quick and easy appetizers. It's just a little something extra to show that you're glad they came.

CREAM CHEESE DIP
SERVES 2–4

1 3-ounce package cream cheese
½ cup grated Cheddar cheese
2 tablespoons white wine

1 teaspoon Worcestershire sauce
½ teaspoon mustard
dash cayenne pepper

Blend all the ingredients until fluffy and light. Thin with a little more wine, if necessary. Heap in a bowl and serve with potato or corn chips.

AVOCADO-SEAFOOD DIP
SERVES 4–6

1 avocado, peeled and mashed
1 tablespoon lemon juice
1 tablespoon grated onion

½ teaspoon salt
½ teaspoon pepper
½ cup tomato sauce

Blend all the ingredients thoroughly and chill. Serve as a dip for shrimp, crabmeat, or other seafood.

HERRING DIP
SERVES 6–8

2–3 mild pickled herrings
  without cream sauce
2 ounces ground slivered
  almonds
1 teaspoon mustard
½ teaspoon horse-radish

few drops lemon juice
dash each cayenne pepper,
  white pepper
2–3 drops Worcestershire sauce
½ cup heavy cream, whipped

Mince the herring. Mix the ground almonds with the seasonings, blending well, and add to the herring. Fold the whipped cream into the mixture last. Serve with buttered bread fingers or crackers.

GARLIC-CHEESE DIP
SERVES 4–6

1 3-ounce package cream
  cheese
½ pint sour cream
1 small clove garlic, minced

½ teaspoon salt
¼ teaspoon cayenne pepper
1 tablespoon vinegar

Combine all the ingredients and blend thoroughly. Serve with strips of raw carrots, celery, green pepper, and/or other vegetables.

AVOCADO SPREAD
SERVES 6–8

1 cup creamed cottage
  cheese, sieved
1 avocado, peeled and mashed
1 teaspoon minced onion

1 teaspoon lemon juice
dash Worcestershire sauce
salt to taste

Blend all the ingredients well together. Serve as a spread for toast fingers or crackers.

OLIVE SPREAD
SERVES 6–8

½ cup finely chopped black
olives
¼ cup finely chopped green
olives
4 hard-boiled eggs, chopped
4 slices bacon, cooked and
crumbled

3 tablespoons mayonnaise
dash Worcestershire sauce
dash Tabasco
dash paprika
salt to taste
sour cream, if needed

Mix all the ingredients, adding sour cream if the mixture is too thick to spread. Serve with fingers of rye or black bread.

CREAM CHEESE–ORANGE SPREAD
SERVES 2–4

1 3-ounce package cream cheese
frozen orange juice

¼ cup chopped toasted
almonds or hazelnuts

Combine the cream cheese with the frozen orange juice to taste. The mixture should be of a smooth, spreading consistency. Stir in the chopped almonds or hazelnuts and serve with nut or banana bread.

ALMOND SPREAD
SERVES 4

4 slices bacon, cooked and
chopped fine
1 small tomato, peeled and
chopped
½ cup finely chopped
almonds

1 teaspoon mustard
dash white pepper
⅓ ounce cream cheese
dash celery salt
1 tablespoon sour cream,
if needed

Mix all the ingredients together, adding the sour cream if it seems too firm. Serve with crackers or potato chips.

HUNGARIAN CHEESE SPREAD
(*Körözött Liptói Túró*)
SERVES 6-8

8 ounces cream cheese
2 tablespoons sour cream
1 teaspoon mustard
2 ounces Roquefort cheese
½ teaspoon anchovy paste
1 teaspoon Worcestershire
    sauce

⅛ teaspoon caraway seeds
dash cayenne pepper
½ teaspoon paprika
2-3 little green onions or
    chives, minced
salt, if needed

Blend all the ingredients very well and add salt, if needed. Serve with dark bread fingers or crackers.

ROQUEFORT SPREAD
SERVES 4-6

¼ pound Roquefort cheese
½ stick sweet butter
¼ clove garlic, minced
white part of 1 green onion,
    minced

⅓ cup cognac
dash each cayenne pepper,
    white pepper

Mix all the ingredients together thoroughly and serve with toasted white bread fingers or tiny, fresh slices of dark bread.

Extra-special Hors d'Oeuvres

I like to make happy movies, movies that make you feel the world isn't such a bad place after all, and I like to have happy dinner parties. These are some of the hors d'oeuvres I often serve as a first course at the table, to make my guests and friends start smiling and say, "Oh, Joe, this is so *good!*" I particularly like the little filled pancakes to start with—they come as a delightful surprise to so many people. You can make the batter and the filling ahead of time and then fry the little cakes quickly, stuff them, and set them in the oven to finish cooking while you attend to the rest of the dinner.

PANCAKES FOR APPETIZERS
2 DOZEN
PANCAKE BATTER FOR APPETIZERS

2 cups plus 4 tablespoons flour, sifted	2 tablespoons melted butter
3 eggs	2 tablespoons cognac
2 cups milk	dash salt

Combine the flour, eggs, and milk. Add the butter, cognac, and salt. Let this batter sit for 1 hour, and then pour it through a fine sieve. To fry the pancakes, follow the cooking directions for blinis on page 15.

FILLINGS FOR PANCAKES

Here's where you (and I) can use creative imagination! I make fillings from leftover roasts, ham, mushrooms, tongue, eggs, or cheese—in fact, almost anything with a flavor to it.

Meat Filling

Grind the meat and add 1 small minced onion, a few drops of Worcestershire sauce, pepper, a dash of cayenne pepper, salt to taste, and enough sour cream to make a thick mixture.

Fill each pancake and roll, fastening with a toothpick. Place side by side in a baking dish, brush with melted butter and sprinkle with grated Parmesan cheese. Brown in a 370° oven for about 20 minutes. Be sure to remove the toothpicks before serving.

Cheese Filling

Mix cream cheese with grated Cheddar cheese. Season with a little dill, pepper, cayenne pepper, a few drops of Worcestershire sauce, ¼ teaspoon mustard, and salt. If the filling needs moistening, add a little sour cream. Fill the pancakes and place in a baking dish. Pour more sour cream over them and bake in a 400° oven for 20 minutes.

Egg Filling

Hard-boil 3 or 4 eggs. Shell them and put them through a fine sieve. Mix in ¼ teaspoon anchovy paste, a dash of cayenne pepper, ¼ teaspoon white pepper, ¼ teaspoon mustard, and 1 tablespoon heavy cream. Fill the pancakes and sprinkle with freshly grated Parmesan cheese. Put them under the broiler for a few minutes until the Parmesan is golden.

Mushroom Filling

Wash and mince ½ pound mushrooms. Sauté with a tiny minced onion in butter, but do not let them brown. Add 2–4 tablespoons heavy cream and continue to sauté until all the liquid has been absorbed. Season with red paprika, salt, white pepper, and plenty of minced parsley. Fill the pancakes and sprinkle them with Parmesan cheese. Place under the broiler until golden.

STUFFED EGGS AU GRATIN
SERVES 6

Right about now you are saying, "That's all very well for you, Joe Pasternak, to take *some* of this and *some* of that, but I don't know my way around a kitchen as well as you do. I want a real recipe!" We Hungarians have a saying, "Patience has its own reward—a long white beard!" But I know that isn't what you want, so here is a *real* recipe!

6 hard-boiled eggs	⅔ tablespoon sour cream
1 teaspoon minced chives	½ pint sour cream
salt, pepper, cayenne pepper	grated Parmesan cheese
1 tablespoon mustard	
½ teaspoon Worcestershire sauce	

Shell the eggs, slice them lengthwise, and slip the yolks into a bowl, reserving the whites. Mash the yolks with the chives, seasonings, and the ⅔ tablespoon sour cream. Stuff the whites with this mixture and arrange them side by side in a baking dish. Pour ½ pint sour cream over the eggs and sprinkle with grated Parmesan cheese. Bake for 25 minutes in a 350° oven.

EGGS IN ASPIC
SERVES 6–8

I don't know why this elegant appetizer isn't served more often in America. It's a lovely beginning for a luncheon or dinner in the hot summer, and is as common in Europe as the uninspired dish of carrot sticks, celery stalks, and radishes on crushed ice is in America. I much prefer to serve it, too, because I get compliments on it—and so will you.

2 10½-ounce cans consommé
   or chicken broth
tarragon, cayenne pepper
2 envelopes plain gelatin

½ cup sherry
6–8 hard-boiled eggs
watercress or lettuce

Prepare an aspic with the consommé and a dash each of tarragon and cayenne pepper, and simmer for 5 minutes. Soak the gelatin in the sherry, add to the hot consommé, and mix well. Simmer 2 or 3 minutes longer. Strain and cool.

Place the shelled, hard-boiled eggs in small individual custard cups. Pour the cooled aspic over them and refrigerate until set. Unmold the eggs onto beds of watercress or lettuce leaves.

CRAB MEAT IN SKILLET À LA BERCY
SERVES 6–8

1–1½ pounds fresh lump
   crab meat
2 tablespoons butter
juice of ½ lemon

salt, pepper, cayenne pepper
½ jigger cognac
paprika for garnish

In a skillet heat the butter, lemon juice, and seasonings. Add the crab meat and cook for about 5 minutes, shaking the skillet so that the flavors mingle. Add the cognac, let heat through, and flame it if you like. Dust with paprika and serve on buttered toast.

RUSSIAN MUSHROOMS
SERVES 4-6

1 medium onion, minced	salt, pepper, chives, cayenne
2 tablespoons butter	pepper to taste
½ pound fresh mushrooms	tomato slices for garnish
1 tablespoon sour cream	green pepper rings for garnish
1 tablespoon lemon juice	caviar (optional)

Sauté the onion in the butter until soft, add the mushrooms, and cook for 2–3 minutes on each side, or until lightly browned and tender. Stir in all the other ingredients, except the caviar and the garnishes, and chill. Arrange in the center of a large glass plate. Circle them with tomato slices and green pepper rings. Cover the mushrooms with a *good* caviar if you like, but it is not necessary. The mushrooms are delicious even without it.

BOUCHÉES
SERVES 6-10

Bouchées are a wonderful "emergency" appetizer to know about, since you can make them out of almost anything you might happen to have on hand in the cupboard or refrigerator, and they neither look nor taste like "last-minute" morsels. The list of ingredients for *bouchées* is not nearly so formidable as it looks. Most of them you can find in your own cupboard, right now. And that is why *bouchées* are one of my favorite appetizers for impromptu gatherings.

Basically, *bouchées* are made from a meat- or seafood-based mixture, moistened and well seasoned. The mixture can be stuffed into little hollowed-out rolls or spread on rounds or fingers of bread, and baked—or it can be formed into small balls, dipped in batter, and deep fried. *Bouchées* are always served sizzling hot, with a sauce either served on the side or used as a dip.

1–1½ pounds cooked crab, lobster, shrimp, ham, tongue, or leftover meat
lemon or lime juice
2–3 tablespoons sour cream
salt
dash dry mustard
pinch nutmeg
Tabasco
pinch cayenne pepper

dash angustora bitters (optional)
½ cup toasted bread crumbs
butter
small rolls *or* fingers or rounds of bread
grated cheese (optional)
paprika (optional)
minced parsley (optional)

Start out by mincing the meat or seafood, whichever you use. Then moisten with lime or lemon juice, add 2–3 tablespoons sour cream, and season with salt, dry mustard, nutmeg, Tabasco, cayenne pepper, and angustora bitters, if you like, to taste. The mixture should be a savory one.

In a small frying pan, toast the ½ cup of bread crumbs in butter until golden, and add to the meat mixture. Check again for seasoning.

Now that you have prepared the filling, you can finish the *bouchées* in any of the following ways.

1. Hollow out tiny little round dinner rolls (the ones about 1½–2 inches across), leaving just the crust and a thin layer of bread inside. Brush the inside with melted butter, fill with the meat or fish mixture, and brush all over in melted butter. Sprinkle with grated cheese and place on a greased cookie sheet. Bake until crisp in a 350° oven.

2. Take a loaf of unsliced white bread and trim off all the crust. Cut the loaf in half, lengthwise. Lay each half flat and cut in half once more, again lengthwise. Then cut across into fingers of bread. Mix the meat or fish mixture with a little Curry Sauce (see page 260) or Cream Sauce (see page 258) and heap on each finger. Sprinkle with grated cheese, paprika, and/or minced parsley, place on a greased cookie sheet, and bake until crisp and golden in a 350° oven.

3. Proceed as for Step 2, but instead of cutting the bread in half lengthwise, cut it into four long, even slices. Out of these, cut rounds with a cookie cutter and proceed from there as for Step 2.

4. Form the meat mixture into small balls and dip in the following batter:

2 eggs   dash white pepper
½ cup milk   vegetable shortening or oil
1 cup sifted flour   for deep frying
½ teaspoon salt

Note: I might add that I never use oil for deep frying, but this is a personal preference. I use a pure vegetable shortening instead.

Mix the eggs with the milk, then stir in the flour, which has been sifted with the salt and pepper, and stir until smooth.

Heat the fat to 370° and fry the small balls until golden. You should fry only a few at a time, never overcrowding them in the fat and removing them with a slotted spoon or spatula when they are golden. Let them drain on absorbent paper in a warm oven while you continue to cook the others.

Bouchées may be served with any one of the following sauces:

Bottled cocktail sauce
Tomato Sauce (see page 268), seasoned a little more highly than usual
Curry Sauce (see page 260), seasoned a little more highly than usual
Cream Sauce (see page 258), seasoned a little more highly than usual

TARTAR STEAK SANDWICH
SERVES 4

½ pound raw fillet of beef salt, pepper, paprika
 or sirloin steak   egg yolk
finely chopped onion   capers or caviar for garnish
finely chopped green pepper

Use only the best cut of beef for this. Just before serving, grind—or better yet, scrape—the meat, discarding all the fat and membrane. Mix with finely chopped onion and green pepper, and season with salt, pepper, and paprika. Blend in the egg yolk and spread on thin slices of bread or toast. Sprinkle with capers or caviar.

CRAB-MEAT DELIGHT
SERVES 4-6

2 pounds crab or lobster, cooked
2 grapefruit, peeled and sectioned
4 stalks celery, scraped and minced
4 ripe olives, minced
4 green olives, minced
½ green pepper, peeled and minced

2 pearl onions, minced
1 small head lettuce, crisped and shredded
1 cup mayonnaise
1 teaspoon sugar
3 tablespoons chili sauce
1 tablespoon vinegar
1 tablespoon lemon juice
pepper, salt, cayenne to taste

Cut the crab or lobster into bite-sized pieces. Arrange the meat and the peeled grapefruit sections on a bed of shredded lettuce. Season the mayonnaise with the rest of the ingredients and top the meat and fruit with it. Garnish with the avocado slices and sprinkle with minced parsley.

FRIED SHRIMP
SERVES 4-6

Use 1 pound medium-sized shrimp. Remove the shells, split in half lengthwise, and rinse out the dark vein. Dry on paper towels. Dip in one of the following batters. The first batter will make a very thin, delicate coating. The second batter is heavier and thicker, but, because of the egg, has its own kind of lightness.

Batter #1
1 cup sifted flour
1 tablespoon cornstarch
½ teaspoon salt
½ teaspoon baking powder
2–3 tablespoons milk

Batter #2
1 egg, beaten
2 tablespoons flour
1 tablespoon milk
pepper, salt, paprika

Mix either batter well, and after dipping the shrimps, drain off the excess batter. Fry in plenty of deep fat at 370° until golden. Drain off excess fat on paper towels before serving with a seafood or cocktail sauce.

3

BOUNTY IN A BOWL

Soup, Beautiful Soup

I got fired from one of my first jobs in America because I knew too much about soup! It happened like this:

There were six of us at home in Hungary, and my Uncle Geza, who had no sons, lived in Philadelphia. His pleas for one of us to come live with him were hard for my parents to withstand, but none of us wanted to leave—until one night, when a great drunken lout assaulted my father for being a Jew. I in turn assaulted the lout—with the biggest rock I could find. Although the lout didn't die—and I don't think I would have cared if he had—we all knew I'd have to leave town. And besides, I no longer wanted to stay in a place where so gentle, kind, and harmless a person as my father could suffer such indignities. So, at the age of seventeen, I was off to America.

America was disappointing at first (there were poor people here, too), but I finally got a job in a cafeteria that was open twenty-four hours a day. The job not only involved being a cook, but also being busboy, boss, dishwasher, waiter—everything. A real one-man operation, and I was the one man. But the pay seemed good, and it was right around the corner from a movie house. I found that if I gave the ushers bigger portions of food, they gave me passes to the movies. Before I knew what was happening, I was movie-struck. I was suddenly determined to be an actor, somehow, someday.

Everything went fine with my job for a while. Then the owner began complaining that my cooking was too expensive (when I made pea soup I made it much better than his way, and when I made chicken soup I just couldn't fake it). So I was fired because I cooked too well. Just like W. C. Fields, complaining loudly that somebody had been putting orange juice he said *was* orange juice in the thermos, the boss was complaining I put too much soup in the soup! I really didn't care about being fired, because I had enough money saved up to enroll in a school that promised to make me a movie star. My usher friends were sorry, though, because they knew good cooking when they tasted it, and now there'd be no more of my *real* soup.

Soups at home used to make up entire meals, and they still do today, in many European countries.

In my mother's kitchen there was always a pot of good, rich stock bubbling on the back of the stove. We made all sorts of wonderful soups, sauces, and gravies from it. Nothing was ever wasted in that kitchen, and our food was all the more delicious and nourishing because of it. We had wonderful beef and chicken soups, fish soups, *gulyás* soup, bean soup, yellow pea soup—even sauerkraut soup! These soups were often enriched with bits of ham or wieners, or further strengthened with vegetables, cheese, cream, eggs, or sour cream. Very often meat cooked in the soup was served alongside it, rounding out the meal. So don't be afraid to use your imagination when you make soup—it can be a marvelous meal in itself.

Today I always keep soup stock in my kitchen, as my mother did. I save the bones and scraps from meat in my freezer, and when there is enough for a good rich stock, I brew it. I make fish stock, too, from the bones, heads, and trimmings of raw fish, but this must be made up immediately, and then used only in fish dishes.

HOW TO MAKE STOCK

SERVES 8–12

4–5 bones (marrow bones, rib and shank bones, roast bones)	1 teaspoon salt
	10 peppercorns
4–6 cups meat scraps (beef, veal, or pork—you can mix them)	1 slice fresh ginger
	1 onion
3–4 quarts water	1 clove garlic

Put all the ingredients in a big pot with 3–4 quarts of water and simmer gently for 2 hours. When it is done, strain it 2 or 3 times to make it nice and clear. Then cool it thoroughly and put it in the refrigerator.

VEGETABLE SOUP FROM STOCK
SERVES 6-8

6–10 fresh mushrooms, sliced
¼ cup green peas
¼ cup green string beans,
   in 1 inch pieces
4 stalks celery, scraped and
   sliced thin

1 carrot, scraped and diced
4–6 cups stock
herb bouquet
1 tablespoon butter
2 tablespoons flour

Boil all the vegetables gently in the stock with the herb bouquet (parsley, bay leaf, thyme, sweet marjoram, and a few peppercorns tied together in a little square of cheesecloth). When the vegetables are done, thicken the soup with a roux. To make the roux, melt 1 heaping tablespoon butter or shortening in a skillet or small saucepan. Add 2 generous tablespoons flour and cook together until lightly browned, stirring constantly. Dilute with 1 cup cold water added slowly while continuing to stir. When it is creamy, add it to the soup and taste for seasoning. Remove the bouquet before serving.

Don't let the simplicity of this soup fool you. It's delicious!

BEEF SOUP HUNGARIAN STYLE
SERVES 6-8

2 pounds beef brisket
2–3 pounds short ribs
1 teaspoon salt
8 peppercorns

1 slice fresh ginger
1 medium onion
1 clove garlic
3–4 quarts water

Put all the above ingredients in a big pot and cook slowly for 2–3 hours. While it cooks, prepare your vegetables.

3 carrots
1 parsnip
1 leek
1 bunch parsley

1 tomato
1 green pepper
4 stalks celery

Wash, clean, and slice the vegetables. When the meat is done, add them to the soup and continue to simmer gently for 30 minutes. Carefully remove the meat and vegetables and strain the broth 2 or 3 times until it is clear. Pour a little broth over the meat and vegetables to keep them moist, and keep warm in the oven.

Before serving, prepare Farina Balls (see page 59), Matzo Balls (see page 61), or thin noodles (see Noodle Dough, page 57), and cook them in the broth. (You can use rice, barley, or packaged noodles instead.) Serve the broth with its garnish very hot. On a separate platter, serve the meat, nicely sliced, with the vegetables around it. Mustard Sauce (see page 264), Parsley Sauce (see page 265), or Horse-radish Sauce (see page 262), served separately in a sauce boat, is very good with this dish.

CHICKEN SOUP HUNGARIAN STYLE

SERVES 6–8

5-pound hen, cleaned and soaked	1 clove garlic
	1 small onion
chicken neck and gizzard (but *not* the liver)	8–10 peppercorns
	1 piece ginger
1 teaspoon salt	2–3 quarts water

Put all the above ingredients in a large pot, adding more water if needed to cover the chicken. Bring to a boil and simmer for 1½ hours. While the chicken cooks, prepare the vegetables.

2–3 carrots	1 tomato
1 parsnip	handful green peas
few stalks celery	1–2 leeks
1 green pepper	

Clean and slice the vegetables and add them to the soup when the chicken is tender. Continue to cook for 30 minutes longer.

While the vegetables are cooking, make Matzo Balls (see page 61).

When the vegetables are tender, remove both vegetables and chicken and keep warm in the oven. Strain the broth 2 or 3 times until it is clear. Then boil the matzo balls in the broth and serve very hot.

Slice the chicken into pieces and serve with the vegetables around it. Tomato Sauce (see page 268), Mushroom Sauce (see page 264), or Dill Sauce (see page 260) is very good with the chicken.

GENUINE FRENCH ONION SOUP
SERVES 6–8

8 cups rich beef stock
8–10 red onions
1/4 cup cooking oil
5 tablespoons butter

1/2 teaspoon sugar
8 toast rounds
8 tablespoons freshly grated Parmesan cheese

In a saucepan, heat the stock. While it heats, slice the onions thinly and sauté very gently in the oil. When they are tender but not brown, add the butter and sugar. (The onions must not be allowed to brown at all.)

Heap the onions into hot soup plates. Pour in the sizzling hot soup. Top with rounds of toast and 1 tablespoon of the freshly grated Parmesan cheese. Work fast, for this soup must be served very, very hot. If you want to use individual casseroles, you can run them under the broiler for a moment or two to lightly brown the cheese.

BLACK BEAN SOUP
SERVES 4–6

1 cup black beans, soaked overnight
1 ham bone or ham shank
1 bay leaf
10 peppercorns
3 stalks celery

1/2 onion
1/2 green pepper
1 clove garlic
1 quart water

Put all the above ingredients in a pot, tying the vegetables up for easy removal, and cook for 1 1/4 hours, or until the beans are tender. Discard the vegetables and bones.

Put the beans and liquid through a sieve or puree in a blender. Then continue with the following ingredients:

2 tablespoons butter
½ tablespoon flour
salt, cayenne pepper

Croutons (see page 59)
ham or wiener slices (optional)

Melt the butter, stir in the flour, add a bit of the soup, and stir to blend. Add to the rest of the soup and bring to a boil. Season with salt and cayenne pepper.

While the soup simmers, make the croutons.

If you use a ham shank with meat on it, you can add slivers of the ham to your soup, or you can add wiener slices, cooked 2 or 3 minutes to heat through, to the soup. Add the croutons to each portion of soup just before you serve it.

POTATO-CHEESE SOUP

SERVES 6–8

2 cups raw potatoes
1 onion
½ green pepper
3 stalks celery
1 leek
1 carrot
3 cups cold water
1 teaspoon salt
dash each pepper and cayenne
    pepper

2 tablespoons butter
1 tablespoon flour
2–3 cups milk or light cream
2 tablespoons grated Parmesan
    cheese
1 tablespoon minced parsley
Croutons (see page 59)

Cook the potatoes with the other vegetables and seasonings in the 3 cups of cold water until tender. Drain, reserving the liquid. Discard the other vegetables and put the potatoes through a sieve. Heat the butter in a saucepan, add the flour, and brown lightly. Add the liquid and the sieved potatoes, then the milk or cream, then the grated cheese. Heat slowly, stirring constantly. Taste for seasoning. Serve hot, garnished with minced parsley and croutons.

SAUERKRAUT SOUP

SERVES 6-8

Don't be alarmed by this soup. If your family or friends like "sauerkraut and weenies," they'll like this. Since "sauerkraut and weenies" seems to be a staple of American cookery, I urge that you try this very delicious version of it.

1 ham hock	salt, paprika
1 pound pork	2 quarts water
4 slices bacon	1 1-pound can sauerkraut,
1 onion	washed
1 clove garlic	½ pint sour cream
1 tomato	1 tablespoon flour
1 green pepper	sliced wieners or sausages
⅛ teaspoon caraway seeds	(optional)
10 peppercorns	additional sour cream
3 sprigs parsley	

Put the ham hock, pork, bacon, vegetables, and seasonings in 2 quarts water and cook for 1 hour or until the meat is tender. Remove the meats, strain the stock, and cut the meats in pieces. Replace them in the stock and add the washed sauerkraut. Simmer gently for 30 minutes longer. Then mix the sour cream with the flour and add to the soup. Heat thoroughly, but do not allow to boil. Just before serving, add a few slices of sausage or wieners. Serve hot, with additional sour cream on the side.

BORSCHT

SERVES 8-12

3 pounds beef brisket	6 stalks celery
3-4 marrow bones or soup	1 green pepper
bones	1 small head cabbage
water to cover	1 leek
salt	4 tomatoes, peeled
8-10 peppercorns	parsley
8 beets, 4 peeled and	1 onion
4 scrubbed	1 clove garlic
2 parsnips	sour cream
3-4 carrots	

Trim the excess fat from the beef brisket. Soak the marrow or soup bones in salted water for 1 hour. Put the meat and bones in a large pot and cover with cold water. Add salt to taste, the peppercorns, and the 4 peeled beets, cut julienne (in little narrow strips). Boil for 1½–2 hours.

In the meantime, peel and cut into noodle-size slices the parsnips, carrots, celery, green pepper, cabbage, leek, and tomatoes. Add these to the soup along with the parsley, whole onion, and garlic. Continue boiling gently for 1 hour more. Cook the 4 scrubbed beets, whole, in the soup for another 30 minutes.

When ready to serve, remove the onion, garlic, peppercorns, whole beets, and parsley. (If necessary, skim the surface fat from the soup.) Serve your soup very hot with the other vegetables and the meat cut into serving pieces. Serve the sour cream on the side.

VICHYSSOISE SOUP
SERVES 6

When the great French chef Louis Diat was a little boy, he pulled plump tender leeks from the family garden so that his mother could make leek and potato soup. And this memory never left him, for years later he refined that French country kitchen dish into the very elegant and cooling vichyssoise, one of his now-classic creations.

It is a very easy soup to make, and I often keep it chilled in the refrigerator, to drink from a glass in the morning when I don't feel like a hearty breakfast. And in the winter it's equally good hot, so try it both ways.

2 bunches leeks (white part only)	½ pint heavy cream
	¼ teaspoon white pepper
2 tablespoons butter	¼ teaspoon Worcestershire sauce
2 Idaho potatoes, thinly sliced	dash nutmeg
3 stalks celery	salt
1 small bunch parsley	chives, finely minced
1 carrot	paprika for garnish
3 cups chicken broth	

Clean the white parts of the leeks, chop very fine, and put into a soup pot with the butter. Cook over very low heat until the chopped leek is limp. Add the potatoes, celery, parsley, carrot, and chicken broth. Simmer for 30–40 minutes. Remove the parsley and force the rest through a fine sieve or blend in an electric blender. Add the cream, white pepper, Worcestershire sauce, nutmeg, salt to taste, and the finely minced chives. Serve hot or cold, sprinkled with paprika.

BEEF VEGETABLE SOUP
SERVES 8–10

2 pounds beef brisket	2 parsnips
2 pounds short ribs	3–4 carrots
marrow bones	1 small stalk celery with top
1 teaspoon salt	1 green pepper
10–12 peppercorns	1 tomato
1 small piece whole ginger	1 bunch parsley
1 clove garlic	1 leek
½ onion	garnish
pinch saffron	

In a soup kettle, cover the meat and bones with cold water. Add the salt, peppercorns, ginger, garlic, onion, and saffron. Boil slowly until the meat is tender, about two hours, then add the cleaned vegetables and simmer gently for 30 minutes to 1 hour longer. Remove the meat and vegetables and keep warm.

Strain the stock two or three times, until it is clear, and taste for seasoning. Now, if you like, you can serve the clear soup hot, with the marrow (see page 58) from the bones as a garnish. Or cook one of the following in the broth: Matzo Balls (see page 61); Liver Dumplings (see page 58); Farina Balls (see page 59); noodles (packaged or see Noodle Dough, page 57), rice, or barley.

Serve the meat and vegetables separately, as a second course. Slice the meat neatly and arrange it on a large, hot platter, garnished with the vegetables. Serve Tomato Sauce (see page 268) or Mushroom Sauce (see page 264) with this course.

OXTAIL SOUP
SERVES 4–6

1 oxtail
salt, pepper, flour
2 tablespoons shortening
beef stock or water
1–2 beef bouillon cubes
2–3 carrots
2 stalks celery
1 onion
1 clove garlic

2 parsnips
1 green pepper
1 leek
2 tomatoes
parsley
1 tablespoon Worcestershire
   sauce
dash sugar

Cut the oxtail in pieces at the joints. Dredge with salt, pepper, and flour, and brown in the shortening in a large pot. Add beef stock or water to cover and simmer for 2–3 hours.

Remove the bones and strain the soup. Add 1–2 beef bouillon cubes and the cleaned vegetables, cut julienne (in long, narrow strips), along with the Worcestershire sauce and sugar. Simmer until very hot, and taste for seasoning. If the soup is too thick, thin with water or beef broth. Serve piping hot.

RAGOUT SOUP
SERVES 4–6

Let me explain what I mean by the first of these ingredients, the "small pieces" of chicken. These are the wing-ends (or even the whole wings, if you don't want to use them another way), the backs, necks, and the neck skins. And when I say giblets, I mean the gizzards and hearts, but not the livers. I also save chicken fat from my chickens and add it, for its delicate richness, to this soup.

giblets and small pieces of
   2 chickens
½ cup long grain rice, washed
2–3 tablespoons butter
1 tablespoon flour
½ onion
½ green pepper
1 clove garlic
1 carrot

2–3 stalks celery
2 tablespoons minced parsley
½ pound fresh mushrooms,
   sliced
4 cups water or broth from
   chicken bouillon cubes
salt, white pepper, cayenne
   pepper

Cut the giblets and the chicken meat into small pieces. Sauté with the rice in the butter and flour for 5 minutes.

Mince the onion, green pepper, garlic, carrots, celery, and parsley. Add these, with the sliced mushrooms, to the meat and rice. Add the water or chicken broth, or a mixture of both. Season with salt, white pepper, and a dash of cayenne pepper. Simmer gently for 1 hour or more, or until the meat and rice are done.

CELERY-RICE SOUP

SERVES 6

5 tablespoons butter
½ cup long grain rice, washed
3 stalks celery, minced
1 quart chicken broth

2 egg yolks
3 tablespoons heavy cream
parsley for garnish

Melt 3 tablespoons of the butter in a saucepan and add the rice. Brown lightly. Add the minced celery. When the celery is limp, add the chicken broth and bring to a simmer. Simmer for 30 minutes.

In a double boiler beat the egg yolks, the remaining butter, and the cream until well mixed. Pour this into the hot soup and cook over low heat, stirring for 3 minutes. Season to taste and serve hot, sprinkled with parsley, with hot toast or garlic bread on the side.

Note: The above soup can be made with other vegetables such as carrots, cauliflower, etc. Simply substitute them for the celery.

ITALIAN MINESTRONE SOUP

SERVES 8–12

I can't give you an exact recipe for this soup, for it is a taste-and-add-as-you-go kind of thing, much depending on the kinds of meat you use. But you start with:

1 large veal knuckle,
   2–4 pounds

1 beef shinbone
water to cover

a few marrow bones
rib roast or steak bones
any kind of leftover meat
   and bones
herb bouquet:
   1 piece whole ginger
   15–20 peppercorns
   1–2 cloves garlic
   1 bay leaf
   marjoram, thyme, oregano
1 quart solid-pack tomatoes
4 small onions, sliced
tops of 1 bunch celery

2 bunches spinach, cut coarsely
1 carrot
1 parsnip
4–5 stalks celery
1 medium cabbage, shredded
1–2 cups mixed green
   vegetables (green beans,
   peas, zucchini)
1 bunch parsley
2 cups well-soaked pink beans
1 cup long grain rice
grated Parmesan cheese
paprika for garnish

Wash, soak, and clean the bones, place in a large soup pot, and cover with water. In a cheesecloth square, tie the ginger, peppercorns, garlic, bay leaf, and a dash each of marjoram, thyme, and oregano. Add the bouquet to the soup. Bring to a boil, then let simmer for 3 hours, stirring frequently.

Remove the meat and strain the broth twice. Cut the meat into small pieces and return to the broth.

Clean the vegetables and slice when necessary. Add them to the soup, with the drained, soaked beans. Simmer slowly for another 3 hours and add the long grain rice. Taste, correct the seasoning if necessary, and continue cooking for 30 minutes, or until the rice is done. Remove the bouquet before serving.

Serve the soup with plenty of freshly grated Parmesan cheese and sprinkle with paprika. This is a long, time-consuming project, but it's worth it!

SPLIT PEA OR NAVY BEAN SOUP WITH HAM BONE

SERVES 6–8

That leftover ham bone makes a wonderful, hearty soup, very satisfying to have in the refrigerator for a late-night snack, or for a lunch with a green salad and some garlic bread.

1 ham bone
3 quarts cold water
1 pound soaked split peas
  or navy beans
1 large green pepper
1 onion
1 clove garlic
3–4 stalks celery
1 small bunch parsley

10 peppercorns
1 bay leaf
salt, if needed
1 tablespoon butter
1 tablespoon flour
2–3 sliced wieners
minced parsley
cayenne pepper

Place the ham bone in a large kettle, cover with about 3 quarts cold water, and add the split peas or navy beans, the vegetables, and the peppercorns and the bay leaf (tied up with the vegetables for easy removal). Simmer for 1½–2 hours.

Remove the bone, peppercorns, bay leaf, and vegetables. Puree the beans or peas through a sieve or in a blender. Make a smooth blend of the butter and flour and add to the puree. Add more water and salt if needed. Cut the ham from the bone in little pieces and add to the soup. Add the sliced wieners and continue simmering for 30 minutes. Taste and correct the seasoning.

When ready to serve, sprinkle with minced parsley and cayenne pepper.

FISHERMAN'S SOUP (*Halászlé*)

SERVES 6–8

2–3 pounds fish bones and
  trimmings
4 stalks celery
2 carrots
1 large onion
1 clove garlic
1 bunch parsley
juice of 1 lemon or lime

1 bay leaf
1 small piece ginger
10 peppercorns
salt, pepper, paprika
2–3 pounds fish fillets in
  serving pieces
fresh vegetables in season
2 quarts water

Cook all the ingredients, except the fish fillets and the fresh vegetables in season, in the 2 quarts water for about 1 hour, skimming frequently. Strain, discarding the bones and vegetables, and place the stock in a clean pot.

Bring to a simmer and add the diced fish fillets and whatever vegetables you like, cut julienne (in long, narrow strips). When the fish is tender, taste for seasoning and add salt, pepper, paprika, or any other seasonings you may like.

Here are a couple of ways to dress up a plain chicken broth or a clear bouillon, which you can buy already prepared if you prefer not to make them yourself.

CONSOMMÉ MONTE CARLO

Just before serving the soup, drop into it little Farina Dumplings (see page 58) and a few leaves of chervil. Top each serving with a small spoonful of whipped cream and serve with a lemon slice or wedge.

CONSOMMÉ VERT-PRÈS

Parboil some spinach leaves for a few seconds, then press in a sieve with a wooden spoon to extract the bright green juice. Add this to a hot soup to make it green. Just before serving, add finely chopped mixed herbs. Serve hot or cold.

Garnishes for Soups

Like making a movie, making a soup requires lots of ingredients, carefully chosen and carefully blended. Then one adds one's own touches and garnishes to make the whole thing a finished composition. Almost all soups are better for these garnishes, and these are my favorite recipes for adding to the interest of my soups.

The garnishes for cream soups and thick soups such as tomato, celery, pea, bean, potato, and so on are usually served separately. I like plain butter-toasted Croutons (see page 59) or Cheese Croutons (see page 59) best for these soups.

The thin soups—chicken broth, for instance, or bouillon or beef vegetable, or any consommé—are the ones that benefit most from an added garnish, such as the ones I give on the following pages. These are for soups that otherwise might seem too plain. All are equally good with any clear soup, but should be chosen to harmonize with the rest of your dinner.

One final suggestion is that aside from the Ravioli and Turnovers for Soup, which should be about 2 inches square, and Matzo Balls, which are traditionally about the size of golf balls, the other dumplings and balls should be made quite small. They seem to taste better in little bites.

NOODLE DOUGH
SERVES 6-8 IN 2 SOUPS

2–3 eggs
1½–2 cups sifted flour

1 teaspoon salt
1 tablespoon cold water

(The size of the eggs and the kind of flour you use make a difference, which is why these proportions must be vague.) Beat the eggs, then add the flour, salt, and water to make a very stiff dough. Knead it thoroughly, and roll out very thin. Let the dough dry for a few minutes. Then, with a sharp knife, cut into noodle strips or, if you prefer, into small squares.

NOODLE PUFFS
SERVES 6-8

Prepare Noodle Dough, rolling it very thin. Fold it over once, and with a thimble cut small rounds or puffs. Don't make your dough too stiff or dry, for the two little halves must stick together. Fry the little rounds in hot fat in a saucepan or a frying basket. When done, drain them on absorbent paper and serve them in chicken broth, bouillon, or any thin soup.

FARINA DUMPLINGS
SERVES 6–8

2 eggs
¼ cup butter
¼ teaspoon salt

dash white pepper
⅔ cup farina

Cream the eggs with the butter, salt, and pepper, then blend in the farina. Let stand 1 hour or longer. Shape into small dumplings or drop from a teaspoon into soup or salted water. Boil gently, covered, for 25–30 minutes.

LIVER DUMPLINGS
SERVES 6–8

¼ pound liver
2 eggs, beaten
1 tablespoon shortening
½ teaspoon minced onion
salt and pepper to taste

1 tablespoon minced parsley
dash ginger
1 tablespoon flour
3 tablespoons fine bread crumbs

Remove the membranes, veins, and skin from the liver and scrape it. Cream the scraped liver with the beaten eggs, shortening, minced onion, salt and pepper, minced parsley, and ginger. Add the flour and bread crumbs and let stand for ½ hour. If the paste seems too soft, add more bread crumbs. Drop a teaspoonful at a time into the boiling soup and continue boiling for 8–10 minutes. Then cover and keep warm. Do not allow the soup to boil again.

MARROW DUMPLINGS
SERVES 6–8

raw marrow bones
1–2 eggs, separated
salt, pepper, cayenne pepper

1 tablespoon minced onion
2 tablespoons flour
2 tablespoons fine bread crumbs

Remove the marrow from the bones before you cook them in your soup. Cream the marrow with 1–2 egg yolks (depending on the amount of marrow), salt, pepper, a dash of cayenne pepper, the minced onion, and the flour. Beat the egg whites and fold them into the mixture, then add about 2 tablespoons fine bread crumbs to make a paste that is not too stiff. Let stand for ½ hour. Then, if the paste seems thin, add more bread crumbs. Drop a teaspoonful at a time into boiling beef or chicken soup and continue boiling for 8–10 minutes longer. Then cover the soup and keep warm. Do not allow it to boil again.

FARINA BALLS

SERVES 6–8

2 eggs, separated
1 tablespoon butter
dash salt and pepper

½ cup farina
1 tablespoon flour

Cream the egg yolks with the butter, salt, pepper, and farina. Beat the egg whites and fold them in lightly. Let stand for 1 hour.

Form a small ball or drop a teaspoonful of the dough into boiling soup. If it separates, add 1 tablespoon flour to the dough. Prepare all the balls and boil for 10–12 minutes, then cover and keep warm. Do not allow the soup to boil again.

CROUTONS

1 thin slice white bread
 per serving

butter

Remove the crusts from the bread and cut the bread into small dice. Sauté them gently in a little butter until golden on all sides, or toast them in the oven. Add to each portion of soup just before serving.

CHEESE CROUTONS

1 thin slice white bread
 per serving

grated cheese
butter

Trim the crusts from the bread and spread with butter. Cut the bread into dice and sprinkle generously with grated cheese. Toast on a baking sheet in the oven until golden, and add to each portion of soup just before serving.

STEAMED DUMPLINGS À LA COLE

SERVES 4–6

This recipe comes from Bill Cole, a young friend who likes to cook and to eat almost as much as I do. When he found out I was writing a cookbook, he insisted that I try this family recipe of his, and I liked the dumplings so well that they're now a part of my regular collection of garnishes for soup. I hope you'll like them that well, too.

1 cup sifted flour	1 egg
½ teaspoon salt	milk
1 tablespoon baking powder	1 tablespoon cooking oil

Sift together the flour, salt, and baking powder. Put the egg in a measuring cup and add enough milk to measure ½ cup. Add the oil to the mixture in the cup and beat lightly. Pour into a mixing bowl and add the sifted dry ingredients. Blend thoroughly.

Butter the top of a double boiler. Drop the batter into it according to the size dumplings you want. Cook, covered, over boiling water for 17–20 minutes. Do not remove the cover until done.

Note: You can vary this recipe by adding fresh chopped parsley, caraway seeds, or poppy seeds. You can also use half flour and half white cornmeal. But if you vary the recipe, add just a little more milk to keep the dumplings light.

RAVIOLI AND TURNOVERS FOR SOUP

SERVES 4–6

Prepare the basic Noodle Dough (see page 57). Roll it out very thin and cut in 2-inch squares. Prepare the following filling:

1 cup cooked meat (chicken
breast, ham, lung, or brains)
2 eggs, separated
1 tablespoon shortening

salt, pepper, paprika
1 tablespoon minced onion
1 tablespoon minced parsley

Grind the meat finely. Mix with the egg yolks, shortening and seasonings. Blend well and fold in the beaten egg whites.

Place a small teaspoon of filling on each noodle square, fold over and press the edges together firmly, so they do not separate in the cooking. Boil 12–15 minutes in the soup.

MATZO MARBLES
SERVES 6–8

½ cup shortening
½ cup water
1 cup of matzo meal

salt and pepper to taste
3 eggs

In a saucepan, bring the shortening and water to a boil. Add the matzo meal and mix well with a fork. Add salt and pepper and beat in the eggs. Remove from the heat. Wet your hands and shape little marbles from the dough. Place them on a well-greased cookie sheet and bake at 450° for about 30 minutes, or until golden. Serve the marbles in soup.

MATZO BALLS FOR SOUP
SERVES 6–8

4 eggs, separated
1 tablespoon shortening
salt, pepper

¼ teaspoon ground ginger
2 matzos
4 tablespoons matzo meal

Cream the egg yolks with the shortening. Add salt and pepper to taste, and the ginger. Soak the matzos in water. Press them out firmly and add to the egg mixture. Add the matzo meal and blend thoroughly. Fold in the egg whites, stiffly beaten. Let stand for 1 hour. (If the batter seems too soft, add 1 more tablespoon matzo meal.)

Wet your hands and shape the batter evenly into balls. Boil them 12 minutes, covered, in chicken or beef broth and then let stand over low heat an additional 10 minutes without boiling.

4

DELECTABLES FROM THE DEEP

Fish and Shellfish

When a very good friend of mine first came to America, he had—as who doesn't?—troubles with the language. And if I interrupted him with a problem of mine when he was working, he'd look up and say, "Go away, Joe, I got other fish under foots, or do I mean in the works?" So now we've got fish under foots or in the works, or even to bake, broil, or fry.

Jonathan Swift once wrote, "He was a bold man that first eat an oyster." But in truth, man was probably picking shellfish off rocks before he figured out how to chase game and gnaw meat. Yet today we in America are way behind the rest of the world in knowing the wonderful world of seafood cookery. It's high time we caught up, since it is now possible—thanks to quick-freezing processes—to purchase a great variety of fresh seafood anywhere and at any time of year.

All varieties of seafood have *very* delicate flesh fibers. This is extremely important to remember both when you're buying seafood and when you're preparing it. It means that, to be good, (1) your fish or shellfish has got to be *really* fresh, (2) you must always treat it with tender loving care, and (3) you must be careful *never* to overcook it. There are many, many ways to prepare fish and shellfish. But no matter how you decide to do it, take it easy, gently, carefully—and keep the delicate morsels delicate.

Now let me give you some pointers about fish cookery (we'll talk more about *shell*fish cookery when we get to the shellfish recipes).

Fish

To begin with, fish need very little cooking. So little, in fact, that the Chinese, the Japanese, and the Mexicans make delicious dishes with raw slices of fish. At the table, they briefly cook translucent fillets in hot broth or marinate and "cook" them in lime juice, thereby retaining all the elusive flavors.

I've discovered an excellent trick for preparing fish. After scaling and washing the fish properly, I soak it in ice water with a lemon or lime (or both), the rind as well as the juice. This helps bring out its natural flavor and kills excessive "fishiness." I never use vinegar for soaking since it makes some fish coarse.

A fish kettle with a trivet in it is a very handy piece of equipment to have for the poaching of large fish. But you can improvise with a roasting pan, wrapping the fish in cheesecloth for easy handling after it is cooked.

I prefer deep fat frying to pan broiling for smaller fish, because they absorb much less fat this way. I always dredge the fish in cornmeal or a mixture of cornmeal and seasoned flour before frying.

If you are going to broil your fish, always be sure that the grill is hot and well greased before you put the fish to the fire. Otherwise, it may stick to the grill and break and tear.

Don't overcook your fish! *All* fish is done when the flesh flakes easily at the touch of a fork. Overcooking will destroy the delicate and distinctive flavors.

Sometimes I think (to paraphrase) that God must have loved fish, He made so many kinds of them. Most of the meat we eat comes from only four animals and two fowls, but a *lifetime* isn't long enough to sample the tremendous variety of our edible finny friends. Of course, we *can* do our best. So, in the words of De Lawd in *Green Pastures*, "Now let de fish fry proceed."

We'll take the little fishes first.

FRIED SMELTS

Wash and clean the fish, removing the heads. Shake them in a paper bag with flour, salt, and pepper. Deep fry in hot fat until crisp, and serve garnished with lemon wedges and parsley.

BAKED SMELTS IN WHITE WINE SAUCE
SERVES 4-6

2 pounds smelts	½ cup white wine
1 cup chopped celery	salt, pepper, paprika to taste
1 cup sliced mushrooms	½ cup bread crumbs
¼ cup minced parsley	¾ stick butter

Wash and clean the smelts, removing the heads, and draw them. Combine the celery, mushrooms, and parsley and spread evenly on the bottom of a shallow baking dish. Lay the fish on this savory bed, add the wine and seasonings, then sprinkle with bread crumbs. Dot with the butter. Bake in a 425° oven, basting frequently, for 20 minutes, or until the smelts are tender.

SMELTS WITH MUSHROOMS
SERVES 6–8

3 pounds smelts	1 clove garlic, minced
1 stick butter	juice of 1 lemon
1 cup sliced mushrooms	½ teaspoon salt
1 tablespoon minced parsley	pepper, nutmeg, paprika

Wash and clean the smelts, removing the heads, and draw them. Place in a single layer in a shallow baking dish. Melt the butter in a saucepan and add the rest of the ingredients. Simmer gently for a few minutes, then pour over the fish. Bake in a 425° oven, basting frequently, for 20 minutes, or until the fish are tender.

PAN-FRIED TROUT
1 PER SERVING

Clean, wash, and dry the fish, then dust inside and out with cornmeal or a mixture of cornmeal and prepared seasoned flour. Season with salt and pepper.

Use a very large skillet and heat enough oil to half cover the fish. The oil should be hot but not sputtering. Fry the trout until golden on one side, then turn and cook the other side. Turn only once and do not overcook.

DEEP-FRIED SMALL TROUT
1–2 PER SERVING

Prepare as for pan frying, but place in a frying basket and fry in deep fat at 350° for 3–6 minutes. When tiny stream trout are cooked this way, they are completely edible—bones and all.

LARGE TROUT

½ PER SERVING

Have the fish filleted, then clean and prepare for cooking. Sprinkle with lemon or lime juice and dust with seasoned flour. Lay in a well-greased shallow pan and bake at 425° for 30–40 minutes, adding a little butter for basting during the cooking.

BROILED FISH

½ POUND PER SERVING

This broiled fish recipe is another example of the simple dish made just a little special by a little more effort. The herb butter adds a subtle but important flavor difference. And if you have the butter made up in advance, it's a marvelous "last-minute" dish with glamour.

small trout, sand dabs, fillet of sole, or any small fish
1 cup cooking oil

2–3 tablespoons lemon juice
few drops Worcestershire sauce
salt, pepper, paprika

Prepare the fish for cooking and arrange on a well-greased broiler rack. Combine the oil, ½ cup lemon juice, Worcestershire sauce, and seasonings, and brush the fish well. Broil 6–7 minutes on each side, brushing at least twice more with the mixture.

HERB BUTTER (*Have this ready in advance.*)

1 stick butter
1 tablespoon parsley
few drops lemon juice

salt and pepper
1 tablespoon herbs

Mix the butter with the parsley, lemon juice, salt and pepper, and 1 tablespoon of any of the following herbs: basil, marjoram, thyme, oregano, or chives. Reshape the butter and chill until firm, then cut in small squares.

Serve the fish hot, with a square of the herbed butter and a slice of lemon on each piece.

Next in the size scale will be:

Steaks and Fillets

BROILED HALIBUT STEAK

1 halibut steak per serving
pinch salt
dash pepper and paprika
2 tablespoons melted butter

few drops lemon juice
2 drops Worcestershire sauce
lemon wedges and parsley for
garnish

Place the washed and dried steaks in a well-greased, shallow baking pan and season lightly with salt, pepper, and paprika. Blend the melted butter with lemon juice and Worcestershire sauce and pour over the steaks. Broil under the flame, 3–4 inches from the heat, for 8 minutes on each side, basting with the pan liquid several times during the cooking. Transfer to a hot platter and serve garnished with lemon wedges and parsley.

HALIBUT STEAK ITALIAN STYLE

1 halibut steak per serving
1 tablespoon olive oil
dash salt and pepper
1 sliver garlic, minced
1 teaspoon minced green onion
pinch oregano

white wine mixed with water
2 tablespoons bread crumbs
2 tablespoons grated Parmesan
cheese
parsley and lemon slices for
garnish

Wash and dry the steaks and rub with olive oil. Season with salt and pepper, then place in a well-greased shallow baking dish. Sprinkle with the minced garlic, green onion, and oregano. Add a mixture of equal parts water and white wine, filling ¼ inch of the pan. Mix the bread crumbs and cheese and sprinkle over the steaks. Bake, uncovered, at 400° for about 30 minutes, or until the fish flakes at the touch of a fork. Serve with parsley and lemon slices.

BAKED SALMON STEAK

1 salmon steak per serving   tomato slices
lemon or lime juice   bacon
salt, pepper, cayenne pepper lemon wedges and parsley
onion slices   for garnish

Wash the steaks in salted water with a little lemon or lime juice. Dry and sprinkle with more juice, then season with salt, pepper, and cayenne pepper. On the bottom of a greased baking pan, place a layer of thin onion slices, then a layer of thin tomato slices, then the fish. Top with bacon strips and bake in a 350° oven for about 45 minutes, or until the fish flakes easily. Garnish with lemon wedges and parsley and serve with Tartare Sauce (see page 267) or Parsley Sauce (see page 265).

VENETIAN SOLE

SERVES 2

2 sole fillets   1 tablespoon minced onion
salt, pepper, paprika, flour few drops vinegar
oil   ¼ cup slivered almonds

Wash and dry the fillets. Sprinkle them with the seasonings and flour. Brown lightly on both sides in a small amount of oil. Transfer to a shallow baking pan and keep warm in a 300° oven while making the sauce.

Sauté 1 tablespoon or so minced onion in the pan in which you browned the sole. When the onion is tender, sprinkle with a little vinegar and add the slivered almonds. Heat until bubbling, then pour over the fillets and bake, uncovered, at 350° for 10 minutes.

SOLE À LA MAXIM

SERVES 8

½ cup minced green onions   8 thick sole fillets
2 tablespoons minced herbs   buttered bread crumbs
   (parsley, chives, basil)   ½ cup dry vermouth
pepper, paprika   1 cup heavy cream

Spread the green onions and herbs in a shallow, well-greased baking dish and season with pepper and paprika. Place the sole fillets on top and sprinkle with buttered bread crumbs and paprika. Bake in a 450° oven for 12–20 minutes, according to size of fillets.

Remove the fish to a warm platter and keep warm. Add the vermouth and cream to the pan in which it was baked and heat. Serve the sauce separately.

FISH FILLET À LA VENDÔME

½-pound fish fillet per
   serving
salt, peppercorns, parsley
1 ounce butter per serving
dash dry mustard

few drops lemon juice
1 tablespoon minced parsley
   and chives, mixed
lemon wedges for garnish

Clean, wash, and dry the fish fillets. In a large saucepan, bring enough water to a boil to cook the fish. Add salt, a few peppercorns, and a few sprigs of parsley and poach the fish gently for 6–8 minutes. Remove from the heat, leaving the fish in the water.

Meanwhile, melt the butter. Add the mustard, lemon juice, minced parsley, and chives and heat through. Transfer the fish fillets to a large warm platter and pour the seasoned butter over them. Serve garnished with lemon wedges.

FISH FILLET À L'AMBASSADOR

SERVES 4–6

1 2- to 3-pound whitefish
1 onion
1 carrot
parsley
salt, pepper
½ cup dry white wine
½ pound minced mushrooms

1 tablespoon minced parsley
½ stick plus 2 tablespoons
   butter
2 tablespoons flour
2 egg yolks
2–3 tablespoons grated
   Parmesan cheese

Have the fish filleted, but ask the fishmonger to give you the head, skin, bones, and trimmings. Make a stock by boiling them in water with the onion, carrot, parsley, and salt and pepper for 30 minutes. Strain and reserve this stock.

Place the fillets in a buttered baking pan. Pour 1 cup of the fish stock and the white wine over them. Cover with foil and bake for 15 minutes at 375°. Remove the fish carefully to a heated dish and keep warm.

Sauté the mushrooms and 1 tablespoon parsley in the ½ stick butter. Add the flour and brown slightly. Remove from the heat and add the egg yolks, mixing very well. Dilute with enough of the fish stock to make a medium thick sauce. Put about half of this sauce in the bottom of a casserole, add the fish fillets, and top with the remaining sauce. Dot with the remaining 2 tablespoons butter and sprinkle with grated cheese. Bake in a 450° oven for 15 minutes to heat through and brown a little. Serve at once.

ALBACORE

Albacore is a delicious white fish, mild and moist, when properly prepared. It should be skinned before cooking, and the dark red meat that runs along the backbone should be removed to eliminate any possibility of a strong taste.

The bones and skin of an albacore make a very fine fish stock. Put them in a pot with plenty of water, some onion, celery, parsley, peppercorns, bay leaves, and a dash each of ginger, rosemary, and thyme. Simmer well, then strain and cool. Refrigerate for chowder, sauce, or fish aspic. (To make an aspic, dissolve 1 or 2 envelopes unflavored gelatin in a little cold water, mix into the hot broth, and pour into a mold to set.)

BAKED ALBACORE WITH HERBS

albacore (½ pound per
    serving)
salted water
lemon or lime juice
salt, pepper, ground ginger,
    rosemary

melted butter
tomatoes, sliced very thin
onions, sliced very thin

Prepare the albacore for cooking. Simmer the whole fish in salted water for 3–5 minutes, then remove from the water, being careful not to break it. (If you don't have a poaching kettle, wrap the fish in cheesecloth for easier handling.) Drain and place in a buttered baking pan.

Sprinkle with the lemon or lime juice and season. Baste generously with melted butter. Alternate rows of very thinly sliced tomatoes and onions across the top of the fish and sprinkle with more melted butter. Bake in a 425° oven, basting frequently with more butter, just until it flakes. For a fish of 2–3 pounds, bake 11 minutes per pound; 4–10 pounds, bake 7–8 minutes per pound.

Slice and serve the fish with Tartare Sauce (see page 267), or Parsley Sauce (see page 265), on the side. Leftover albacore is delicious cold for salads or creamed dishes.

BAKED ALBACORE

SERVES 6–8

1 4-pound albacore
2 cups dry white wine
salt, pepper
1 cup minced onion

herb bouquet (tie 1 bay leaf, a little basil and thyme, a few stalks of celery and parsley, and some thin lemon slices in cheesecloth)

Prepare the albacore for cooking. Wash and dry it carefully. Marinate in the wine in the refrigerator for a few hours, then transfer the fish and wine to a baking pan. Sprinkle with salt and pepper. Add the onion and the herb bouquet. Bake in a 425° oven, basting frequently, for about 35 minutes, or until the flesh flakes easily. Carefully remove the fish to a warm platter and keep warm while you make the following sauce.

ALBACORE SAUCE

MAKES 1–2 CUPS

3 tablespoons butter
1½ tablespoons flour

albacore baking liquid
parsley for garnish

Over low heat, blend the butter and flour until smooth. Skim the fat from the albacore liquid and add the liquid slowly to the butter and flour mixture. Cook gently for 5–10 minutes. Taste for seasoning, then pour over the fish and serve sprinkled with fresh minced parsley.

ALBACORE STEAMED IN CREAM
SERVES 4–6

2 pounds albacore fillets	1 cup bread crumbs
½ cup flour	3–4 tablespoons melted butter
1 teaspoon salt	1 cup cream
1 teaspoon paprika	
¼ teaspoon ginger or curry powder	

Wash and dry the fillets. Mix the flour with the seasonings and bread crumbs and coat the fillets with the mixture. Place the fish in a greased baking pan and pour the melted butter over the fish. Pour the cream around the fish and bake, uncovered, in a 375° oven for about 30 minutes, basting occasionally. Serve very hot.

STUFFED BAKED FISH À LA NEGRESCO
SERVES 8–10

The Negresco in Nice is a beautiful Victorian wedding cake of a building, romantic and very elegant. The atmosphere is perfect for glamorous lady spies and sinister, monocled adventurers, but I have never been fortunate enough to encounter any lurking among the potted palms. I have had superb food there, however, and this is one of my favorite Negresco dishes. (Naturally, I've added a few touches of my own. No Hungarian can resist *that* temptation in any creative endeavor!) If possible, use a freshwater fish for the authentic French flavor.

1 4-pound fish	¼ cup grated pecans
salt, lime juice, pepper, paprika	dash rosemary
1 cup raw rice	4 tablespoons butter
1 cup minced mushrooms	watercress and lemon or lime
½ cup minced onion	slices for garnish

Soak, wash, and dry the cleaned fish and rub, inside and out, with salt, lime juice, pepper, and paprika.

Boil the rice in salted water for 20 minutes, or until tender, then rinse. Sauté, in butter, the minced mushrooms and onions until limp, then add the pecans, the rosemary and the rest of the butter. Mix the rice with the mushrooms, onions, pecans, rosemary, and butter, and season with salt and pepper. Stuff the fish lightly with this mixture and fasten the opening with skewers. Lay the fish in a buttered baking pan and pour a little melted butter over it. Bake in a 350° oven for 1 hour, or until done. Serve garnished with watercress and lemon or lime slices.

BAKED WHITEFISH HUNGARIAN STYLE
SERVES 6–8

While I was making the movie *Anchors Aweigh*, I knew that, when Friday night rolled around, I could usually expect a particular dinner guest. Gene Kelly would knock at the door, and say, grinning, "Any baked fish?" (He knew that if the day's shooting had been good, he was pretty sure of getting what he wanted.) Sometimes Frank Sinatra would come along, but I couldn't feed Sinatra much, except French onion soup or maybe some leftover lasagne! Frankie just didn't like to eat, but Gene did, and this is the dish he enjoyed so much.

1 3- to 4-pound whitefish	1 teaspoon flour
salt, pepper	1 teaspoon paprika
4 medium potatoes, peeled, boiled, and sliced	4–6 slices bacon, fried and crumbled
2 green peppers, peeled, boiled, and sliced	1 pint sour cream
3–4 tomatoes, sliced	2 tablespoons butter

Ask the fishmonger to fillet the fish or cut it in half lengthwise, removing the head and backbone. Remove as many other bones as possible, then soak and wash the fish and dry it thoroughly. Season with salt and pepper.

Arrange a layer of cooked potato slices on the bottom of a greased baking dish. Add a layer of green pepper slices and then one of sliced tomatoes. Season with 1 teaspoon salt and ½ teaspoon pepper and arrange the fish on top. Sprinkle with flour and paprika. Cover with the crisp bacon bits and another layer of tomato slices. Pour the sour cream over and bake in a 400° oven for 15 minutes. Sprinkle about 2 tablespoons butter over the dish and continue baking for 5 minutes more, or until the fish is cooked. Serve with a green salad.

POACHED FISH

SERVES 6–8

3 pounds whitefish, cut in
   serving pieces
salt, lime or lemon juice
1 bay leaf
1 bunch parsley
3–4 stalks celery
1 carrot
½ onion
½ green pepper
1 clove garlic
dash cayenne pepper

water to cover
½ pound fresh mushrooms,
   sliced
4 tablespoons butter
1 tablespoon flour
1 cup sour cream
thyme, rosemary
1 cup cooked shrimp (may be
   canned)
minced parsley and paprika for
   garnish

Soak the fish for 1 hour in ice water with lime or lemon juice and salt, then rinse.

Put the bay leaf, parsley, celery, carrot, onion, green pepper, and garlic into a large saucepan with salt and a dash cayenne pepper and add water to cover. Add the fillets and poach gently for 10–15 minutes, or until the fish is tender. Transfer to a warm platter and keep hot.

While the fish poaches, make the sauce. Sauté the mushrooms in 3 tablespoons of the butter. When they are tender, add the remaining butter and the flour and stir well. Add the sour cream and a dash each thyme and rosemary and heat carefully, but do not boil.

Serve the fillets on a platter surrounded with the cooked shrimp and pour the sauce over. Sprinkle with minced parsley and paprika.

JELLIED WHITEFISH

SERVES 8–12

2 2½- to 3-pound whitefish
juice of 1 lemon or lime
1 medium onion
1 clove garlic
3 stalks celery
1 bay leaf
1 carrot
½ parsnip

handful parsley
½ green pepper
1 tomato
10 peppercorns
dash each ginger and rosemary
½ teaspoon salt
2 quarts water
2 envelopes unflavored gelatin

For Decoration:
sliced cooked carrot
sliced hard-boiled egg

parsley
sliced lemon

You may use one large fish for this recipe, but I prefer to use two smaller ones, since they are not so fat.

Soak, clean, and dry the whole fish and season inside and out with salt and pepper.

Put all the rest of the ingredients except the gelatin and decorations into a large pot and cook for 30 minutes. Add the fish and continue cooking for 10–15 minutes, or until the fish flakes when tested with a fork.

Remove the fish to a large platter. Remove the skin, heads, and backbones and return these to the kettle. Continue cooking for 30 minutes more.

Mix the gelatin with a little cold water and stir into the liquid, cooking until the gelatin is completely dissolved. Remove from the heat and let cool.

Remove as many bones as possible from the fish, keeping the fish as whole as you can. Also, remove the fat and brown spots.

Next, rinse but do not dry an oblong ovenproof casserole. Pour in enough strained, cooled liquid to fill ¼ inch of the casserole. Chill until the liquid sets to jelly. On the jelly, arrange your decorations as attractively as you can, since this will be the top of the finished dish. Place the fish, white side down, on top of the design. Taste the liquid and correct the seasoning. Strain the liquid very carefully, so as not to disturb the design. Now let the dish cool completely, then refrigerate overnight.

Before you serve the fish, prepare the following sauce:

SAUCE FOR JELLIED WHITEFISH

2 tablespoons prepared
  horse-radish
1 teaspoon mustard
dash each salt, white pepper,
  cayenne pepper

1 teaspoon sugar
2 tablespoons finely ground
  blanched almonds
1 cup whipped cream
lemon juice (optional)

Mix all the ingredients together in the order listed, adding the cream last. Taste for seasoning, adding a little lemon juice if it seems too bland.

When ready to serve, remove the fish from the refrigerator. Place a large platter upside down over the casserole containing the fish and invert both together to unmold the fish. If it sticks, loosen the sides delicately with a spatula, or place a cloth soaked in hot water over the dish containing the fish for a few seconds. Garnish the platter with fresh watercress or parsley and serve the sauce separately.

Note: If you prefer, have the fish filleted for you, but be sure to get the heads, skins and bones to use in the gelatin. Cooking time for filleted fish will be shorter, too, so be careful not to overcook.

JELLIED SALMON (*Bauer au Lac, Zurich*)
SERVES 6–10

You can use the Jellied Whitefish recipe to make a Jellied Salmon as it is served in France. Follow the recipe exactly, but use a 3- to 4-pound whole salmon or the center cut of a very big one. When the fish is tender, remove at once from the broth and let cool. Skin it, returning the skin, head, and bones to the broth to cook a little longer.

In France, the broth is often strained and jelled separately and not poured over the fish. After it is jelled, it is cut into dice and arranged as a garnish around the cold salmon. Serve with

Rémoulade Sauce (see page 266), Mayonnaise Sauce (see page 263) or Tartare Sauce (see page 267). Cucumber Salad (see page 242) or Potato Salad (see page 241) is an excellent accompaniment to this dish.

HUNGARIAN PAPRIKA FISH (*Hal Paprikash*)

SERVES 6-8

1 3-pound mirror carp	2 tomatoes
1 pike	2 tablespoons shortening
1–2 small freshwater fish	1 tablespoon paprika
salt, pepper	¼ teaspoon salt
2 medium onions	½ teaspoon, pepper
2 cloves garlic	2–3 potatoes, thinly sliced
1 green pepper	water to cover

Have the butcher slice the carp for you, saving the head and tail. Scale and wash the other fish, dry and season.

Sauté all the vegetables except the potatoes until tender in the shortening.

Place the cleaned carp head and tail, the small fish, and the pike in a large pot. Add all the vegetables (except the potatoes), the paprika, salt, pepper, and just enough water to cover. Cover with a lid and simmer gently for about 1 hour. Remove and reserve the fish and the carp head and tail.* Strain the liquid into a wide saucepan, forcing the vegetables through a sieve. Arrange the carp slices on top and bring to a boil. Do not stir. Simmer gently for 5–8 minutes, or until the carp flakes when tested with a fork.

Transfer the carp slices to a hot platter and pour some of the liquid over them. Keep warm while you cook the thinly sliced potatoes in the remaining broth until tender. Serve the carp on its warm platter and the soup and potatoes in a separate dish.

* *Note*: If you are not afraid of the fish bones, the reserved fish and the carp head and tail are delicious, too. And some people do not strain and separate the soup. They cook the potatoes in it without straining and serve the whole dish right from the oven—fish, potatoes, soup, and all. My way is more work, but looks more attractive.

SHAD PAPRIKA
SERVES 4-6

1 tablespoon butter or
   shortening
1 large onion, chopped
1 tablespoon paprika

salt, pepper
1 cup water
2-3 pounds shad, cut into
   serving portions

Melt the butter in a saucepan and sauté the onion until transparent. Remove from the heat and add the paprika, mixing well. Add salt and pepper to taste and the 1 cup cold water. Bring to a boil.

Place the shad in the pan with the above mixture and simmer gently for about 30 minutes. Shake the pan occasionally, but do not stir or break the fish. Add a little more water if necessary. When the shad is done, place it in a deep platter. Before serving, pour the gravy over.

HALIBUT MOLDS
SERVES 2-4

1 pound fresh halibut
¼ cup parsley
2-3 stalks celery
1 carrot
1 small onion
water to cover

½ teaspoon salt
¼ teaspoon white pepper
1½ teaspoons lemon juice
½ cup heavy cream, whipped
3 egg whites, stiffly beaten

Cook the halibut, with the vegetables, in water to cover until it flakes. Remove the fish from the broth and rub the fish through a sieve. Season with the salt, pepper, and lemon juice. Carefully fold in the whipped cream and stiffly beaten egg whites. Turn this mixture into 6-8 small buttered molds.

Place the molds in a pan half filled with water. Cover with buttered paper and bake in a 375° oven for 20-25 minutes. Unmold and arrange on a hot platter. Serve with Hollandaise Sauce (see page 261) in a separate dish.

BAKED WHITEFISH (*Garnished with Vegetables*)
SERVES 6–8

1 3- to 4-pound fish (I prefer whitefish, but you can use haddock, pompano, halibut, or sea trout)	butter or oil
	1 lemon, sliced
	2 potatoes, sliced
	3 tomatoes, peeled and sliced
1 teaspoon seasoned salt	1 green pepper, sliced
½ teaspoon pepper	1 onion, sliced
½ teaspoon paprika	parsley for garnish

Clean the fish, left whole, and rub inside and out with the seasoned salt, pepper, and paprika. Place on a large broiling platter or in a pan lined with a double thickness of heavy-duty aluminum foil. Slice the fish almost, but not quite, through into serving pieces and brush with butter or oil. Separate the pieces with thin slices of lemon. Arrange the sliced vegetables around the fish and dust with seasoned salt. Brush with oil and bake 10 minutes in a 400° oven, then reduce the oven heat to 350° and continue baking for 45–50 minutes, or until the fish and vegetables are done. Garnish with parsley and serve sizzling hot.

FROGS' LEGS À LA HORCHER
SERVES 6–8

While I have never liked German food, thinking it too heavy and *gelumpen*, with its *Kartoffel Klösse* and *Kartoffel*-this and *Kartoffel*-that, the Horcher in the days when Berlin was the wildest, wickedest—and saddest—city in the world had really memorable dishes. This is one that I have always liked in particular, and even people who are dubious about frogs' legs find them delicious when cooked in this savory sauce.

2–3 pounds frogs' legs, disjointed	1 bay leaf
milk	1 6-ounce can sliced button mushrooms, drained
salt, cayenne pepper, flour	3 tablespoons white wine
1 stick butter	4 tablespoons sherry or Marsala
1 clove garlic, crushed	minced parsley for garnish
6 green onions, finely chopped	

Dip the frogs' legs in milk, then dust with salt and cayenne pepper and dredge in flour.

In the butter, sauté the garlic, onions, bay leaf, and mushrooms. Sauté the frogs' legs in the butter mixture until they are a delicate brown, then transfer to a hot platter and keep warm.

Add the white wine to the skillet and bring to a simmer. Return the frogs' legs to the skillet and let simmer for 5–10 minutes. Remove the legs and the mushrooms and strain the sauce through a sieve. Return the sauce to the pan and stir in the Marsala or sherry. Return the frogs' legs and mushrooms to the sauce and simmer 5 minutes longer. Serve hot, garnished with parsley, on a warm platter.

Note: Frogs' legs are also delicious when prepared as directed for Fried Chicken (Rántott Csirke) (see page 97). Serve very hot, sprinkled with parsley, and serve Mustard Sauce (see page 264) on the side.

They are equally delicious with Dill Sauce (see page 260) or Tomato Sauce (see page 268), seasoned quite highly and garnished with the following:

FRENCH-FRIED PARSLEY

small bunches of parsley   fat for deep frying

Dip the little bunches of parsley into deep fat at 350° to 370° for just a few seconds, until they turn a bright dark green and become crisp. They are delicious!

Shellfish

I have learned that gentle treatment and some attempt at understanding works wonders when dealing with the ladies. As a motion picture producer, I've had to learn to understand their moods, their idiosyncrasies—and their mysterious charms. The same, strange as it may seem, can be said of lobsters.

The ladies among my readers may think that I know no more about them than do the other befuddled members of my sex, and granted—it's not too gallant of me to compare the Lady with the Lobster. But when one is both a producer and a cook, one learns that ladies and lobsters have certain definite affinities. Both are tender and lovely. And both have protective shells that are pretty hard to crack sometimes.

But the only important thing, after all, is that the Lobster, like the Lady, is tender and lovely—and so, you will find, are the shrimp, the oyster, the crab, and all other shellfish. For this reason, never plunge a lobster (or any other shellfish) into boiling water. This instantly toughens the meat. Instead, place it in cool or lukewarm water and gradually increase the heat, a soothing treatment that will lull the lobster gently to sleep without stiffening the muscles.

I understand that there is a new school of thought that advocates dropping shellfish into wine or even stronger brews and getting them, in effect, drunk as well as cooked. While I've known a few actors who might have preferred this method had they been shellfish, I still prefer to use salted water with a little lemon or lime juice, and to drink the wine myself with the dinner.

But more of lobster later. Let's start off with shrimp.

Shrimp, which require the same gentle handling as lobster, can be cooked either with or without their shells. I usually shell them and remove the sand vein before cooking. They should not be boiled at all if they are to be fried or broiled.

SHRIMP WITH LEMON (*Scampi*)

SERVES 4

1 pound medium-sized shrimp	1 teaspoon salt
1 stick butter	⅛ teaspoon pepper
juice of 1 lemon	1 clove garlic, minced

Clean and shell the shrimp, leaving on the tails. Melt the butter in a saucepan and add the lemon juice, salt, pepper, and garlic. Toss the shrimp in this mixture to coat well. Turn into a broiler pan and broil 3 inches from the flame for about 5 minutes, or until pink and tender. Tomatoes broiled in the same pan with the shrimp are delicious.

FRIED SHRIMP
SERVES 4

½ cup flour
½ cup cornstarch
1 teaspoon baking powder
¼ teaspoon salt
¼ teaspoon monosodium
    glutamate

1 egg
⅔ cup water
1 pound medium or
    jumbo shrimp
lime juice
fat for deep frying

Mix the dry ingredients in a bowl. Beat the egg with the water and stir into the dry mixture. Let the batter stand for an hour before using.

Shell the shrimp, leaving on the tails, and remove the sand vein with a sharp knife, splitting the shrimp almost, but not quite, in two. Rinse them in cold water, then flatten out on paper towels and pat dry. Sprinkle with lime juice.

Heat the fat to a depth of 2–3 inches in a wide pan. Dip the shrimp into the batter, coating thoroughly. Fry a few at a time, turning once, until golden brown. Serve with Tomato Sauce (see page 268) or your favorite bottled cocktail sauce.

FRENCH FRIED SHRIMP
SERVES 6–8

¼ cup lemon juice
¼ cup mayonnaise
½ teaspoon salt
⅛ teaspoon cayenne pepper
1–2 cloves garlic, crushed
2 pounds medium shrimp,
    cleaned and shelled

1 cup buttermilk pancake mix
1 cup water
salt, pepper
fat for deep frying

Combine the lemon juice, mayonnaise, salt, cayenne pepper, and garlic. Add the shrimp and let stand for 1 hour.

Combine the pancake mix with 1 cup water and a dash of salt and pepper. Beat with a rotary beater until very smooth.

Heat 2–3 inches of shortening or oil in a deep kettle. Dip the shrimp in the batter, coating them evenly, and fry a few at a time, turning once, until golden. Serve with Mustard Sauce (see page 264) or Tartare Sauce (see page 267).

SHRIMP CURRY

SERVES 6–8

1½ pounds raw shrimp
1 bunch parsley
4 peppercorns
½ green pepper
1 onion
1 apple
1 clove garlic
½ stick butter

¼ cup flour
1 tablespoon curry powder
1 teaspoon salt
1 tablespoon shredded fresh or candied ginger
2 cups fish stock or chicken broth
2 tablespoons lemon juice

Clean and shell the shrimp, remove the sand vein, and cook in salted water with the parsley, peppercorns, and green pepper for 3–5 minutes, or until pink. Remove the parsley, peppercorns, and green pepper and drain the shrimp.

Chop the onion, apple, and garlic and sauté in the butter until limp. Add the flour and curry powder and stir well, then add the remaining ingredients and cook until smooth, stirring constantly. Taste for flavor, and add more curry powder if you like a hotter curry.

Put the shrimps into the sauce and let stand overnight. Reheat in a double boiler and serve with plenty of hot, fluffy rice. Traditional accompaniments for curry are chutney, crisp bacon bits, fried onion bits, chopped hard-boiled eggs, coconut, chopped nuts, shredded orange peel, raisins, and chopped green onions. Any and/or all add a great deal to the dish.

LOBSTER THERMIDOR

SERVES 2–4

In the days of gaslight and red plush, when opulent ladies glittered with diamonds and fluttered with ostrich feathers, this was a favorite dish, often served in private dining rooms after the theater. We don't need all those fancy trappings today. Lobster

Thermidor is just as delicious served at an informal buffet, on a cool summer patio, or even in a winter dining room.

2 ½-pound lobsters	½ cup heavy cream
¾ stick butter	½ cup sliced mushrooms
¼ cup flour	2 tablespoons sherry
1 teaspoon salt	½ cup bread crumbs
1 teaspoon paprika	1 tablespoon grated Parmesan
½ teaspoon dry mustard	cheese
dash cayenne pepper	lemon wedges for garnish

Buy cooked lobsters for this dish. (Or you can cook them yourself according to the directions in the introduction to this section. Simmer them only until they are red.)

Remove the meat from the cooked lobsters, keeping the shells intact and the meat in bite-sized pieces when possible.

Melt ½ stick of butter over low heat, then blend in the flour, salt, paprika, mustard, and cayenne pepper. Cook for a few minutes, but do not let the flour brown. Then add the cream gradually, stirring constantly, until the sauce is thick and smooth. Next add the mushrooms and sherry, then the lobster meat, and heat through. Spoon into the lobster shells. Combine the bread crumbs with the remaining butter, then spread over the shells. Sprinkle with the cheese and put under a broiler until golden brown. Serve with lemon wedges.

FRENCH OYSTERS

½ dozen oysters per serving	Worcestershire sauce
(at the very least)	salt, paprika
garlic	buttered bread crumbs
coarse salt	lemon wedges for garnish
butter	

Shell the oysters and put them in a bowl, reserving the deeper halves of the shells and discarding the shallow ones. Wipe the shells clean and dry and rub well with garlic. Fill a tin pie plate or a shallow baking dish level with coarse salt. Press the shells down in this bed and put an oyster in each shell.

Melt plenty of butter and add a little Worcestershire sauce, salt to taste, and paprika. Pour this over the oysters in the shells and then sprinkle with buttered bread crumbs. Brown in a hot oven (450°–500°), until the edges of the oysters curl. Serve with lemon wedges and eat them as fast as they come out of the oven.

CRAB CURRY
SERVES 2–4

½ cup chopped onion
1 clove garlic, minced
4 tablespoons butter
2 teaspoons curry powder
2 tablespoons flour
2 cups light cream
1½–2 pounds cooked crab meat
½ teaspoon salt

dash cayenne pepper
pinch thyme
hot rice
crisp, crumbled bacon
chopped hard-boiled eggs
chopped green onions
chopped peanuts

Sauté the onion and garlic in the butter until limp but not brown. Add the curry powder and cook over low heat for 3 minutes. Blend in the flour and cook for a few minutes, then gradually add the cream, stirring constantly, until smooth and thick. Remove from the heat, strain into the top of a double boiler, and place over boiling water. Add the crab meat, salt, cayenne pepper, and thyme and leave over the water until heated through. Serve with hot rice, and sprinkle with crisp, crumbled bacon. In separate dishes serve chopped hard-boiled eggs, chopped green onions, and chopped peanuts.

SEAFOOD BOUILLABAISSE
SERVES 6–8

No one can possibly hope to make an authentic bouillabaisse, as it is made in Marseilles, anywhere but near that seaport city.

Traditionally, it contains several varieties of fish obtainable only there. But we can make a very good interpretation of the basic idea, as witness the following:

¼ cup oil	4 cups water
2 medium onions, minced	2 tablespoons lemon juice or
2 cloves garlic, minced	sherry
1 pound shrimp	½ teaspoon paprika
1 pound fresh crab meat	¼ teaspoon each pepper, thyme
1 pound fresh lobster meat	1 bay leaf
1 #2 can tomatoes	

Heat the oil in a kettle, add the onions and garlic, and simmer slowly for 10 minutes. Add the rest of the ingredients and simmer 15–20 minutes over low heat.

Pour into soup bowls and serve with toasted French bread.

BOUILLABAISSE NEW ORLEANS
SERVES 4–6

I have the distinction of having produced the only picture that the great French director René Clair made in America. Since I had worked with him in Europe, I knew his inimitable flair for satire, but our picture, *Flame of New Orleans*, pleased neither the critics nor the bookkeepers at my studio. (To this day, I suspect that had it been imported, with French subtitles, the critics would have given it a different reception!) But several good things did come out of this venture. One was that, in the course of my research, I discovered the wonderful food of New Orleans, with its French and Creole traditions. The following recipe displays these characteristic touches in a more elaborate version of Marseilles' famous specialty.

2 medium onions, sliced	1 lobster, cut into pieces
1 carrot, sliced	6 clams (or more)
2 tomatoes, peeled	6 oysters (or more)
pinch each saffron, allspice	1½ pints water
¼ teaspoon paprika	5 tablespoons olive oil
dash cayenne pepper	1 pint white wine
1 pound fish fillets	

In a large kettle, place all of the ingredients in the order listed, except the wine, sprinkling the oil over all. Bring to a boil and simmer gently until the fish flakes. Just before removing from the fire, add the wine and heat thoroughly. Serve with thin buttered toast in the serving dishes.

5

THERE ARE BIRDS IN MY KITCHEN

Poultry and Game Birds

Chicken

Eight years after I arrived in America as an immigrant in steerage, I was sent back to Europe by Carl Laemmle, to produce pictures there. "Uncle Carl," who had been an immigrant himself, understood my request to go back like a king— first class on the *Mauretania*, preceded by a fanfare of pomp and publicity.

It was wonderful to see my parents again, to return home as The Boy Who Made Good in America. But Berlin, where I had to work, was a sick and dying city, restless and wild with a feverish vitality that made me uneasy.

When Hitler came to power, I knew I couldn't stay in Germany any longer. As an American citizen I was personally safe, but my gorge rose uncontrollably at the sight of gentle, ancient men being kicked into the gutters by arrogant bullies.

Of all the cities I knew, I loved Budapest the best. Since I could no longer stomach Berlin, I moved our film-making operation to this enchanting city, full of chic, beautiful women and dashing men who could be very diverting companions. And everybody had an additional virtue: They were all Hungarian.

When I was in Budapest, the Hungarian who couldn't rustle up a chicken, a bottle, and a little music in order to entertain a lady was presumed sick in bed, if not fixing to die. I ought to know, because many a signature that read "Joe Pasternak" went on a check for a dinner I didn't order. Once, when I complained to one of the most frequent signers, I was met with an outraged explosion. "But Joe, who else is making your kind of money? What does it matter what I spend, anyway? You are paying for it and you can afford it. I can't!"

Somehow, in that gay and enchanting city this made sense. And when I consider the many wonderful ways we had of cooking chicken, it still makes sense—but possibly only to a Hungarian.

In Europe, you went to the market, picked out your chicken, and had it prepared for you—but not, I'm sorry to say, with the care that your nearby supermarket gives your chicken today. Prepared under rigid governmental standards, your supermarket chicken is virtually guaranteed "ready to cook" no matter what form you buy it in—whole, split, or in parts. Nevertheless, when I get a chicken home, I singe it over an open flame to make sure that all pinfeathers are removed, paying particular attention to the wings. Then I wash it inside and out, to be certain that the cavity is completely cleaned of all bits of fat and membrane. Finally, I soak the chicken for an hour in a big pan of ice water with a little salt and lemon juice in it. These details add that little extra "something" that makes the difference between just a good chicken dish and a wonderful one.

PAPRIKA CHICKEN WITH SOUR CREAM
(*Transylvanian*)
SERVES 6–8

2 2- to 3-pound broilers	2–3 tablespoons paprika
salt, pepper	1 tablespoon tomato paste
2 tablespoons shortening	1 cup water
2 medium onions, minced	1 cup sour cream
1 green pepper, minced	minced parsley for garnish
1 tomato, peeled and minced	

Clean and soak the chickens, then salt and pepper them. Cut into serving pieces and sauté in the shortening until golden. Add the minced vegetables and continue sautéing gently for 30 minutes.

Remove from the heat and stir in the paprika and tomato paste. Add the water and return to the heat. Simmer gently for about 15 minutes, adding a little more water if needed. If necessary, stir, but very carefully—a gentle shaking of the pan from time to time should be enough.

Just before serving, add the sour cream thinned with 1–2 tablespoons water and heat through but do not boil. Serve sprinkled with minced parsley.

CHICKEN PAPRIKASH (*Hungarian*)
SERVES 4

A couple of years ago, I made a movie called *Where The Boys Are* with a delightful singer named Connie Francis, as pert and cute and vivacious a star as any producer could hope for. It isn't easy for a top recording artist suddenly to become an actress, but Connie far exceeded my hopes. And then she came for dinner. What to feed her, this very American girl?

Well, I've never known a lady yet who didn't enjoy a *paprikash*, so I made this Chicken Paprikash for Connie. She took one bite, and said solemnly (and honestly) that she would make a picture for me any time if I would teach her how to make it. So now I've got a deal with her—she's making *Looking For Love* for me, and I'm giving her a bigger salary and three cooking lessons. This arrangement's going to continue—a salary boost and more cooking lessons for each picture. Any girl smart and talented enough to be successful at both singing and acting deserves it—and should turn out to be a wonderful cook as well.

1 3-pound chicken	1 tomato, seeded and chopped
salt, pepper	2 tablespoons paprika
3 tablespoons shortening	1 tablespoon tomato paste
2 medium onions, minced	1 cup water
1 green pepper, minced	green pepper rings for garnish

Clean and soak the chicken, cut into serving pieces and season with salt and pepper. Melt the shortening in a skillet and sauté the vegetables until golden but not brown. Add the chicken pieces and continue sautéing for 30 minutes.

Remove from the heat and stir in the paprika. Allow to stand for a few minutes, then add the tomato paste and the water. Cover and return to the heat. Continue to cook for 15 minutes, or until tender, adding a little more water if necessary.

Place the chicken pieces on a hot serving platter and strain the gravy over them, forcing the vegetables through a sieve. Garnish with green pepper rings and serve.

STUFFED SPRING CHICKENS HUNGARIAN STYLE

SERVES 6–8

4 small spring chickens	lemon or orange juice
salt, pepper	8 slices white bread

water or milk
3 egg yolks
½ stick butter
white part of 2 green onions,
   minced
3 sprigs parsley

½ clove garlic, minced
white pepper, ginger, cayenne
   pepper
3 egg whites, beaten
paprika
3 tablespoons melted butter

Clean and soak the chickens for 30 minutes in ice water with salt and a little lemon or orange juice. Dry them well. Next, very carefully loosen the skin of each chicken from its flesh. Use your fingers and work gently, being very careful not to tear the skin, just moving your fingers between skin and flesh. This sounds difficult, but is surprisingly easy if you start where the neck has been cut off. Season the chickens inside and out with salt and pepper and let them stand while you make the stuffing. Before you make the stuffing, see the note on page 99.

Trim the crusts from the bread and soak the bread in a little water or milk, then squeeze as dry as you can. Mix with the egg yolks and the butter. Add the minced green onions, parsley, and garlic and season with white pepper, a dash each of ginger and cayenne pepper, and salt to taste. Finally, fold in the beaten egg whites.

Now you're ready to stuff the chickens, but note—the stuffing goes between the skin and the flesh, not in the cavity. Use a teaspoon, and again be very careful not to tear the skin. From the outside, using your fingers, smooth the stuffing in an even layer so that the entire chicken is covered between skin and flesh— back, breast, legs, and wings. Shape the chickens so they look nice and plump. Fold the neck skin back, fasten with skewers, and tie the legs to the tail.

Wipe the skin clean with a wet paper towel and place the chickens, breast up, in a baking pan. Sprinkle them with paprika and pour a little melted butter over them. Roast, uncovered, for 1 hour in a 350° oven, basting frequently. Increase the oven heat to 450°–500° and continue baking for another 15 minutes to make the chickens very crisp, but be careful not to burn them.

Do try this—it is one of my very favorite recipes. Putting the stuffing next to the flesh adds an amazing amount of flavor to the little birds!

FRIED CHICKEN (*Rántott Csirke*)

SERVES 6-8

Several years ago my wife and I planned the biggest party we'd ever attempted—some three hundred people were invited, and I did all the cooking. But our party was scheduled for the night that the terrible Bel Air fire broke out, raging through the hills and ravishing millions of dollars' worth of homes and property before it could be quelled.

With the area blocked off by police, only the few people who lived in the neighborhood could reach our house, and even then it was around three in the morning before they came. Almost everybody had gone out to fight the fire until they were sent away.

But my beautiful food wasn't wasted. I sent most of it to hospitals and orphanages the next day. That night, I served the dishes that would be just as good cold as hot.

First to arrive was Elizabeth Taylor, who lived just across the street at the time, and eventually thirty or forty people were there—tired, smoke-stained, and starving for food. The sight of Sir Laurence Olivier and David Niven, smoky, grimy, and grinning at each other over a great platter of fried chicken, is something I'll long remember. And so are Olivier's words as he turned to me. "Bless you for this," he said. "God bless you."

This is the chicken which was so appreciated on that terrible night.

2–3 small chickens	1 cup bread crumbs
salt, pepper	2–3 pounds shortening
½ cup flour	parsley for garnish
1–2 eggs, beaten with 1	
tablespoon water or milk	

If you can, buy the very young, very small spring chickens, but not the squab chickens. Soak, clean, and dry them and cut in serving pieces. Salt and pepper them. Coat the pieces first in flour, then in beaten egg, and finally in bread crumbs.

Heat the shortening in a large skillet. When it is hot, put in a few pieces of the chicken. Cover and fry until golden on one side, then uncover and turn. Fry, uncovered, on the other side until golden, then remove to paper towels to absorb excess fat. Place the cooked pieces on a baking sheet in a 200° oven to keep warm, and continue cooking the rest of the chicken in the same way. Serve on a hot platter garnished with fresh parsley.

FRIED CHICKEN FRENCH STYLE

SERVES 4–6

2 small broilers	3 pounds shortening
1 cup flour	2 eggs
½ teaspoon salt	½ cup milk
½ teaspoon paprika	minced fresh dill or parsley
½ teaspoon pepper	for garnish

Clean and soak the chickens, dry, and cut into quarters. Put the flour, salt, paprika, and pepper in a paper bag and shake the pieces well to thoroughly coat them.

Heat the shortening in a large skillet. Dip each chicken piece in the eggs beaten with the milk. Cover and fry them, a few pieces at a time, until one side is nicely browned, then fry them uncovered until the second side is done. When the pieces are done, arrange them in a large flat casserole. Sprinkle with the minced fresh dill (this is traditional but you can substitute parsley), and place in a 200° oven to keep warm until serving time.

Of course, you don't have to add the dill or parsley flavor touch. But this is just another one of those "little extras" that, I feel, make the difference between an average dish and a really good one.

STUFFED CHICKEN

To stuff any bird, fill the body and neck cavities, folding the skin over the openings and securing it with skewers. Turn the tips of the wings so that they meet across the back and tie the leg ends to the tail with string. Roast, breast side up, on a rack in a shallow pan and do not cover, but brush with shortening and baste frequently with the drippings. When your bird is about three-quarters done, cut the string between the legs. Mix ½ cup water with 2 tablespoons vinegar and sprinkle the bird with this mixture a few times during the remaining cooking time. A few minutes before removing the chicken from the oven, brush it with butter so the skin will be crisp.

Squabs and pigeons are roasted in the same manner as the small, very young chickens.

Once your chicken has been soaked, cleaned, and stuffed and trussed, bake in a 350° oven for 1–1½ hours, or 25–30 minutes per pound.

Roast stuffed chicken is a traditional American dish, and a marvelous tradition it is, too. Nothing is better than a good bread stuffing, and I'm going to give you a simple, savory recipe for this favorite. But some unusual stuffings are every bit as good. I think you'll like my Chestnut, Apple-Rice, and Mushroom-Rice Stuffings—maybe they'll become traditions in your home, too!

Note: Before the days of modern refrigeration, the greatest care and caution was essential, in dealing with food, to sidestep the dangers of food poisoning. In the past, many an unsuspecting husband—or perhaps even an unwanted one—expired of botulism from the food his wife prepared.

Today we don't face the food hazards that our grandmothers faced. But it is still wiser, even now, to prepare your stuffing for a bird or a roast in advance, refrigerate it, and then do the actual stuffing just before cooking. And it is equally sensible to remove the stuffing after the meal and refrigerate stuffing and meat separately, since a warm bread mixture is the perfect culture for mold. A bonus: if separated, both stuffing and meat will keep better and taste better when re-heated.

BREAD STUFFING (*For 2 Chickens*)

SERVES 6–8

6 slices white bread	salt, pepper, ground ginger,
water or milk	cayenne pepper
¼ stick plus 2 tablespoons butter	1 tablespoon minced parsley
	1 teaspoon minced onion
2 egg yolks	2 egg whites, beaten

Soak 4 slices of the bread in a little water or milk, then squeeze out the liquid.

From the other 2 slices, cut and discard the crusts. Cut the bread into small dice and sauté, with the 2 tablespoons butter, in a skillet until golden.

Cream the ¼ stick butter with the egg yolks and the soaked, squeezed bread. Add the seasonings, the minced parsley, and the minced onion and mix well. Fold in the beaten egg whites and then the toasted, diced bread.

Now the stuffing is ready to use.

CHESTNUT STUFFING

Use the ingredients and method of preparation you used for Bread Stuffing, but, for the toasted, diced bread, substitute:

1 cup cooked chestnuts
¼ cup white raisins, cleaned and washed

APPLE-RICE STUFFING

Use the ingredients and method of preparation you used for Bread Stuffing, but, for the toasted, diced bread, substitute:

½ cup cooked rice   ½ cup thinly sliced apples
½ cup finely ground pecans

MUSHROOM-RICE STUFFING

2 tablespoons chopped onion   1 tablespoon parsley
2 tablespoons butter   salt, pepper
½ pound fresh mushrooms,   ½ cup or more cooked rice
  finely sliced

Sauté the onion in the butter with the mushrooms, parsley, salt, and pepper until the mushrooms are tender. Mix well with the cooked rice.

CHICKEN STEW   (*Csirke Becsinált*)

SERVES 4-6

2 young chickens   1 green pepper, minced
1 small onion, minced   1 small carrot, minced

2 stalks celery, minced
1 clove garlic, crushed
2 tablespoons butter or
   shortening
salt, pepper, paprika

1 tablespoon flour
1 cup cold water
lemon juice
minced parsley for garnish

Clean and soak the chickens, then cut into serving pieces. Sauté the vegetables in the butter until soft. Season the chicken pieces, add to the vegetables, and sauté for 10 minutes. Sprinkle with the flour and continue to cook for 2 minutes more. Add the cold water, cover, and simmer gently for 40 minutes, or until tender. Taste and correct the seasoning, adding a little lemon juice for an extra snap.

Remove the chicken to a hot platter and strain the gravy over it. Serve hot, garnished with minced parsley.

CHICKEN FRICASSEE

SERVES 4–6

A clever friend of mine once said, "I can cook very good fancy food, but plain food's real hard because the ingredients are so simple and it has to taste *right!*" Chicken Fricassee is a good example of this, because it is basically a very simple dish, delicious and satisfying when right—and pretty awful when wrong. This is the recipe I think is right.

1 3-pound chicken, cut into
   serving pieces
salt and pepper
1 small onion, minced
4 stalks celery, minced

1 small clove garlic, crushed
butter
2 tablespoons flour
1 egg yolk
2–3 tablespoons heavy cream

Salt and pepper the cleaned, soaked chicken pieces. Sauté the minced vegetables in a little butter until soft but *not* brown, then sprinkle with the flour. Cook, stirring, until the flour is a pale gold. Add the chicken pieces and pour in enough freshly boiled water to just barely cover them. Cover and simmer gently over low heat until the chicken is tender, about 1 hour.

Remove the chicken pieces to a platter and strain the gravy.

Mix the egg yolk with the cream and add to the gravy, off the fire. Blend carefully. Place the chicken in a clean pot and pour the gravy over. Cook over a low flame to heat through and serve with Steamed Dumplings à la Cole (see page 60), Bread Dumplings (see page 211), or Matzo Balls (see page 61).

CHICKEN AU GRATIN
SERVES 2

2 small whole chicken breasts
¼ onion, minced
1 stick butter
¼ cup sherry or Marsala
salt, pepper
4 small potatoes

1 package frozen peas
3 eggs
1 cup heavy cream
3 tablespoons grated Parmesan
    cheese

Remove the meat from the bones and cut the chicken breasts into small dice. Sauté the minced onion and chicken in the butter and wine for 20 minutes, or until tender. Add salt and pepper to taste.

Boil and mash the potatoes. Cook the green peas according to package directions and mix in with the chicken.

Beat the eggs and mix in the cream. Place the chicken-pea mixture on the bottom of a buttered casserole. Cover with the mashed potatoes and top with the egg-cream mixture. Sprinkle with the cheese and bake in a 350° oven for 15–20 minutes.

Note: This dish can also be made with fillet of beef or veal, and all three are equally delicious.

CHICKEN CASSEROLE SUPREME
SERVES 4–6

4 small whole chicken breasts
1½ cups chicken broth
white part of 2 green onions,
    minced
4 stalks celery, minced

1 leek, minced
1 bunch parsley, minced
½ green pepper, minced
salt, pepper
½ stick butter

¼ cup flour
1 cup light cream
½ teaspoon pepper
½ teaspoon salt

dash cayenne pepper
4 cups hot, cooked rice
1 avocado and pimiento strips
   for garnish

Cook the chicken breasts in the chicken broth with the minced vegetables for 20 minutes, or until tender, adding salt and pepper to taste. Remove the chicken, strain and reserve the broth. Dice the chicken when cool enough to handle.

Melt the butter, mix in the flour, and stir until the flour is golden. Remove from the heat and add the strained broth, cream, and seasonings. Return to the heat, stirring constantly, and taste for seasoning. Cook gently until medium thick, add the chicken, and blend thoroughly. Transfer to a double boiler and keep hot over simmering water.

To serve, place the hot cooked rice around the outside of a large platter. Fill the center with the chicken in its sauce. Cut long thin slices from the avocado and place around the edge of the platter, putting a strip of pimiento between each avocado slice. Serve hot.

CHICKEN PINWHEEL

SERVES 2–4

½ cup milk
1½ cups biscuit mix
1 cup chopped, cooked chicken
   breast
¼ cup chopped mushrooms

¼ cup minced onion
¼ teaspoon salt
⅛ teaspoon pepper
⅓ cup sour cream
butter

Stir the milk into the biscuit mix to form a soft dough. Turn onto a lightly floured board and knead gently, then roll into a rectangle ¼ inch thick and about 12 inches long.

Mix the chopped chicken meat with the rest of the ingredients and spread the mixture over the dough. Roll up like a jelly roll and place on a greased baking sheet, trimming the ends neatly. Brush the top with butter and bake until golden, about 1 hour in a 375° oven.

CHICKEN WITH MUSHROOMS IN CASSEROLE

SERVES 2

½ cup raw rice
2 small whole chicken breasts
1 small onion
1 green pepper
½ pound fresh mushrooms
3 tablespoons butter or
  shortening

salt, pepper, paprika
2–3 tomatoes
2 tablespoons grated Parmesan
  cheese

Boil the rice in salted water for 20 minutes, or until tender, and drain.

Cut the chicken breasts into thin slices and pound between sheets of waxed paper until very thin.

Mince the onion, green pepper, and mushrooms and sauté in the butter. When they are soft, add the meat and continue cooking for 20 minutes, or until the meat is tender. Add the seasonings and taste. Add more if needed.

Line the bottom of a 2-quart casserole with a layer of the boiled rice. Add a layer of the meat. Alternate until all the rice and meat are used. Top with peeled, sliced tomatoes and sprinkle with the cheese. Bake in a 375° oven for 30 minutes.

HERBED CHICKEN

SERVES 4–6

2 small young chickens
2 tablespoons flour
¼ teaspoon salt
dash each rosemary, basil,
  paprika
3–4 tablespoons butter or
  shortening

1 cup dry white wine
2 tablespoons water
2 tablespoons sour cream
  (optional)
parsley for garnish

Cut each chicken into 4 pieces. Mix the flour, salt and herbs in a paper bag and shake the chicken pieces to coat them. Melt the butter in a skillet and sauté the chicken pieces on all sides until golden. Add the wine and cook until tender, about 45 minutes.

Remove the cover and transfer the chicken pieces to a hot platter. Add the 2 tablespoons water to the pan and heat. You can add 2 tablespoons sour cream, if you wish to make a thicker and richer gravy. Pour the gravy over the chicken and serve sprinkled with parsley.

CHICKEN DELIGHT
SERVES 4–6

1 pound chicken livers or
   1 goose liver
4 tablespoons butter
2 pounds chicken breasts, boned
4 slices white bread
water or milk
1 small onion
1 clove garlic
½ green pepper
8–10 sprigs parsley, without
   stems

2 egg yolks
salt, pepper, paprika
1 teaspoon mustard
1 tablespoon Worcestershire
   sauce
1–2 tablespoons sour cream
1 egg, beaten
2 tablespoons or more water
3 tablespoons hot shortening

Sauté the livers in 2 tablespoons of the butter for a few minutes, but do not add salt. Put the chicken breasts through a grinder twice. Soak the bread in water or milk and squeeze dry.

Mince the onion, garlic, green pepper, and parsley and put through the grinder with the squeezed bread. Combine this mixture with the ground meat and sauté in the rest of the butter for a few minutes, then put in a mixing bowl and blend in the egg yolks, salt, pepper, and paprika to taste, mustard, Worcestershire sauce, and sour cream. Mix thoroughly.

Remove the mixture to a board and flatten it out. Place the livers on top and form the mixture around them in the shape of a stuffed meat loaf. Place the loaf in a baking pan and brush with beaten egg. Pour about 2 tablespoons water into the pan around the meat and pour 3 tablespoons hot shortening over the loaf. Sprinkle with paprika.

Bake in a 375° oven for 1 hour. During the baking, brush the loaf with beaten egg once more. It will be done when it is a nice brown. Don't let it overcook and dry out. Remove from the oven to cool, then refrigerate to chill completely. Serve cold in thin slices.

CHICKEN À LA KING

SERVES 4–6

As a businessman (and a producer *is* a businessman, even a Hungarian producer), I have eaten my share of chicken *à la king* at luncheons and I have often wondered what they do to it in the kitchen to make it so *bad*. Even when I was a waiter at the Paramount studios on Long Island in the early days of movies, I wouldn't have dreamed of serving anything that I hadn't tasted, or even, if the truth be known, added a little something to make it better. If *I* liked it, then I thought Gloria Swanson or Thomas Meighan would, too—and they did! But the unending yards of wallpaper paste with a little stringy maybe-chicken in it that passes for chicken *à la king* at most banquets is something I find very depressing. Because I'd rather be cheerful, I worked out a recipe for a delicious chicken *à la king*—tender bites of flavorful chicken in a rich and succulent sauce.

1 3- to 4-pound chicken	2 tablespoons butter
water to cover	2 tablespoons flour
1 teaspoon salt	1–2 egg yolks
10 peppercorns	½–1 cup heavy cream
dash each ginger, saffron	1 2-ounce jar minced pimientos
1 small onion	1 4-ounce can whole
1 clove garlic	mushrooms, drained
4 stalks celery	white pepper, paprika
2 carrots	4 cups hot cooked rice or
½ parsnip	hot mashed potatoes
1 tomato	grated Parmesan cheese
1 leek	slivered almonds (optional)
1 green pepper	½ cup sherry (optional)
1 bunch parsley	

In a large pot, place the chicken in just enough water to cover, with the salt, peppercorns, ginger, saffron, and vegetables. Simmer gently until very tender, about 1–1½ hours. Remove and skin the chicken, saving the broth. Reserve the vegetables. Save the bony pieces of the chicken, too, and cut the meaty parts into bite-sized pieces. (You can use the vegetables and bony pieces for a luncheon dish tomorrow.)

Mix the butter and flour and sauté in a skillet until golden. Add the broth slowly, stirring until smooth and creamy. Stir the egg yolks into the cream and add very carefully, off the fire, to the mixture in the skillet. Return to the heat to thicken, but do not let boil. Add the pimientos and mushrooms, a dash of white pepper, paprika, and salt. Taste and correct the seasoning. Finally, add the chicken and keep warm over very low heat, or in a double boiler.

Put the potatoes or rice into a ring mold and turn out onto a hot platter. Fill the center of the ring with the creamed chicken and serve sprinkled with Parmesan cheese and slivered almonds. If you want to add the sherry, stir it into the chicken and sauce just before turning into the mold.

JELLIED CHICKEN
SERVES 6–8

1 4- to 5-pound roasting chicken	½ green pepper
1 teaspoon salt	1 bunch parsley
1-inch piece fresh ginger	1 bay leaf
10 peppercorns	6½ cups water
2 carrots	2 envelopes unflavored gelatin
1 parsnip	hard-boiled egg slices for garnish
3–4 stalks celery	carrot slices for garnish
1 leek	lemon slices for garnish
1 small onion	pickle slices for garnish
1 clove garlic	parsley and paprika for garnish
1 tomato	

Boil the chicken and the vegetables in 6 cups water until tender, about 1½ hours. Remove the chicken and continue to cook the broth down until only 4 cups remain.

Dissolve the gelatin in ½ cup gold water and mix into the

broth. Simmer a few minutes longer and remove from the heat. Put through a fine strainer, discarding the vegetables.

Skin the chicken and remove the meat from the bones. Cut the meat into small dice and arrange in a deep serving platter. Add decorations of sliced hard-boiled egg, carrot rounds, parsley, thinly sliced lemons and thinly sliced pickles.

Carefully pour the broth over the chicken platter and let it stand until cool. Then refrigerate for at least 4 hours. Sprinkle with paprika and garnish with sprigs of fresh parsley.

CHICKEN LOAF (*Warm or in Aspic*)

SERVES 6–8

1 4-pound roasting chicken	½ stick butter
¼ small onion	2 egg yolks
¼ green pepper	1 cup heavy cream
1 clove garlic	2 envelopes unflavored gelatin
2 tablespoons minced parsley	sliced hard-boiled eggs for
1 teaspoon salt	garnish
⅛ teaspoon pepper	sliced pickles for garnish
dash nutmeg	parsley for garnish

Ask the butcher to remove the bones from the chicken. Save the bones, skin, gizzard, heart, and liver if you want to make an aspic.

Grind the boned chicken meat with the onion, green pepper, garlic, parsley, and seasonings. Cream the butter with the egg yolks until smooth and creamy, then add the ground meat-vegetable mixture and lastly the cream, stirring well together. Form into a loaf and bake in a greased loaf pan at 350° for 1½ hours.

To serve hot, slice and serve with Mushroom Sauce (see page 263).

To serve in aspic, make a stock with the bones, skin, and gizzard (see page 251). Dissolve 2 envelopes unflavored gelatin in a little cold water and add to the hot broth. Simmer until the gelatin is completely dissolved, then cool slightly. Garnish the cold loaf with sliced hard-boiled eggs, pickle slices, and parsley. Carefully pour the cooled and strained gelatin liquid over the loaf and chill until firm.

In my travels I have eaten in many a famous restaurant or hotel. Whenever I found the food intriguing or different, I consulted with the chef afterward, employing every wile that I, presumably a wily Hungarian, possess to get the secret of the recipe. These are the best of the chicken dishes that took so much friendly persuasion to collect. Each one, never before published, is the creation of a famous chef.

COQ AU VIN (*Duc Royale*)
SERVES 6

6 small whole chicken breasts
1 stick butter
½ medium onion, finely chopped
2 tablespoons finely chopped parsley

1 bay leaf
tarragon, thyme, basil, salt, pepper, paprika
1 cup Chablis or sherry
parsley or green pepper rings for garnish

Sauté the chicken breasts in the butter until golden brown, remove from the pan, and skin and bone them. Place in a casserole and pour the pan butter over them. Add the vegetables and seasonings. Pour the wine over the whole and simmer, covered, on top of the stove or bake in a 350° oven for 1–1½ hours. Baste frequently and add more wine, if necessary. Serve from the casserole, garnished with parsley or green pepper rings.

BREAST OF CAPON (*Grand Hotel, Vienna*)
SERVES 4

4 whole capon breasts
2 sticks butter
½ medium onion, minced
½ green pepper, minced
1 small clove garlic, minced
½ bay leaf

½ pound mushrooms, sliced
1 stalk celery, minced
2 cups champagne or dry white wine
1 pint heavy cream
salt, pepper, cayenne pepper

Put the capon breasts into a casserole with three-quarters of the butter, the onion, green pepper, garlic, bay leaf, mushrooms, and celery. Cover and bake for 45 minutes in a 400° oven.

Remove from the oven and transfer the meat to a hot platter.

Keep warm. Strain the gravy from the casserole into a clean saucepan, using a fine sieve, and then add the champagne or dry white wine to this liquid. Simmer, uncovered, until the liquid is reduced by half. Add the cream and stir well. Return the breasts to the sauce, cover, and simmer gently on top of the stove for 10–15 minutes. Remove the meat and whip the remaining butter into the sauce. Taste and correct the seasoning. Strain the sauce over the capon and serve at once with rice.

FRENCH ROYAL CHICKEN (*Café de Paris, Paris*)
SERVES 4

4 whole breasts from small young chickens or squab chickens	salt, pepper
	1 small onion, minced
	1 clove garlic, minced
½ stick butter	⅔ cup sour cream
½ cup plus ⅓ cup dry white wine	1 teaspoon lemon juice
	¼ cup brandy

Sauté the chicken breasts in the butter until golden. Add the ½ cup dry white wine and cook until tender, about 30 minutes. Season with salt and pepper to taste. Remove to a silver platter and keep warm.

To the butter remaining in the pan, add the onion and garlic (and a little more butter if it seems dry). Cook gently until the onion is translucent. Mix the remaining ⅓ cup wine with the sour cream and lemon juice and add to the pan over very low heat. Allow to heat through but do not boil. Taste and correct the seasoning. Force the sauce through a sieve or puree it in a blender and pour over the meat. Serve hot, flamed with warmed brandy poured around the edge of the platter.

SAUTÉED CHICKEN BREAST
(*Hotel Imperial, Vienna*)
SERVES 3–6

3 whole chicken breasts, halved lengthwise	salt, pepper, cayenne pepper, pinch saffron
1 onion, sliced thin	½ cup white wine
1 carrot, sliced thin	water to cover

4 tablespoons butter
2 tablespoons flour
1 egg yolk

3 tablespoons heavy cream
minced parsley

Place the chicken breasts, onion, carrot, seasonings, and wine in a saucepan with just enough water to cover. Put a lid on the pan and simmer gently until the chicken is tender, about 1 hour. Remove the chicken and keep warm, reserving the broth.

Melt 2 tablespoons of the butter and stir in the flour. Cook until golden, then gradually add the strained broth from the chicken, adding enough water, if necessary, to make 1 cup. Continue cooking until thickened, stirring constantly. Add the remaining 2 tablespoons butter and stir well. Combine the egg yolk with the cream and stir into the hot sauce but do not allow it to boil. Heat thoroughly, then pour over the chicken and serve garnished with finely minced parsley.

CHICKEN LIVER PILAF
(King David Hotel, Jerusalem)
SERVES 2–4

3 tablespoons butter
1 tablespoon chopped ripe
  olives
1 eggplant, cubed
1 green pepper, chopped
½ pound mushrooms, sliced

dash curry powder
¼ teaspoon cayenne pepper
1 pound chicken livers
2 tablespoons sherry
salt, if needed

Melt the butter, add the vegetables, and sauté for 15 minutes, or until the eggplant is tender. Add the seasonings and the chicken livers and continue to cook, stirring, for 3 minutes, or until the livers are done. Add the sherry and taste. Add salt if needed. Serve with Baked Saffron Rice (see page 216).

CHICKEN LIVERS WITH MUSHROOMS
(Albergo Savoy, Florence)
SERVES 2–4

1 tablespoon chopped onion
1 tablespoon minced green
  pepper
½ cup mushrooms

3 tablespoons butter
salt, pepper, cayenne pepper,
  paprika
1 pound large chicken livers

1 tablespoon flour
3 tablespoons chicken broth,
　water, or white wine

1 tablespoon minced parsley
　for garnish

Sauté the chopped onion, green pepper, and mushrooms in the butter until soft. Add all the seasonings *except* the salt at this time. Then add the livers and cook, stirring or turning over and over with a spatula, until done, about 3 minutes. Remove the livers to a warm plate. Add the flour to the vegetables and brown lightly. Then add the broth or water (or even white wine) and bring to a boil. Now add the salt and taste for seasoning. Strain the sauce over the livers and serve sprinkled with parsley.

Turkey

This is the timetable for roasting turkey: Allow 25 minutes per pound.

Ready-to-Cook Weight	Oven Temperature	Approximate Cooking Time
4–8 pounds	325°	3–4 hours
8–12 pounds	325°	4–4½ hours
12–16 pounds	325°	4½–5½ hours
16–20 pounds	300°	5½–7 hours
20–24 pounds	300°	7–8½ hours

On a larger bird, allow an extra 30 minutes of cooking time. All turkeys should "rest" for 20–30 minutes after cooking and before carving.

I think hen turkeys are the most tender, juicy, and flavorful. Select a nice plump one and carefully remove all pinfeathers. Wash it well inside and out, then rub it with cornmeal. Rinse and then put it in a large pan of cold salt water with the juice of a lemon or lime as well as the skin of the fruit. Let it soak for 1 hour, dry it well, and season inside and out with salt and pepper, crushed garlic, a little poultry seasoning, and the juice of an orange. Refrigerate it until ready to stuff. Allow ½ cup of stuffing per pound of bird.

And before you make the stuffing, see the note on page 99.

STUFFING FOR A 12–16 POUND TURKEY

SERVES 8–12

14 slices white bread	4 egg yolks
butter for toasting	½ pound butter
water or milk	salt, pepper, paprika
½ onion, finely minced	½ cup minced parsley
1 clove garlic, finely minced	4 egg whites, beaten
1 stalk celery, finely minced	

Trim the crusts from 8 slices of the bread and cut the bread into dice. Toast the dice in plenty of butter until golden. Soak the remaining 6 slices in milk or water, then squeeze dry.

Sauté the onion, garlic, and celery in more butter. (You can use shortening, but butter has the best flavor by far, and I usually use about ½ pound in all for a 12- to 16-pound turkey.)

Cream the egg yolks with 3 tablespoons butter. Add the sautéed vegetables, the soaked bread, and the toasted diced bread. Season with salt, pepper, and paprika and taste for seasoning. Add the minced parsley and fold the beaten egg whites in last of all.

Stuff the body and neck cavities. Don't pack the stuffing too tightly, for it will expand in cooking. Truss the bird and wipe it all over with a damp paper towel. Place in a shallow baking pan. Sprinkle with paprika and pour a little hot butter over it.

Roast in the oven according to the timetable above, basting frequently with plenty of butter and pan drippings. Let stand at least 20 minutes after cooking and before carving. While the turkey "rests," make the gravy.

GRAVY FOR TURKEY

SERVES 8–12

turkey giblets and neck	1 clove garlic
2 stalks celery	3–4 cups water
½ green pepper	2 tablespoons flour
2 slices onion	

While the turkey roasts, boil the giblets and vegetables in 3–4 cups water until the gizzard is tender. Cut the giblets into small dice, and reserve 2 cups of the strained liquid.

After you have taken the turkey from the roasting pan, pour the drippings into a bowl. Allow the fat to rise to the surface and skim it off, reserving it.

Measure out 2 tablespoons of the fat and put back in the roasting pan. Stir in the flour and let it brown lightly, stirring constantly. Add the broth and finely cut giblets and continue to stir until thickened. Taste for seasoning and, if necessary, add a little more of the fat. Serve very hot in a separate bowl or gravy boat.

Garnish your turkey, roasted crisp and golden, with broiled orange or grapefruit halves placed around the platter. Serve with cranberry jelly and cranberry sauce, the traditional accompaniments, as well.

Store the leftover turkey and stuffing separately. Both will keep longer this way, and both are delicious served cold the second day. And for the third day try:

CURRIED TURKEY
SERVES 6-8

4 cups cooked wild (or regular) rice	2 tablespoons lemon juice
4 cups diced cooked turkey	1 tablespoon curry powder
4 hard-boiled eggs, diced	salt, pepper, cayenne pepper
1 cup minced parsley	1¼ cups undiluted evaporated milk or light cream
5 tablespoons melted butter	paprika

Place the rice, turkey, eggs, parsley, butter, and lemon juice in a large bowl and sprinkle with the seasonings. Toss lightly until well mixed and taste for seasoning. Turn into a buttered 3-quart casserole and pour in the milk or cream. Sprinkle with paprika and bake for 35–40 minutes in a 350° oven.

TURKEY ARMAGNAC
SERVES 6-8

Here is a splendid—and spectacular—dish that will delight barbecue buffs and cognac connoisseurs alike!

1 young hen turkey, 6–8 pounds
butter
salt, pepper, poultry seasoning,
    ginger, cayenne pepper
1 clove garlic, mashed
1 cup cooked chestnuts
1 apple, sliced

½ cup plus 2 tablespoons
    butter
1 cup Armagnac
5–6 shallots
2 tablespoons flour
turkey stock or chicken broth
½ cup heavy cream

Rub the turkey inside and out with butter and season with salt, pepper, poultry seasoning, ginger, cayenne pepper, and garlic. Stuff the cavity with the chestnuts, sliced apple, and the 2 tablespoons butter, generous ones. Truss as usual.

Roast the turkey on a spit over a charcoal fire for 2–3 hours, or until the legs move easily and the juice runs clear when the thigh is pierced with a fork. While it cooks, make a stock from the gizzard, neck, and giblets (see page 44).

When the turkey is done, remove from the spit and place in a large pan. Pour the Armagnac over it, heat slightly, and then flame. Remove the turkey to a platter and take out the chestnuts and apple, reserving them. Keep the turkey warm, and combine the pan juices with any drippings that were caught while the bird roasted.

Mince the shallots and cook until wilted in the ½ cup butter. Add the flour, the pan juices, and enough turkey stock or chicken broth to make 1½ cups gravy. Simmer for 5 minutes, then add the cream and salt and pepper to taste. Add the chestnuts and apples that were cooked in the turkey and heat through. Serve in a gravy boat, with the turkey. Make sure your plates are very hot.

Goose, Duck, and Game Birds

I don't know about you, but I like to serve the unexpected at festive dinners, instead of always relying on turkey, ham, or roast beef, wonderful as they are. My guests like surprises, too. My actor friends might be able to fake pleasure convincingly when they *see* a golden roasted goose being served. But I don't think that even a Sir Laurence Olivier could fake the pleasure of eating it to the extent of asking for three helpings, as some of them have!

So if you share my pleasure in providing the unexpected to please, consider the fine fat goose, the delicious duck, or the flavorful pheasant, partridge, or quail, birds that have been considered delicacies for centuries. Once you try them, you'll know why!

Timetable for roasting goose: Allow 25 minutes per pound.

ROAST GOOSE
SERVES 4–6

1 6- to 8-pound goose	1 green pepper, sliced
salt, pepper	½ stalk celery
1 clove garlic	1 tablespoon butter
1 onion, sliced	2 tablespoons melted shortening

Wash, clean, and soak the goose as any other fowl. Dry it, season with salt and pepper, and rub the inside well with a clove of garlic. Place the vegetables and butter in the cavity and skewer and truss as usual. Place, breast side up, on a rack in a shallow baking pan and pour the melted shortening over. Bake, covered, in a 400° oven for 30 minutes. Reduce the oven heat to 375° and continue baking for 1 hour longer. Now remove the cover and bake for about 2 more hours, basting frequently and skimming the excess fat from the roasting pan, leaving only enough to prevent burning. During the last 30 minutes of cooking increase the oven temperature to 450°, to crisp the skin.

Remove the goose to a warm platter and keep it hot while you make a pan gravy (see directions for Turkey Gravy, page 119). Serve the gravy, in a separate boat, with the sliced goose.

STUFFED GOOSE
SERVES 4–6

Roast the goose according to the preceding recipe, but instead of vegetables in the cavity, use one of these stuffings. And before you make the stuffing, see the note on page 99.

BREAD STUFFING

¼ cup minced onion
¼ cup minced celery
½ cup minced parsley
½ stick butter
2 cups diced bread, toasted
   in butter

salt, pepper, cayenne pepper,
   thyme
2 eggs, beaten
4 slices white bread, soaked
   in milk and squeezed dry

Sauté the minced vegetables in butter. Add the remaining ingredients and mix very well. Stuff and truss as usual.

RICE STUFFING

1 cup cooked rice
1 small onion, minced
1 stick butter
½ cup diced ham

1 cup sliced fresh mushrooms
½ cup dry white or red wine
salt, pepper, paprika, ginger

Mix well together. Stuff and truss as usual.

FRUIT, NUT, OR CHESTNUT STUFFING

1 tablespoon minced onion
½ cup minced celery
2 cups diced bread, toasted
   in butter
2 cups diced fruit (apples,
   prunes, apricots, or cooked
   chestnuts)

3 tablespoons lemon juice
1 stick butter
salt, pepper, paprika

Mix well together. Stuff and truss as usual.

GOOSE RAGOUT WITH RICE (*Rizses Liba*)

SERVES 4–6

backbones, neck, giblets, and
   legs of 1 goose
1 onion
1 clove garlic
1 carrot, sliced
3–4 stalks celery, diced

10 peppercorns
½ inch slice ginger
½ bay leaf
1 cup long-grain rice
saffron, white pepper, salt
2 tablespoons minced parsley

Put the pieces of goose in a large soup kettle with enough water to cover. Add the vegetables and make a little cheesecloth bag for the peppercorns, ginger, and bay leaf. Simmer for 2 hours, or until the goose is tender. Then remove the vegetables and the cheesecloth bag.

Wash the rice and add to the liquid with the other ingredients. Continue simmering for about 15 minutes. Then transfer to a casserole, cover, and bake in a 350° oven for 30 minutes. Serve hot directly from the casserole.

BREAST OF GOOSE, HASHED   (*Vagdalt Liba Mell*)
SERVES 4–6

1 whole goose breast	¼ green pepper
2 slices white bread	1 egg yolk
milk or water	3–4 tablespoons shortening
½ clove garlic	salt, pepper, cayenne pepper,
½ small onion	paprika
4–5 sprigs parsley	

Remove the skin from the goose breast, in one piece if possible, and reserve it. Cut the meat from the bone and save the bone, too. Grind the meat.

Trim the crusts from the white bread. Soak the bread in milk or water and squeeze dry. Chop the garlic, onion, parsley, and green pepper. Put the soaked bread through a fine sieve, then mix it with the ground meat, vegetables, egg yolk, 1 tablespoon of the shortening, salt, pepper, and cayenne pepper to taste. Blend well and taste for seasoning. Then reshape the mixture on the breast bone, molding it to its original shape. Cover with the skin and fasten in place with skewers.

Pour 2–3 tablespoons melted shortening over the breast and sprinkle with paprika. Bake in a 375° oven for about 1½ hours, basting frequently. If the skin is not crisp at the end of this time, increase the oven heat to 450° for a few minutes.

If you don't want to replace the skin on the hashed breast of goose, simply shape the meat mixture back on the bone, brush it with a beaten egg and pour 2 tablespoons melted shortening on it. Then bake until crisp, as above.

Serve on a hot dish with the following pan gravy in a separate boat.

PAN GRAVY

2 tablespoons pan drippings	1 cup water
1 teaspoon bread crumbs	seasonings

To make the gravy, remove excess fat from the baking pan, leaving about 2 tablespoons in the bottom. Add the bread crumbs and the water. Simmer to a smooth texture, put through a fine strainer, taste and correct the seasoning. Serve at once.

ROAST DUCK

Duck is similar to goose and can be prepared in the same way, allowing a little less cooking time since it is a smaller bird. For the average bird, 20–25 minutes to the pound in a 350° oven is about right.

ROAST DUCK WITH ORANGE SAUCE

SERVES 4

1 4- to 5-pound duck	herb bouquet of parsley, thyme,
2 tablespoons salt	marjoram, bay leaf
2 tablespoons vinegar	2½ cups water
salt, pepper, paprika	1 cup chicken broth
2 onions, 1 large	(approximately)
2 green peppers	juice of 1 orange
1 tomato	rind of 1 orange
2 tablespoons hot shortening	1 teaspoon flour or
duck giblets	bread crumbs
1 carrot	1 wineglass Curaçao
3–4 stalks celery	

Wash and clean the duck and soak for 1 hour in ice water with 2 tablespoons salt and 2 tablespoons vinegar. Remove and dry. Rub it inside with salt, pepper, and paprika.

Place on a rack in a large roasting pan. Add the smaller onion, 1 green pepper, and the tomato. Pour hot shortening over the duck and sprinkle with paprika. Cover and bake in a 375° oven for 1½ hours. Remove the cover and continue roasting until tender, about 30 minutes, basting frequently. When almost done, increase the oven temperature to 450° to crisp the skin.

While the duck is roasting, start the sauce. Cut up the giblets (but not the liver), neck, and other small pieces. Put them in a large pot with the carrot, celery, remaining green pepper, large onion, herb bouquet, and 2 cups of the water. Simmer slowly for 2 hours, and as the liquid is reduced, add the chicken broth.

Take the juice from 1 orange and reserve it. Cut the orange rind (without the white membrane) into very thin little strips and simmer for 5 minutes in ½ cup water. Set aside.

When the duck is done and crisp, take it from the pan and keep warm in a slow oven, leaving the door open. Place the roasting pan on top of the stove and skim off the fat, saving the bottom drippings. Sprinkle in about 1 tablespoon flour or bread crumbs and simmer, stirring. Then add the boiled vegetables with the giblets, the orange rind, and the liquid in which the orange rind was simmered. Simmer for 5 minutes, then strain through a fine sieve into a saucepan. Add the orange juice and the Curaçao. Taste, correct the seasoning, and heat through.

Carve the duck into serving pieces and serve the sauce separately.

PAPRIKA DUCK HUNGARIAN STYLE

SERVES 4

1 4- to 5-pound duck	1 tomato
salt, pepper, paprika	1 tablespoon shortening
1 large onion	1 cup cold water
1 green pepper	

Wash, clean, and soak the duck according to the directions in the preceding recipe. Cut into serving pieces and season with salt, pepper, and paprika. Chill for at least 1 hour in the refrigerator.

Peel and mince the vegetables and sauté in the shortening until soft but not brown. Remove from the heat, add 1 tablespoon paprika and the duck pieces. Pour the cold water into the pan, cover, and simmer for 1–1½ hours, adding more water if necessary and stirring frequently to prevent burning. When the duck is tender, taste and correct the seasoning. Serve very hot.

PAPRIKA DUCK WITH SAUERKRAUT
SERVES 4

ingredients as above, plus:

1 1-pound can sauerkraut, rinsed	3–4 tablespoons sour cream

Proceed as in the above recipe. When the meat is tender, add the rinsed and drained sauerkraut. Continue cooking for 30 minutes. Just before serving, stir in the sour cream.

Note: Try this recipe substituting a cored cabbage cut into wedges for the sauerkraut, and adding a little more water if necessary.

ROAST APPLES FOR GOOSE OR DUCK
SERVES 6–8

These spicy, sweet, rum-flavored apples aren't any more trouble to make as a garnish to fowl than the more common applesauce, and they are infinitely more interesting to eat. You can prepare them ahead of time, waiting till the last minute to pop them under the broiler—or you can bake them in the oven as you roast your bird.

6 tart apples	1 cup water
1 cup brown sugar	1 cup sugar
juice and grated rind of 1 lemon	½ cup dark rum
2 whole cloves	cinnamon and nutmeg
1 stick cinnamon	

Peel, core, and quarter the apples. Place them in a baking dish and cover with the following syrup:

Boil together the brown sugar, lemon juice, cloves, stick cinnamon, and water until syrupy. Pour this over the apples and bake in a 350° oven for 30 minutes.

When the apples are tender, remove the stick of cinnamon and the cloves. Mix together the sugar, rum, grated lemon rind, and a dash each of cinnamon and nutmeg. Sprinkle over the apples and place under the broiler until the sugar begins to caramelize.

PHEASANT IN COCOTTE
SERVES 2-4, DEPENDING ON SIZE OF PHEASANT

1 pheasant, prepared for cooking	1 wineglass meat glaze
4 large mushrooms	½ pound chicken livers
2 wineglasses Madeira or sherry	butter
	2 slices bacon, cooked and diced

Clean, wash, and soak the bird as you would any fowl. Roast according to the rules for chicken (see page 96), and while it is cooking, prepare the following gravy, which will be added 30 minutes before the pheasant is done.

Cook the mushrooms for 8 minutes in a saucepan with the wine and meat glaze. Transfer the mushrooms to the pan in which you will finish cooking the pheasant.

Sauté the chicken livers in butter for 3-4 minutes, then add the bacon and the wine–meat glaze mixture. Blend well and add to the pan with the mushrooms. Transfer the bird to this pan and roast for 30 minutes longer, basting frequently. Remove the bird to a warm platter and serve the gravy separately.

Note: This recipe can be used for partridge, quail, squab, or chicken as well.

ROAST PHEASANT
SERVES 2-4, DEPENDING ON SIZE OF PHEASANT

1 pheasant	thyme, bay leaf, cayenne
salt, pepper, paprika	pepper, pepper
butter or shortening	1 wineglass brandy
1 cup chicken livers	

Clean, wash, and soak the bird as you would any fowl. Season inside and out and place, breast side up, in a baking pan. Pour a little hot butter or shortening over it and roast at 450°, basting frequently. A 2½- to 3-pound bird will take 45 minutes to 1 hour of cooking time to turn golden and crisp. Remove the roasted bird to a hot platter and keep warm.

Sauté the chicken livers with the seasonings in 3 tablespoons butter for 3–4 minutes, then add the brandy. Remove the bay leaf and put all the rest through a sieve. Add to the pan in which you cooked the bird and mix well, stirring on top of the stove, to pick up the browned bits in the bottom. Taste and correct the seasoning. Serve the gravy hot, in a separate dish, with the roasted bird.

ROAST PARTRIDGE
SERVES 4

4 1-pound birds (1 per serving)	bacon
salt, pepper, paprika	1½ cups water
onion, sliced	½ cup sour cream
green pepper, sliced	1 teaspoon mustard
parsley sprigs	1 teaspoon lemon juice
butter	2 tablespoons sherry or Marsala

Clean and soak the birds as any other fowl. Season inside and out with salt, pepper, and paprika. Into each bird put 1 slice onion, 1 slice green pepper, a few sprigs parsley and a pat of butter. Truss the birds and fasten bacon slices over them. Place them in a roasting pan and pour ½ cup water into the pan. Roast, uncovered, in a 450° oven for 30 minutes.

Remove the bacon and the vegetables from inside the birds and continue roasting, basting frequently, until the birds are golden brown and crisp.

Remove the birds to a hot platter and keep them hot in the oven, with the door open. Transfer the roasting pan to the top of the stove and add 1 cup water to the drippings. Simmer gently, stirring the bottom and sides of the pan. Mix the sour cream with the remaining ingredients and add to the sauce off the fire. Reduce the heat and put the pan back to heat through again.

Taste before serving to correct the seasoning. Serve the gravy in a separate boat.

ROAST QUAIL

1–2 birds per serving   bacon
salt, pepper, butter, parsley,   paprika
   green onions

Clean and prepare the little birds as you would any other fowl. Dry and season with salt and pepper. In each bird place about ½ teaspoon butter, 1–2 sprigs parsley, and the white part of a green onion. Truss the birds and wrap each in a slice of bacon. Place in a roasting pan, sprinkle with paprika, and add water to almost cover them. Roast, uncovered, in a very hot oven (550°) for 10 minutes.

Remove from the pan. Take off the bacon and wipe the birds dry. Place in another pan side by side. Sprinkle with paprika and a little melted butter. Pour into the pan, but not over the birds, 1 cup of the liquid from the roasting pan. Roast in a 450° oven for about 30 minutes, basting frequently, until they are crisp and golden. Quickly remove and discard the vegetables from inside the birds. Serve the birds hot, without gravy, but with currant or cranberry jelly on the side.

BAKED RABBIT OR HARE (*Hasen Braten*)
SERVES 4–6

Since we're on the subject of game birds, I'll include here my favorite recipes for the game animal everyone says tastes like chicken, a domestic bird. You may not follow my Hungarian logic, but if you follow my Hungarian recipes, I think you'll agree that rabbit has a distinctive and fascinating flavor of its own and can be just as delicious as chicken.

I never bake the entire rabbit—only the back and legs. The rest of it is turned into *Hasenpfeffer* (see next recipe) a couple of days later.

saddle and back legs of 1 rabbit
  or hare
2 tablespoons salt
juice of 1 lemon or 2
  tablespoons vinegar
salt, pepper, paprika
½ cup water
1 stick butter

2 tablespoons white wine
1 clove garlic
½ onion
½ green pepper
1 pint sour cream, at least
1 tablespoon prepared mustard
1–2 anchovies, minced
½ teaspoon capers

Wash the meat carefully and remove all the skin, both inside and out. Soak for 1 hour in ice water with 2 tablespoons salt and the juice of 1 lemon or 2 tablespoons vinegar. Dry with paper towels and sprinkle all over with salt, pepper, and paprika. Place in a baking pan and pour ½ cup water into the pan. Add the butter, white wine, garlic, onion, and green pepper. Wrap the bony leg ends in foil and place the pan, uncovered, in a 450° oven. When the meat is lightly browned, pour the sour cream over it and continue cooking, basting frequently, until the meat is nicely browned.

Transfer the meat to a hot platter and keep warm while you make the gravy. Mix a few tablespoons of the pan drippings with the mustard, anchovies, and capers. Return to the pan and simmer, stirring, then taste for seasoning, adding a little more sour cream or lemon juice if it seems to need it. Serve the meat and gravy separately, with Bread Dumplings (see page 211).

HASENPFEFFER (*Rabbit or Hare Stew*)

SERVES 2–4

smaller and less meaty pieces
  of rabbit or hare
1 clove garlic, minced fine
1 onion, minced fine
1 carrot, minced fine
1 green pepper, minced fine
1 bay leaf

salt
5 peppercorns
½ teaspoon mustard seeds
vinegar and water
1 stick butter
1 cup sour cream or heavy cream
parsley for garnish

Clean and soak the rabbit pieces according to the directions in the preceding recipe and place in a bowl. Add the garlic, onion, carrot, green pepper, and seasonings. Cover with half vinegar and half water and refrigerate, covered, for 2 days.

Remove the meat from the marinade (reserving the marinade) and brown all over in the butter, turning often. Then add 1 cup of the strained marinade and continue cooking, basting frequently, for 1–1½ hours or until tender. If necessary, it can simmer gently until time for serving. Just before serving, stir in the cream, off the fire. Return to the stove to heat through, but do not boil. Serve very hot with Bread Dumplings (see page 211) and sprinkled with parsley.

6

EVERYMAN'S MEAT

Beef, Plain and Fancy

In civilizations throughout the ages, cattle have proven themselves the most useful animals on four legs! Milk, butter, cheeses, leather, and perhaps best of all, an enormous variety of delicious meats—all these products come from one marvelous animal.

My birthplace was once one of the major cattle-producing areas of Europe. (And the intrepid horsemen who rode the wide, grassy plains of Hungary told just as many tall tales as did the American cowboys.) The largest cattle-breeding country in the world is now in South America, but nowhere is beef finer than it is here in America.

It's so good that people don't like to meddle with it. And I agree that you can't do much to improve the best cuts of steaks and chops; light seasoning and careful broiling is all they really need. *But*—I don't believe in serving steaks and chops to groups larger than my family and maybe one or two guests, unless I'm presiding over a traditional Western barbecue. Serving steak to large groups is not only expensive, it's unimaginative. If you do, it won't help you earn a reputation as a great hostess, and it won't help you become a great cook. Even your family will tire of steak if you don't vary your beef menus with exciting and unusual dishes.

In my not-so-modest opinion, the beef recipes I'm going to give you are truly exciting and unusual. These Continental dishes —goulash, pot roast, roast beef in different styles, and many more—are my party-day and everyday favorites. In this chapter, too, you'll find recipes to make steak a little different (yes, you can even gild the lily a little), recipes for some of the most wonderful stews, and recipes using cuts of beef you've probably never used before. These recipes are the very best of the Continental way with beef, and that doesn't necessarily mean the most expensive, either. (Yes, even producers are conscious of a budget!)

We'll start with some practical information.

THE VARIOUS CUTS OF BEEF

ROASTS:

Standing Rib—a tender, juicy meat that should be well marbled with fat. The rib is not removed and there should be a layer of fat on the outer surfaces. *Cooking method:* roast.

Rolled Rib—the same cut as the standing rib, but with the rib removed and the meat rolled and tied. *Cooking method:* roast.

Chuck (bone in)—a juicy, well-flavored meat. Both the blade-bone pot roast and the arm-bone cut contain moderate amounts of fat. *Cooking method:* braise, which is the same as pot roasting.

Rump—triangular in shape, sold either with the bone or boneless. It is juicy, tender, and has a moderate amount of fat. *Cooking method:* braise.

STEAKS:

Club—cut from the rib end of the short loin. It is triangular in shape, smaller than a T-bone, and has little or no tenderloin. *Cooking method:* broil or pan-broil.

T-bone—adjoins the club steak, but is larger and includes some tenderloin. It is cut from the center section of the short loin and identified by its T-shaped bone. It should be well marbled with fat. *Cooking method:* broil or pan-broil.

Porterhouse—cut from the sirloin end of the short loin, the tenderest section of a side of beef. It is fine grained, well marbled with fat, and includes a large portion of tenderloin. *Cooking method:* broil or pan-broil.

Sirloin—cut from the loin end. Sirloin steaks vary in size, shape, and bone size. The wedge-bone steak is the largest. Others are the round-bone, pin-bone, and double-bone steaks. *Cooking method:* broil or pan-broil.

Round—cut from the leg. It is practically all lean meat, oval in shape, with a small, round bone. *Cooking method:* braise or grind for patties and loaves.

Chuck—cut from the shoulder section of the beef. Chuck comes in either round-bone or blade-bone steaks. The muscles are small and run in different directions. *Cooking method:* braise.

Flank—a lean, flat steak with no bone. There is only one to a side of beef. The meat fibers run lengthwise. *Cooking method:* score on both sides, stuff, and bake covered, or braise.

New York Cut Steak or Roast—a very juicy, fine meat cut from the loin. It is equally delicious as steak or roast. *Cooking method:* broil, pan-broil, or roast.

BUDGET CUTS:

Ground—ground beef may come from the chuck, shoulder, or flank. (I like my hamburgers of ground sirloin or round steak.) *Cooking method:* form into patties and broil or pan fry, or form into loaves and bake.

Stew—beef stew may be made of chuck, shank, flank, or brisket. (I use sirloin or rib steak for my stews.) *Cooking method:* simmer slowly and gently in water or other liquid, first browning the meat in fat.

Short Ribs—cuts from the ribs and plate. They contain layers of lean meat and fat with the fat rib bones. *Cooking method:* boil for soup or braise.

Brisket—layers of fat and lean beef with or without bone. *Cooking method:* braise, boil, or cure as corned beef. For corned beef, simmer slowly in water with vegetables and seasonings until tender.

Plate—layers of fat and lean beef with the end of the rib bones. *Cooking method:* braise or simmer slowly in water until done.

And now, on with the recipes. . . .

ROAST BEEF (*Savoy Hotel, London*)

SERVES 6-8

The roast beef of Olde England has been famous for centuries, and most justifiably so. At the very elegant Savoy Hotel in London they serve a superb roast of beef. And this is the way they do it.

3 rib "standing rib" roast or	1 onion, chopped
3–4 pounds sirloin, New	1 clove garlic, chopped
York cut or fillet	½ green pepper, chopped
3–4 slices bacon	1 tomato, chopped

Roast beef will never be any better than the meat itself, so tell your butcher you want the very best roast of whichever cut you choose. Prime grade meat is the top quality, but a *good* choice-grade cut can be almost as delicious.

Trim the excess fat from your roast and wipe the meat with a damp paper towel. Place 3–4 slices of bacon on the bottom of a roasting pan and put the roast on top of them.

Preheat the oven to 500° for 5 minutes, and while it heats, add the onion, garlic, green pepper, and tomato to the roasting pan. Slide the roast into the hot oven for 5–10 minutes, then lower the oven heat to 300°–350° and continue roasting, basting every 10 minutes, until the meat is done to your liking.

In a 300° oven: 15 minutes to the pound will give you rare meat.

18 minutes to the pound will give you medium-rare and medium meat.

20 minutes to the pound will give you well-done meat.

Serve with Yorkshire Pudding and Pan Gravy.

YORKSHIRE PUDDING (*To Accompany Roast Beef*)
SERVES 6–8

1 cup sifted flour	dash salt and white pepper
2 eggs, beaten	½ teaspoon baking powder
1 cup milk	¼ cup water

Mix all the ingredients and beat thoroughly with a rotary beater. When your roast is done, take it from the oven and let it "rest" under foil. This will distribute the juices and make the roast easier to carve. Turn the oven heat to 450° and strain ¼ cup of the fat from the bottom of the roasting pan into a heated heavy iron skillet. Pour the pudding batter *over* this fat and bake in the 450° oven for 25 minutes, or until nicely browned. Cut in wedges and serve in a separate dish with the roast beef.

PAN GRAVY FOR ROAST BEEF
SERVES 6–8

This is about as simple and delicious a gravy as possible. While the roast "rests" and the Yorkshire pudding bakes, put the roasting pan over a top burner on your stove. Add ½ cup water to it and bring to a boil. Continue boiling until the bubbles are gone. Then strain the contents of the roasting pan through a sieve, mashing the vegetables through with a wooden spoon. Reheat this gravy and serve in a sauce boat.

ROAST STUFFED FILET MIGNON À LA ROYALE

SERVES 6–10

A fillet is a noble dish by itself, roasted rare and served to beef lovers. This is an even more impressive dish, and I suggest that you serve it on an occasion when you want to offer the very best of food.

1 4- to 5-pound filet mignon	3 tablespoons cooked rice
½ pound fresh mushrooms	salt, pepper, paprika
1 clove garlic, minced	bacon strips
½ small onion, minced	2 tablespoons hot shortening
½ green pepper, minced	1 cup dry white wine
3 tablespoons minced parsley	1 cup water
3 tablespoons butter	

Cut a pocket in the side of the filet, but do not slash all the way through the meat.

Make a filling by sautéing the mushrooms, garlic, onion, green pepper, and parsley in the butter. Add the cooked rice, salt, pepper, and paprika to taste.

Fill the pocket in the filet with this stuffing. Fasten with toothpicks or small skewers. Salt and pepper the meat well and wrap in bacon strips. Place in a baking pan and pour the 2 tablespoons hot shortening over it. Pour into the pan, but not over the meat, the dry white wine. Bake in a 375° oven for about 1 hour, or until tender, basting frequently. Transfer to a hot platter and remove the toothpicks and bacon.

Make a gravy by adding 1 cup water to the pan, first removing some of the fat, if you think there is too much. Boil briskly, stirring to pick up pan juices and reduce to gravy consistency. Taste, correct the seasoning if necessary, and put through a strainer. Serve with the roast, in a sauce boat, with mashed potatoes on the side.

CHATEAUBRIAND
SERVES 4–8

This beautiful cut of meat is one of the most delicious, and needs only simple preparation. Marinate the meat at room temperature for several hours in 3 parts of oil to 1 part of wine vinegar, a few slices of green pepper, and a few slivers of garlic. Broil over coals. A 3-inch Chateaubriand weighing 3½–4 pounds should cook to succulent rareness in about 25 minutes over medium coals.

TOURNEDOS

Tournedos of beef are typical of continental cuisine, but Americans love them, too, as a change from the everlasting broiled steak. They are slices of beef tenderloin cut from the center of the heart of the tenderloin, and weigh about 4 ounces each. They are grilled or sautéed (rarely if ever broiled), served with sauce, and garnished with sautéed mushrooms, small glazed onions, brussels sprouts, artichoke bottoms, little browned new potatoes, or any delicate vegetable.

TOURNEDOS BÉARNAISE

1 tournedo per serving
butter
1 round of bread, fried in
  butter, per serving
1 large mushroom, or artichoke
  bottom, per serving

1 cup Béarnaise Sauce
  (see page 258)
½ cup tomato paste

Sauté the little steaks quickly in butter. Place each on a round of toast fried in butter and top with a mushroom or an artichoke bottom. Fill the mushroom or artichoke with Sauce Béarnaise mixed with tomato paste, and serve at once.

FLANK STEAK
SERVES 3–4

This is an inexpensive but delicious cut. Popularly known as London Broil, it is a real lifesaver when the budget gets low and yet you want to feed someone special with a hearty broiled steak. Try it sometime, too, for a steak-and-eggs breakfast—it's pretty sensational, in the best sense of the word.

1 flank steak	salt, pepper
butter	

Have the flank skinned but not scored by the butcher. Brush it with butter, salt, and pepper and broil for 3–4 minutes on each side to keep it rare and tender. Carve in very thin slices, cut diagonally.

MARINADE FOR STEAK

SERVES 6

3 tablespoons oil	1 tablespoon Worcestershire
1 tablespoon mustard	sauce
1 tablespoon catsup	dash cayenne pepper
1–2 cloves garlic, minced	dash white pepper
1 tablespoon vinegar	½ teaspoon salt

Mix these ingredients together thoroughly and brush the meat on all sides with the mixture. Let stand in the marinade from 2 hours to overnight.

Note: This is also a good marinade for a pot roast, if you want to add a little extra flavor.

PEPPER STEAK

SERVES 4

1½- to 2-pound sirloin steak	salt
½ teaspoon freshly ground	
black pepper	

Rub each side of the steak with the freshly ground pepper. Heat a heavy skillet and grease it lightly. Sear the steak until brown on one side, then turn and cook to desired rareness. Sprinkle with salt just before serving.

SWISS STEAK

SERVES 4–6

2 tablespoons flour
dash salt and pepper
2 pounds round or rump steak
3 tablespoons oil
1 #2 can tomatoes

1 teaspoon Worcestershire
  sauce
1 onion, chopped
1 green pepper, sliced in rings

Combine the flour, salt, and pepper. Pound it into the meat. Heat the oil in a Dutch oven and brown the meat on both sides. Add the rest of the ingredients, except the green pepper, and simmer very slowly for 2½–3 hours, or until the meat is tender. Add the green pepper rings and cook 10 minutes longer.

Remove the meat to a serving platter and keep hot in the oven. Strain the gravy, forcing the vegetables through the sieve. Reheat, correct the seasoning, and pour over the meat. Serve with rice, noodles, or potatoes.

STUFFED SIRLOIN STEAK

SERVES 4–6

2 1-pound sirloin steaks
2 green onions
1 clove garlic
½ pound ground pork leg or
  shoulder
salt, pepper, paprika,
  cayenne pepper
1 egg
3 tablespoons cooked rice

prepared mustard
4 hard-boiled eggs
½ carrot, chopped
2 stalks celery, chopped
½ green pepper, chopped
1 onion, chopped
2 tablespoons shortening
1 cup water, at least

Pound the sirloin steaks to flatten and tenderize them.

Mince the green onions and garlic and mix with the ground pork and a dash each of salt, pepper, paprika, and cayenne pepper. Add the raw egg and blend well, then add the rice and mix again. Spread a little bit of mustard on each steak. Divide the meat mixture between them and spread it on each steak over the mustard. On top of the meat mixture place 2 peeled hard-boiled eggs. Roll up the steaks over the stuffing and eggs and fasten with skewers.

Sauté the carrot, celery, green pepper, and onion in the shortening until limp. Sprinkle with the paprika. Add the meat and brown. Then pour in the 1 cup water and cook slowly until tender, about 2 hours. If necessary, add a little more water from time to time.

Transfer the steaks to a hot serving platter. Remove the skewers and slice. Put the gravy and vegetables through a sieve, reheat, and pour over the meat. Serve very hot.

MINUTE STEAKS IN CASSEROLE
SERVES 4–6

6 minute steaks
3 tablespoons flour
salt, pepper, paprika to taste
3 tablespoons shortening
6 small cooked potatoes
1 package frozen peas and
   carrots

1 small onion
1 clove garlic, minced
1 1/2-pound can stewed
   tomatoes

Cut the meat into slices 1 inch thick. Mix the flour and seasonings. Toss over the meat and turn until the meat is well coated. Brown the meat slices in the shortening. Add the remaining ingredients and cover. Simmer for 15 minutes. Serve in the sauce.

HUNGARIAN RIB STEAK WITH POTATOES
(*Lábasos Rostélyos*)
SERVES 4–6

6 thinly sliced rib steaks
salt, pepper
2 medium tomatoes
1 large onion
1 green pepper

2–3 tablespoons shortening
1 tablespoon paprika
2 cups tepid water
4 potatoes
green pepper rings for garnish

Trim the excess fat from the rib steaks. Pound them and season with salt and pepper.

Peel the tomatoes and remove seeds. Cut the tomatoes into thin slices. Slice the onion and green pepper.

Heat the shortening and sauté the steaks lightly on both sides. Add the sliced vegetables and continue cooking for about 10 minutes, or until the vegetables are soft. Remove from the heat and stir the paprika into the fat. Add 1 cup tepid water, cover, and simmer over low heat until the meat is tender, about ½ hour.

Peel the potatoes and slice lengthwise into 4–6 slices each. Place the slices under the meat. Add 1 cup water (or more, if the dish seems dry) and continue cooking until the potatoes are tender, about 15–20 minutes. Taste and correct the seasoning.

Serve on a long meat platter with the meat on top of the potatoes and pour the gravy over the meat. Garnish with thin green pepper rings.

POT ROAST À LA DANIELI
SERVES 6–8

When a man has been promised twenty-four hours in the life of one of the world's most glamorous women, it can give him the headiest of feelings. Some years ago, when Marlene Dietrich had been labeled "box-office poison" and had virtually retired in France, I coaxed her back to Hollywood to make *Destry Rides Again*, the picture that began a great career anew. While we were making the picture, Dietrich, wonderful woman that she is, offered to spend twenty-four hours with me if the picture was successful. I could only dream of that promise until one romantic night in Venice . . .

(But here let me digress. This fabulous woman, who looks like moonbeams and starshine, is an equally fabulous cook—which should certainly inspire some of the women who think that cooking is not glamorous. We did a lot of cooking together when we made *Destry*. She became known as the "Best Pot Roast Cooker" and I was known as the "Best Chicken Paprika Cooker," so, of course, we eventually traded recipes, as all good cooks do.)

And now to return to my story. One year when I went to the

Venice Film Festival, I stayed at the beautiful Royal Danieli in Venice, one of the world's most romantic hotels. When I checked in, I found an invitation waiting for me, an invitation to dine with Dietrich! She greeted me at the door of her suite, looking more beautiful than I had ever seen her, and said she'd been waiting for me—anxiously, eagerly, impatiently. . . .

Oh, well, you can't have everything. She'd been waiting for me to taste the Danieli's pot roast!

1 4- to 5-pound sirloin or rump roast	1 small bay leaf
flour, salt, pepper	dash rosemary
6 tablespoons shortening	2 cups white wine
4 slices bacon	2 cups water
1 onion, minced	1 tablespoon minced parsley
2 cloves garlic, minced	1 teaspoon flour or bread crumbs
½ cup tomato puree	½ cup cognac

Dredge the meat in flour, salt, and pepper. Heat the shortening in a roasting pan and sear the meat on all sides. Cover the meat with the bacon. Add the onion, garlic, tomato puree, bay leaf, rosemary, wine, parsley, and 1 cup water. Cover the pan and bake in a 350° oven for 3–4 hours, basting frequently.

When the meat is tender, remove it so that you can make a pan gravy, and keep it warm in the oven. Scrape the sides of the pan and add the teaspoon of flour or bread crumbs and 1 cup water. Simmer, stirring, on top of the stove until reduced by half. Put the gravy and vegetables through a sieve (or blend in an electric blender) and place in a saucepan. Add the cognac and simmer to heat through.

Slice the meat thin, diagonally across the grain. Place on a heated platter and pour the hot gravy over. Serve at once.

POT ROAST (*with Gravy or Cream Sauce*)
SERVES 8–10

This is my recipe, but I don't mind admitting that I learned a few things about cooking it from Marlene.

3–4 pounds pot roast
  (shoulder, chuck, blade,
  or rump)
salt, pepper
2 tablespoons shortening
1 clove garlic
1 onion

1 carrot
2 stalks celery
1 tomato
1 green pepper
1 10½-ounce can bouillon
½ cup white wine
water, if needed

For the Gravy:
1 tablespoon flour
1 cup water or dry white wine

3–4 tablespoons heavy cream
  or sour cream (optional)

Remove excess fat and bone from the meat. Wipe with a damp paper towel. Season with salt and pepper. Melt the shortening in a heavy iron pot or Dutch oven and sear the meat on all sides until lightly browned. Add the vegetables, bouillon, and white wine and cover tightly. Reduce the heat and simmer very slowly for 2½–3 hours, basting frequently. Add a little water, if necessary (I prefer warm water, not from the tap). You must pour the water under the meat, never over it. When the pot roast is tender, remove to a hot platter and keep warm in a slow oven.

Now make the gravy. Skim excess fat from the liquid and vegetables in the pan. Add the flour and stir well. Add 1 cup water or dry white wine and cook until the liquid is reduced by half. Put the mixture through a sieve, pressing the vegetables through (or use an electric blender), and transfer to a saucepan. Taste for seasoning, and if the gravy is too thick, add a little more water. Heat well and serve with the pot roast, in a gravy boat. Just before serving, you can stir in heavy cream or sour cream to make a cream sauce—with or without, it's delicious!

BEEF STROGANOFF

SERVES 4–6

So many American youngsters seem to grow up on hamburgers and hot dogs that if they even see anything else, they automatically don't like it. I often used to cook in the home of a producer friend who always had lots of the younger actors and actresses around. One beautiful young blonde actress in particular was always saying, "I don't like it," about my dishes without even trying them.

So I made the same deal with her that I often make with my three sons to get them interested in food.

"Just taste it," I said. "And if you don't like it, I'll cook what you do like tomorrow."

So Gloria de Haven tasted my Beef Stroganoff.

"Shall I lie?" she asked me, and then she smiled. "Oooh, I *do* like it!"

And the dish I had to cook the next day was Beef Stroganoff.

This is a technique that has always worked very well for me. So if your kids (or your friends) want the same old things all the time, tell them, "Just taste it! Please, just taste it!" Then watch their surprise when they find they *do* like it!

2–3 pounds fillet of beef
3 tablespoons flour
salt, pepper, cayenne pepper, paprika
6 tablespoons butter
1 cup finely chopped onion
2 cloves garlic, minced
1 pound mushrooms, sliced

1 cup beef bouillon
2 tablespoons tomato paste
1 teaspoon Worcestershire sauce
¼–½ cup sour cream
½ cup fresh heavy cream
1 teaspoon prepared mustard

Cut the meat into thin strips, 2 inches long and ½ inch thick. Mix together the flour, salt, pepper, dash cayenne pepper, and a little paprika in a paper bag. Shake the meat in the bag to coat on all sides.

Melt the butter in a skillet. Add the onion, garlic, and mushrooms and sauté until the onion is translucent. Remove to a saucepan, leaving as much butter as possible in the skillet. Now sauté the meat strips, browning them lightly but leaving them pink in the center. Remove the meat and replace the vegetables. Add the bouillon, tomato paste, and Worcestershire sauce and stir well. Now add the meat and bring to a boil. Reduce the heat and add the sour cream, heavy cream, and mustard. Do *not* allow it to boil now, but heat through gently. Serve with buttered noodles or rice.

PAPRIKA CREAM SCHNITZEL
SERVES 4-6

3 tablespoons shortening
2 pounds sliced sirloin of
   beef (or veal)
2 tablespoons minced onion
6 slices bacon, diced

salt, pepper, paprika to taste
½ cup tomato sauce
1 cup sour cream
parsley or green pepper rings
   for garnish

Heat the shortening and sauté the meat until well browned and tender. Transfer to a hot platter and keep warm.

Add the onion and diced bacon to the skillet and simmer for 5 minutes. Add the seasonings, tomato sauce, and sour cream and continue to simmer very gently for 15 minutes. Serve the gravy over the meat and garnish with minced parsley or green pepper rings.

HUNGARIAN GOULASH (*Gulyás*)
SERVES 6-8

The best customer I have ever had is a man with an appetite as big as he is and a personality as warm and wonderful as his voice. Lauritz Melchior, the incomparable Wagnerian tenor, is every cook's dream, a gourmet who loves everything I cook. But choosing what to cook for him is a dilemma as well as a delight. Whenever I'm in doubt about what to feed him, I make Hungarian goulash, since he enjoys it above all else. And there could be no better reward than the song he sings for me in appreciation.

If you like happy people singing in your house, try this goulash on your friends and see if you get the same results I did with Melchior. No guarantee, you understand, but if they like good food, who knows?

I serve this as a one-dish meal since it is like a very hearty soup, needing only a dessert and good hot coffee to make a complete dinner.

1 2- to 3-pound rib roast or
   similar cut
2–3 pieces marrow or
   shinbones
2 quarts cold water

12 peppercorns
1 clove garlic
1 onion
few sprigs parsley
1 carrot

½ parsnip
1 green pepper
1 tomato
3–4 stalks celery, diced

dash caraway seed
2 tablespoons shortening
1 tablespoon paprika
3–4 potatoes

Wash the meat and dry it. Cut the meat into 1-inch dice, dry them, and set aside. Dice the vegetables.

Put the bone remaining from the roast and the marrow or shinbones in a large soup kettle with the 2 quarts cold water, the peppercorns, garlic, onion, parsley, carrot, parsnip, green pepper, tomato, celery, salt, and caraway seed. Bring to a boil and let simmer while you sauté the diced meat in the shortening.

When the meat is brown, remove the pan from the heat and sprinkle with paprika. Remove the bones and vegetables from the kettle and strain the broth. Combine the meat, vegetables, and strained liquid. Simmer slowly for 1½ hours, or until the meat is tender. While this cooks, peel and dice the potatoes. When the meat is almost tender, add the potatoes and cook for 20 minutes longer.

When everything is done, taste for seasoning and serve very hot in soup plates, accompanied by fresh rye bread.

HUNGARIAN BEEF PAPRIKASH

SERVES 6–8

Not too many Americans know that paprika ranges in strength and taste from very sweet to very hot. What we usually find in our markets is a mild, sweetish paprika. Beef *paprikash* is supposed to be highly spiced, but I prefer to mix the sweet paprika with the hot (which you can purchase in gourmet shops) for a more delicate flavor. While this Hungarian dish is made in various ways, epicures agree that this version is the best.

3 pounds rump or sirloin tip
3 tablespoons shortening
1 large onion, minced
1 clove garlic, minced
1 tomato, peeled and minced
1 green pepper, peeled and
  minced

water, if needed
1 tablespoon paprika
salt, pepper, if needed
green pepper rings
  for garnish

Trim the excess fat from the meat. Wipe with a damp paper towel and dice the meat in 1½-inch pieces. Sear them on all sides in the shortening. Add the minced vegetables and cover. Cook slowly for 2 hours, adding ½ cup water if necessary to prevent sticking and burning. When almost done, remove from the heat and stir in the paprika. Continue cooking slowly, adding a little more water if necessary to make plenty of gravy. When the meat is tender, taste and add salt and pepper if needed. Garnish with green pepper rings and serve very hot with Egg Barley (see page 213), rice, potatoes, or noodles (see Noodle Dough, page 57).

HUNGARIAN BEEF STEW

SERVES 6

2 pounds sirloin tip, cut in
   1-inch slices
¼ cup flour mixed with salt,
   pepper, paprika
1 cup minced green pepper
½ cup minced onion

2 tablespoons butter
1 quart beef soup stock (see
   page 44), water, or broth
2 cups sour cream
green pepper rings or parsley
   for garnish (optional)

Dredge the meat in the seasoned flour and sauté, with the vegetables, in butter until browned. Add the soup stock and simmer slowly until tender, about 1 hour. Fifteen minutes before serving, whip the sour cream until smooth. Remove the pot from the stove and carefully stir in the sour cream. Heat gently, but do not boil, until heated through. Serve very hot with noodles or potatoes. Garnish with green pepper rings or parsley for color, if you like. (You can also serve this stew without the sour cream, as I often do.)

BEEF ROULADES IN RED WINE

SERVES 6

1 2-pound slice of sirloin
salt, pepper, paprika

1 pound pork shoulder
1 anchovy, mashed

3–4 capers
½ teaspoon minced onion
flour
2 tablespoons shortening
1 cup dry red wine

1 8-ounce can tomato sauce
½ teaspoon bread crumbs
1 cup water
2 tablespoons sour cream or
heavy cream (optional)

Cut the sirloin into 6 slices of equal size and pound them out as thin as possible between pieces of waxed paper. Season with salt, pepper, and paprika.

Grind the pork shoulder and mix well with the anchovy, capers, and onion. Using a spatula, spread each piece of sirloin evenly with the mixture. Roll the pieces up and fasten with skewers or toothpicks. Dredge lightly with flour and brown on all sides in the shortening in a hot skillet. Transfer to a Dutch oven or casserole.

In the skillet drippings heat the red wine and the tomato sauce. Mix well and then pour over the roulades. Cover and cook on the top of the stove over low heat until tender, basting frequently. This will take about 2½ hours.

When done, transfer the roulades to a hot platter. Make a gravy in the casserole by adding the bread crumbs and browning for a minute, then adding 1 cup water. Continue cooking until the liquid is reduced by half, then put the gravy through a fine sieve. If you like a thicker gravy, add 2 tablespoons of sour or heavy cream and heat through. Pour over the roulades and serve hot.

BEEF BRISKET À LA VIENNA

SERVES 6–8

Brisket is a cut of beef too little known in America except as corned beef. But this baked brisket, which was a specialty of the very elegant Grand Hotel in Vienna, is an elegant dish indeed. In fact, the eating of beef was a fine art in Vienna at one time. One restaurant served twenty-four different and distinct cuts of *boiled* beef alone, which should give you some idea of how much variety can be created in a gourmet's world.

3–4 pounds beef brisket	1 fresh tomato
salt, pepper, paprika, cayenne	½ carrot
pepper	2–3 stalks celery
1 large onion	3–4 slices bacon
2 cloves garlic	3 tablespoons shortening
1 green pepper	1 cup water

Remove the excess fat and skin from the brisket. Season the meat with salt, pepper, paprika, and cayenne pepper. Place in a roasting pan and add the vegetables and bacon.

Heat the shortening and pour it on top of the meat to sear it. Pour 1 cup water under the meat. Cover and bake in a 350° oven for 2 hours.

Remove the cover and continue baking until tender, basting frequently. It will require at least 3 hours, or more, depending on size.

When it is done, remove to a hot platter and make a pan gravy by putting the liquid and gravy remaining in the pan through a fine strainer, forcing the vegetables through as well (or blend in an electric blender). Serve the meat in thin slices and the sauce in a separate boat.

STEFANIA ROAST

SERVES 6–8

1 pound each ground pork,	dash ginger
veal, and beef	2 pearl onions, minced
minced fresh parsley	1 small clove garlic, crushed
1 teaspoon salt	3 hard-boiled eggs
¼ teaspoon white pepper	melted butter
¼ teaspoon paprika	1 egg, beaten
dash thyme	

Mix the ground meats with the seasonings, reserving the parsley.

On a board, flatten the mixed ground meats into an oblong and sprinkle with minced fresh parsley. Dip the peeled, hard-boiled eggs in melted butter and place them lengthwise in the center of the ground meat. Shape the meat over and around them into a loaf and place in a baking pan. Brush the loaf with beaten egg and pour about 2 tablespoons hot shortening over it. Sprinkle with paprika. Bake in a preheated 375° oven, basting frequently, for 1 hour. Brush again with beaten egg and reduce the oven heat to 350°. Bake for 1 hour longer, or until nicely browned on top.

Serve hot or cold, but always in very thin slices. If you are serving it hot, remove the loaf to a hot platter to keep warm and make this pan gravy.

2 tablespoons hot shortening	1 slice green pepper
paprika	1 cup water

Put the baking pan on top of the stove and add 1 slice of green pepper and 1 cup water. Boil briskly, stirring constantly, until the liquid is reduced by half. Taste, add seasoning if necessary, and strain. Do *not* pour it over the loaf; serve separately in a gravy boat.

GROUND BEEF PERIGNEAUX

SERVES 4

1 pound ground beef	2 eggs
½ cup chopped parsley	salt, pepper, paprika
½ cup chopped onion	1 cup fine bread crumbs
3 tablespoons grated Parmesan cheese	oil or fat for deep frying

Mix all the ingredients except the oil and bread crumbs and shape into patties or balls. Roll in bread crumbs and chill for 1–2 hours. Heat the oil and fry the patties or balls until golden on all sides. Drain on absorbent paper. These can be done half an hour ahead of serving and kept hot in the oven after cooking.

BURGUNDY SPINACH BURGERS

SERVES 4–6

1 package frozen leaf spinach	½ cup Burgundy
2 pounds ground round steak	½ cup grated Parmesan cheese

2 tablespoons finely chopped
  onion
1 clove garlic, minced
1 tablespoon minced green
  pepper

1 tablespoon minced parsley
1 teaspoon salt
½ teaspoon pepper

Cook the spinach according to package directions. Drain thoroughly and chop or grind. Mix in the remaining ingredients and blend well. Shape into patties and broil or pan fry. (These are delicious done over charcoal.) Approximately 6 minutes on each side should be about right for 1-inch thick patties. Serve with the usual relishes for burgers.

DUTCH HASH
SERVES 4–6

1 medium-size eggplant
salt
1 large onion, chopped
1 tablespoon butter, at least

1 pound ground beef
salt, pepper to taste
3–4 tomatoes, sliced
grated Parmesan cheese

Wash the eggplant and slice into ½-inch slices. Sprinkle with salt and set aside.

Sauté the onion in butter until tender. Add the ground beef and continue to sauté until the meat is browned. Add salt and pepper to taste.

Sauté the eggplant slices in additional butter until golden on both sides. Line the bottom of a 3- or 4-quart casserole with a layer of eggplant slices. Add a layer of meat and then one of sliced tomatoes. Finish the casserole with a final layer of eggplant and sprinkle generously with the cheese. Cover with aluminum foil and bake for 1 hour in a 350° oven. Uncover and bake 5 minutes more before serving.

7

FROM SCHNITZEL TO SHISH KEBAB

Veal, Pork, Ham, Lamb

Veal is a delicate, tender, and flavorful meat, highly prized throughout Europe but not, alas, throughout America. In the splendidly gastronomical city that was Vienna before the war, the average citizen would have been just as unhappy without his schnitzel as the average American would be without his steak. "Schnitzel" literally means "little cut," but in Vienna it means a little slice of veal, carefully selected, pounded thin, cooked with one of a variety of delectable sauces, and served with attractive garnishes.

But there is more to veal than Wiener schnitzel. The same little cuts used for schnitzel are used for Italian *scallopini* and dishes from other continental cuisines. Then there are a myriad of delicious dishes in which other cuts of veal are used.

Veal is baby beef, and it lacks the marbling of fat that occurs in mature animals. It needs gentle cooking, and when roasted needs constant basting to keep it juicy and tender. It should never be broiled, because the strong flavor imposed by broiling would overpower its delicacy.

Now I will give you a good-food lover's tour of the world of continental veal cookery. Let's begin with my three favorite schnitzels.

NATUR SCHNITZEL

SERVES 4–6

2 pounds veal steak, cut thin
    and pounded even thinner
salt, pepper, paprika, cayenne
    pepper, flour

4 ounces butter
½ cup water
1 slice green pepper

Most butchers will pound the veal thin for you, but if yours won't you can do it at home. Put the veal between two pieces of waxed paper and pound with a meat mallet or even a heavy saucepan. The schnitzels should be about ⅛ inch thick after pounding.

Cut off the excess fat and skin. Season with salt, pepper, paprika, and cayenne pepper, and dust lightly with flour.

Heat the butter in a skillet. Sauté the schnitzels for 3–4 minutes on each side, until golden brown, and remove to a hot platter. The schnitzels should be almost as thin and delicate as autumn leaves, and when cooked to perfection are the same beautiful golden color.

Make a gravy by adding the ½ cup water and slice of green pepper to the skillet. Cook, stirring, until reduced and slightly thickened, then strain over the schnitzels.

WIENER SCHNITZEL À LA SACHER

SERVES 6–8

The restaurant in the Hotel Sacher was for many years one of Vienna's most glamorous, no small accomplishment in a city of gourmets and good living. The Wiener Schnitzel à la Sacher became world famous—and quite deservedly so, as you'll see when you try it.

2 pounds veal steak, pounded
   very thin into schnitzels
salt, pepper, paprika, flour
2 eggs, beaten

fine fresh bread crumbs
fat for deep frying
lemon wedges for garnish

The schnitzels should be about ⅛ inch thick. Cut off their outside fat and skin, and season them lightly with salt, pepper, and paprika. Dip them in flour on both sides, then in beaten egg, and finally into fine bread crumbs, pressing the coating in well with the heel of your hand.

In a large skillet heat fat about ¼ inch deep. Fry the coated schnitzels in the fat. While frying the first side, cover the pan. Uncover, turn, and fry the second side until crisp and golden. Remove to absorbent paper to drain. Serve hot with quartered lemon wedges. A crisp salad, French fried potatoes, and peas or asparagus are good side dishes.

SCHNITZEL À LA BUDAPEST
SERVES 6

In the early 1930's I loved Budapest, a city full of gypsy music, love, laughter—and other Hungarians, who worked in my pictures, amused me, entertained me, kept me up all night, and borrowed money from me in an endless variety of irresistible ways. This recipe will always remind me, very happily, of those days and those friends.

6 veal slices, pounded thin
salt, pepper, paprika, cayenne
  pepper, flour
butter
1 tablespoon finely minced
  onion
½ pound mushrooms, minced
  or sliced

1 tablespoon catsup
1 cup chicken broth
¼ cup sherry
finely minced parsley for
  garnish

Season the schnitzels with salt, pepper, paprika, and cayenne pepper, and dredge lightly with flour. Brown them gently in butter over moderate heat, until golden on each side. Add the rest of the ingredients, except the parsley, and cover. Simmer for 15 minutes, or until the veal is tender. Remove the schnitzels and keep warm.

To make a gravy, thicken the pan liquid with about 1 tablespoon flour. Boil, stirring constantly, until slightly reduced, and pour over the meat. Sprinkle with parsley and paprika before serving.

VEAL PAPRIKASH
SERVES 4–6

Life for my Hungarian friends in Budapest was always one long struggle to avoid work. Ideally, they rose around five in the afternoon and went to bed in the early morning, when the cafés were at long last closed. But I had to make pictures, which meant shooting from nine in the morning to six in the evening. Their habits combined with my schedules made for the sleepiest collection of actors and technicians ever assembled. Getting home in the pale dawn, they'd bathe and change, swear long and bitterly at me, and come to work when all sensible people of their world were just going to bed.

If I was going to get my work done, I could accept no excuses nor make any exceptions, not even for the men suffering from overindulgence in an especially delicious *paprikash*.

Nowadays, I never make a *paprikash* without thinking of those days, and what fun they were. I hope that this simple but delicately flavored *paprikash* will convey to you some of the magic of the Budapest I remember.

2 pounds veal shoulder
2 tablespoons shortening
1 large onion, chopped
¼ clove garlic
¼ green pepper, chopped

1 fresh tomato, chopped
salt, pepper, paprika to taste
1 cup water
green pepper rings for garnish

Cut the meat into 1-inch cubes. Sauté in the shortening over low heat with the chopped onion, garlic, and green pepper for 5 minutes. Add the tomato and the seasonings, then stir in the 1 cup water. Cover and continue cooking gently until the meat is tender, about 1 hour. If you want more gravy, add a little more water as it cooks. Serve garnished with green pepper rings.

VEAL STROGANOFF
SERVES 4–6

2 pounds boneless veal
3 tablespoons flour
½ teaspoon salt
¼ teaspoon paprika
dash cayenne pepper
4 tablespoons butter
1 clove garlic, minced
½ pound fresh mushrooms, sliced
1–2 dried mushrooms

2 tablespoons tomato paste
½ tablespoon Worcestershire sauce
¼ teaspoon mustard
2 tablespoons lemon juice
1 cup water
1 cup sour cream
½ cup sherry or Marsala
minced parsley for garnish

Cut the veal into thin slices. Mix together the flour, salt, paprika, and cayenne pepper and coat the meat well. Melt the butter in a skillet and add the garlic. Brown the coated meat, then add both the sliced and the dried mushrooms and continue to sauté gently.

In a small bowl, blend the tomato paste, Worcestershire sauce, mustard, and lemon juice with the 1 cup water. Add to the meat and cover. Continue to simmer until the meat is tender, stirring frequently. This will take about 1 hour. Mix the sour cream with the wine. Remove the skillet from the stove and stir in the sour cream mixture. Return to a very gentle heat but do not allow to boil. Heat through and serve sprinkled with minced parsley.

VEAL À LA RUSSE
SERVES 8–10

I couldn't say whether this is an authentic Russian dish or not, but it is one of the best veal dishes I have ever eaten. It was served to me twenty years ago at the Hôtel de Paris in Monte Carlo, and I can still remember the thrill of that first wonderful taste! Luckily, I did get the chef to give me the recipe. Since then I have served it many, many times, always to the kind of acclaim I sometimes wish I could get from a preview audience at one of my new movies.

1 4- to 5-pound fillet of veal	1 tomato
salt, pepper, paprika,	1 cup white wine
dash cayenne pepper	2 cloves garlic, minced
pinch rosemary	1 10½-ounce can chicken broth
8 slices bacon	or 1¼ cups veal broth
1 onion	1 teaspoon flour or bread
1 green pepper	crumbs

Wash and dry the fillet. Season it all over with salt, pepper, paprika, a dash of cayenne pepper, and a pinch of rosemary.

Lard it with the bacon. (Larding may take a little explanation. Butchers use a larding needle to insert thin strips of fat into "dry" roasts, or to give extra flavor. If your butcher looks baffled when you ask him to lard the fillet with bacon, you can do much the same job at home with a very thin, sharp knife, a skewer, and a little ingenuity. Cut the bacon into thin strips. Poke a long hole in the fillet and force a thin strip of bacon into the meat with the skewer. Do this over all the fillet until the bacon is used up.)

Place your roast in a large roasting pan with a lid. Put the onion, green pepper, and tomato on a skewer and stab it into the roast. Around the roast pour the white wine, mixed with the minced garlic, and the chicken or veal broth.

Bake, covered, in a 375° oven for 2 hours. Uncover and baste every 15 minutes, increasing the oven heat to 450°, until the roast is golden brown and tender, about another 30 minutes.

Transfer to a serving platter and keep warm in a slow oven. To make a gravy, skim the excess fat from the roasting pan. Place the pan on top of the stove, add the flour or bread crumbs to the pan and cook, stirring, until reduced to the proper consistency. Put through a fine sieve, forcing the vegetables from the skewer through, too. Reheat and serve in a gravy boat, to be poured over the thin-sliced roast.

VEAL ROAST HUNGARIAN STYLE
SERVES 8–10

The best cuts for roasting are the leg, rib, rib with kidney left in, or shoulder, all of which cook up to a golden deliciousness when prepared this way.

4–5 pounds veal for roasting	2–3 tablespoons sour cream
2 tablespoons salt	3 tablespoons shortening
3 tablespoons vinegar	2 cloves garlic
salt, pepper, paprika, cayenne	1 onion
pepper, thyme	1 tomato
3–4 slices bacon	1 green pepper

Soak the meat in water with the vinegar and 2 tablespoons salt for ½ hour. After soaking, cut off any excess fat or skin and dry with paper towels.

Season the meat with salt, pepper, paprika, cayenne pepper, and thyme. Place in a roasting pan and lay the bacon over it, then spread with the sour cream. Heat the shortening and pour over, then sprinkle with paprika. In the pan, put the garlic, onion, tomato, and green pepper. Cover and roast in a 375° oven for 1–1½ hours. Uncover, increase the oven temperature to 450°, and continue baking for about 30 minutes, or until golden brown.

Serve with pan gravy, either plain or with cream added, as directed in the other roast recipes (see page 132).

VEAL SCALLOPINI
SERVES 4–6

1 teaspoon salt	6 veal slices or cutlets
pepper to taste	½ cup flour
1 teaspoon paprika	1 stick butter
dash nutmeg	1 medium onion, minced
1 tablespoon lemon juice	1 green pepper, minced
¼ teaspoon dry mustard	½ pound mushrooms, sliced
1 clove garlic	1 10½-ounce can chicken broth

Combine the salt, pepper, paprika, nutmeg, lemon juice, mustard, and garlic and blend well. Place the meat flat in a baking pan and pour the mixture over it. Turn the pieces to coat thoroughly and let stand for 15 minutes, then remove the garlic.

Lift the slices from the sauce, dredge in flour, and brown well in heated butter in a skillet. To the sauce, add the onion, green pepper, mushrooms, and chicken broth. Replace the meat in the pan, cover, and cook slowly for 40–50 minutes, or until the meat is tender.

PAPRIKA VEAL STEAK
SERVES 6–8

2–3 pounds veal steak, or sirloin, shoulder, or ribs	½ green pepper, minced
½ cup flour	1 tomato, peeled and chopped
1 stick butter	1 cup water
1 onion, minced	salt, pepper, paprika
1 clove garlic, minced	green pepper rings for garnish

Wash the meat in ice water, dry, and cut into slices. Coat the slices lightly with flour and sauté for 5 minutes in butter. Add the onion, garlic, green pepper, and tomato and sauté lightly. Then add the water and salt, pepper, and paprika to taste. Cover and cook over low heat for 30–40 minutes, or until the meat is tender. Taste and correct the seasonings, adding more water if necessary to make more gravy. Transfer the meat to a hot platter, strain the gravy over it, and serve garnished with green pepper rings.

VEAL ROULADES
SERVES 8–12

12 thin slices of veal steak	½ teaspoon salt
½ pound ground pork	⅛ teaspoon pepper
1 egg	paprika
½ cup finely cut onion,	½ cup butter or shortening
sautéed in butter	½ cup finely minced raw onion
½ cup finely cut mushrooms,	½ cup finely minced green
sautéed in butter	pepper
1 tomato, chopped	½ cup white wine
¼ teaspoon oregano	1 cup chicken or veal broth

Pound the veal slices thin. Blend the ground pork with the egg, sautéed onion, half of the sautéed mushrooms, tomato, oregano, salt, pepper, and paprika. Put a spoonful of the mixture on each slice of meat, roll up and fasten with skewers or toothpicks.

Heat the butter or shortening in a casserole and brown the rolls on all sides for a few minutes. Add the rest of the ingredients and remaining mushrooms, cover and simmer slowly for 1 hour, or until very tender. Transfer the rolls to a hot platter and pour the pan gravy over. Serve with buttered noodles.

VEAL BIRDS
SERVES 8

2 pounds veal steak	16 slices crisp fried bacon
salt, pepper, paprika	or 8 slices ham

8 anchovy fillets
8 hard-boiled eggs
8 thin slices pickle
½ cup butter or shortening
1 medium onion, minced
1 clove garlic
1 green pepper, minced

1 tomato, chopped
1 cup water
1 cup sour cream
¼ cup Marsala
minced parsley or chives for
garnish

Cut the veal into 8 pieces about ½ inch thick. Season with salt, pepper, and paprika. On each piece put 2 slices crisp bacon or 1 slice ham, 1 anchovy fillet, 1 hard-boiled egg, and a thin slice of pickle. Roll up and fasten with skewers or toothpicks.

Brown the rolls in the butter or shortening in a casserole. Add the onion, garlic, green pepper, tomato, and water. Cover and continue cooking for about 1 hour, or until the meat is tender.

Remove the rolls to a saucepan. Put the pan gravy through a fine sieve, forcing the vegetables through, or blend in an electric blender. Mix with the sour cream and Marsala and heat. Pour over the meat and cook, but do not boil, for another 10 minutes. Serve sprinkled with minced parsley or chives, and then with paprika.

STUFFED VEAL BREAST (*Töltött Borjúmell*)

SERVES 6–8

This is an excellent example of what I mean when I say that good food is not necessarily expensive. Breast of veal costs very little as a rule, and this way of cooking it results in a most delicious and unusual dish.

1 2- to 3-pound veal breast
3 tablespoons vinegar
2 tablespoons salt
4–6 slices white bread
milk or water
½ stick butter
3 eggs, separated
¼ teaspoon ginger
¼ teaspoon pepper
dash thyme

dash cayenne pepper
dash paprika
½ teaspoon salt
white part of 2 green onions,
minced
1 clove garlic, minced
3 tablespoons minced parsley
3–4 tablespoons shortening
¼ cup water

Have the butcher make a pocket in the veal breast. Remove any excess fat and skin. Soak for at least 1 hour in ice water with 2 tablespoons of the vinegar and 2 tablespoons salt. Rinse and wipe dry.

(Before you make the stuffing, see the note on page 99.)

While the meat is soaking, trim the crusts from the bread slices and put them to soak in a little milk or water.

Mix the butter with the egg yolks, ginger, pepper, thyme, cayenne pepper, paprika, ½ teaspoon salt, minced onion, garlic, and parsley. Then squeeze the liquid out of the bread and add that, blending the whole together well. Beat the egg whites and fold them into the mixture. Stuff the pocket of the veal with the mixture and sew or fasten with skewers to prevent the stuffing from leaking out.

Place the stuffed breast in a large baking pan. Heat the 3–4 tablespoons shortening and pour over the roast and sprinkle with paprika. Cover and roast in a 350° oven for 1½ hours, basting often. Uncover and sprinkle with 1 tablespoon vinegar mixed with ¼ cup water. Increase the oven heat to 450°–500° and continue cooking and basting for another 1½ hours, or until golden brown.

Remove roast to a warm plater and take out the skewers or string. Keep warm while you make a pan gravy, as directed for the other roasts (e.g., see page 132). Serve everything very hot, with the gravy on the side in a gravy boat.

JELLIED VEAL LOAF
SERVES 4–6

1 veal knuckle	1 carrot
1 pound veal shank meat, diced	1 tablespoon Worcestershire
1 onion, sliced	sauce
1 clove garlic	1 teaspoon salt
6 black peppercorns	dash cayenne pepper
½ bay leaf	1 envelope unflavored gelatin
4 sprigs parsley, minced	3 hard-boiled eggs, sliced
½ green pepper	1 pickle, sliced thin
1 tomato	lettuce

Ask the butcher to crack the knuckle into four or five pieces. Place the bones, the meat, and all the vegetables and seasonings in a large kettle and cover with water. Bring to a boil, reduce the heat, and simmer for 2 hours.

Remove the meat and chop very fine. Strain the broth and discard the vegetables. Soften the gelatin in a little cold water. Put the broth back into the kettle, add the gelatin, and cook it down to 1½ cups. Cool.

Arrange the sliced hard-boiled eggs and the slices of pickle in a pattern on the bottom of a loaf pan lined with a little of the broth. Add the chopped veal and pour the broth over. Chill in the refrigerator until firm. Unmold and serve on lettuce, sliced thin. Creamed horse-radish or pickled beets are very good with this.

Pork

I was born in Transylvania, a country now best known for having produced one of the most famous hams of all time, Count Dracula. But I had to get out into the wide world before I discovered pork, and all the marvelous ways it can be prepared.

One of the most delicious of all meats, pork needs more cooking time than any other, and must always be well done. For the best flavor you should use a little more spices, salt, and other seasonings with pork than you would with other meats.

PORK ROAST (*Loin, Rib, Leg, or Shoulder*)
SERVES 6–8

1 3- to 4-pound roast of pork	1 onion, sliced
1 tablespoon vinegar	2 cloves garlic
1–2 tablespoons salt	1 green pepper, sliced
3–4 slices bacon	1 tomato, sliced
salt, pepper, paprika, caraway seed	2 cups water
	flour or bread crumbs

You should always soak a roast of pork for 2 or 3 hours in ice water, to which you have added 1 tablespoon vinegar and

1-2 tablespoons salt. Then rinse and dry the roast and make crisscross slits on the fat side.

Place the bacon in the bottom of a baking dish and put the roast on top of it. Season and add the vegetables. Pour in 1 cup water, cover, and roast in a 350° oven for 1½ hours, or until tender. Then uncover and increase the oven heat to 400°. Allow about 45 minutes per pound and continue cooking, basting frequently. Just before serving, increase the oven heat to 450°-500° so that the outside of the roast will be beautifully crisp.

When done, remove the roast to a hot platter and keep warm. To make a pan gravy, remove the excess fat from the roasting pan and sprinkle in a little flour or bread crumbs. Sauté for 2 minutes, then add 1 cup of water and cook, stirring, until it is as thick as you like. Strain the gravy, forcing the vegetables through a sieve, and reheat. Taste and correct the seasoning. Serve the gravy separately with the carved roast.

BONELESS PORK LOIN
SERVES 4-6

1 2- to 4-pound boned pork loin	1 teaspoon salt
1 tablespoon dry mustard	pepper, paprika
	½ teaspoon caraway seed

This is quite a different roast, but the taste is wonderful. Rub your roast with the seasonings. Place it on a rack in a shallow pan. Insert a meat thermometer and roast, uncovered, in a 350° oven until the thermometer registers 185°. If you have no thermometer, allow 45-50 minutes per pound.

When the roast is done, remove to a platter and slice thin. Serve hot or cold. Being boneless, this is a very nice dish for a buffet table at a luncheon or cocktail party.

STUFFED PORK CHOPS
SERVES 6

6 double-thick pork chops	½ cup mushrooms
3 tablespoons butter	1 clove garlic, minced
1 tablespoon minced onion	¼ green pepper

salt, pepper, paprika, cayenne
pepper
8 slices bacon fried and
crumbled

½ cup fine bread crumbs,
toasted in butter, or ½ cup
boiled rice
shortening

Have the butcher cut a pocket for stuffing in each of the chops. Melt the butter in a skillet. Add the onion, mushrooms, garlic, and green pepper. Cook for 5 minutes over low heat. Remove from the stove and add the spices, bacon, and bread crumbs or rice. Mix well and stuff the pockets in the chops with the mixture. Fasten with toothpicks or skewers to hold the stuffing in.

Place the stuffed chops in a baking dish or pan and dust with paprika. Heat a little shortening and baste the chops. Bake in a 375° oven for 1½ hours, or until tender, basting frequently with the pan juices.

SPECIAL RIB CHOPS
SERVES 1

2 rib chops
flour, salt, pepper, paprika
2 tablespoons butter

¼ teaspoon oregano
1 tablespoon minced parsley
2 tablespoons white wine

Dust the chops with the flour and seasonings. In a skillet melt the butter and brown the chops on both sides. Sprinkle with oregano and parsley and pour in the wine. Cover tightly and sauté over low heat until tender, about 30 minutes.

CHINESE GLAZED SPARERIBS
SERVES 8–12

The Chinese do superb things with pork, and in fact, after devouring my Chinese Glazed Spareribs, Gene Kelly threatened to expose me as an impostor. I was posing as a Hungarian producer when I was really a Chinese chef!

4 pounds spareribs
salt, pepper
1 8-ounce can tomato sauce
½ cup sherry
¼ cup honey

2 tablespoons vinegar
½ teaspoon Worcestershire
sauce
2 tablespoons minced onion
1 clove garlic, minced

Sprinkle the spareribs with salt and pepper. Put them in a shallow pan and bake in a 400° oven for 1 hour. Pour off the fat.

Mix the tomato sauce with the rest of the ingredients and pour over the ribs. Continue baking at 400° for 1 hour more, basting every 15 minutes with the sauce.

BAKED SPARERIBS
SERVES 8–12

4 pounds spareribs   salt, pepper, paprika
¼ cup water   1 clove garlic, minced
1 8-ounce can tomato sauce

Make sure the butcher has cracked the ribs through the center and cut them into serving-size pieces. Place them in a shallow baking pan, meaty side up, and pour in ¼ cup water. Bake in a 350° oven for 1½–2 hours. Pour off the fat and liquid.

Mix the tomato sauce with the other ingredients and spoon over the ribs. Return to the oven and continue cooking until the ribs are tender, about 30 minutes. Then increase the oven heat to 500° for 10 minutes to crisp the ribs. Cut into 3–4 rib portions and serve.

Ham

Ham, of course, is cured and smoked pork. In America it is the traditional Easter dish, and a beautifully glazed ham is so delicious either hot or cold that many a lavish buffet has been planned around it.

Thanks to modern scientific methods of processing, you can now buy "tenderized" (precooked and treated) ham and boneless ham, which is very easy to carve. These hams are among the most economical of meats.

The country hams are often more expensive and require more work, but they are treasured by gourmets. They must be soaked and scrubbed—there are usually directions on the wrappings for this—before cooking. But they are worth all the extra work, believe me!

COOKING SCHEDULE FOR HAM AT 350°F.

Raw (Unprocessed) Ham	*Processed (Precooked) Ham*
5 to 8 lbs.—2¾ hrs.	8 to 12 lbs.—2 hrs.
8 to 10 lbs.—2½ to 3 hrs.	10 to 12 lbs.—2 to 2½ hrs.
10 to 12 lbs.—3 to 3½ hrs.	12 to 15 lbs.—2½ to 3 hrs.
12 to 15 lbs.—3½ to 4 hrs.	15 to 18 lbs.—3 to 3½ hrs.
15 to 18 lbs.—4 to 4½ hrs.	18 to 22 lbs.—3½ to 4½ hrs.
18 to 22 lbs.—4½ to 5 hrs.	
22 to 24 lbs.—5½ to 6 hrs.	

Ham should roast fat side up on a rack in an open pan. It is not necessary to add water. Bake it in a 350° oven according to the time schedule for its size. Then pour off the drippings, remove any remaining skin, cut the fat into diamond patterns with a sharp knife, and brush with one of the following glazes. Return to a 400° oven and brown for 15 minutes more before serving.

FRUIT GLAZES FOR HAM

1 cup cranberry or currant jelly, heated

or

1 cup crushed pineapple mixed with 1 cup brown sugar

or

1 cup orange or pineapple marmalade

or

1 cup applesauce mixed with ½ cup corn syrup and 2 tablespoons prepared mustard

SHINY GLAZES FOR HAM

1 cup brown sugar mixed with 1 tablespoon dry mustard

or

1 cup honey or corn syrup

BAKED HAM (*A Pasternak Variation*)

SERVES 16–24

1 processed ham, 8–12 pounds	1 tablespoon salt
cloves	pepper, ground ginger, dry
liquid from either sweet or	mustard
dill pickles	hot applesauce

Scrub the ham and remove any remaining rind. Dry it and score the fat into diamond patterns with a sharp knife. Insert a clove in each diamond. Brush it all over with the liquid from a jar of pickles and then rub it with a mixture of the salt and the other seasonings.

Place the ham, fat up, in a baking pan and add about 1 inch of water to the pan. Bake it in a 450° oven for 15 minutes, then reduce the oven heat to 350° and continue cooking for 20 minutes to the pound. Baste with the drippings every 15 minutes. Serve hot, with hot applesauce on the side.

Lamb

When people say they don't like lamb because it has a strong taste, what they really mean is that it hasn't been properly prepared or cooked. The "strong" taste comes from a thin outside skin called the fell, and if you remove that and as much excess fat as possible, the true delicate flavor of the meat will be released.

I always soak a roast of lamb in salt water to which I add a bit of vinegar. And just before it is finished roasting, I put a little butter on it for additional flavor and goodness. These two little secrets will make all the difference in your lamb, so don't forget them.

CROWN ROAST OF LAMB
SERVES 6–8

This is a very impressive dish, and you will need the cooperation of a butcher to produce it. Allow two double ribs per person. This allows four chops per person, which isn't as startling as it seems because rib chops have only a tiny "eye" of meat on each chop—about two bites to a chop—and less than four chops just isn't an adequate serving of meat.

Tell the butcher what you plan to do. He will cut and shape the meat for you.

A crown roast is usually served with a stuffing or filling in its center, which is added after roasting and just before serving. Try Mushroom Rice (see page 217), rice mixed with green peas, or the Potato Stuffing given here, which I confess is my favorite.

To roast the crown, first wash and dry the meat. Rub the exposed bone ends well with garlic. Season the entire roast with salt, pepper, paprika, cayenne pepper, and a dash each of rosemary, thyme, and mace. Then dust it well with a prepared seasoned flour.

Wrap the exposed bone ends in heavy aluminum foil and place the roast, foil-end down, in a pan. Cook, uncovered, in a 350° oven for 1 hour. Then turn the roast right side up, increase the oven heat to 450° and continue cooking until a crisp golden brown, about another 30 minutes, basting frequently with the drippings.

POTATO STUFFING FOR CROWN ROAST

4–6 potatoes	2 tablespoons butter
1 medium to large onion, minced	¼ teaspoon salt
	1 teaspoon paprika

Boil the potatoes in salted water until tender. Peel and dice them. While they cook, sauté the minced onion in the butter until golden. Mix in the salt and paprika, and then add this to the hot diced potatoes and keep warm until just before serving.

When the roast is done, remove to a warm platter. Replace the foil with paper frills, fill the center and serve at once. It does not require a gravy or sauce, but spiced fruit of some kind as a side dish goes very well with it.

ROAST LEG OF LAMB

SERVES 6–8

1 leg of lamb, 3–4 pounds	3–4 slices bacon
½ cup plus 1 tablespoon vinegar	shortening
2–3 tablespoons salt	¼ cup water
garlic slivers	butter
salt, pepper, paprika, cayenne, pepper, rosemary, thyme	

Soak the lamb in ice water with the ½ cup vinegar and salt for 1 hour. Remove all excess fat and skin from the meat and dry it with paper towels. Make several slits in the roast and insert slivers of garlic. Season well all over.

Place the bacon slices on the bottom of a baking pan. Put the roast on them, fat side up. Do not cover or add water, but heat a little shortening and pour over the meat. Bake in a 350° oven, allowing 35 minutes per pound, and baste frequently. When the roast is done, mix the ¼ cup water and the 1 tablespoon vinegar and sprinkle over lamb. Increase the oven heat to 450°, then cook for another 5 minutes. Rub it with a little butter and serve at once.

BAKED LAMB CHOPS

2 chops or 1 double chop
  per serving
salt, pepper, cayenne pepper,
  oregano, minced parsley

thinly sliced onions
thinly sliced tomatoes
thin strips green peppers
½ cup water

Trim the chops and wipe with damp paper towels. Season the chops well on both sides. Place in a shallow baking dish. Cover with the onions, tomatoes, and green pepper. Add the water and bake in a 400° oven for 1 hour. Turn and bake 25 minutes longer, or until well done. Serve very hot.

PAN-BROILED LAMB CHOPS

2 chops per serving
garlic, salt, pepper, paprika

2–3 tablespoons butter

Wipe the chops with damp paper towels. Trim them, but leave on a little of the fat. Rub them well with garlic and seasonings. Melt the butter in a large skillet and sauté the chops for 2–3 minutes on each side over a hot flame. Serve at once on hot plates.

LAMB SHISH KEBAB
SERVES 4

1½-pound leg of lamb, cut in
   1-inch cubes
1 clove garlic, crushed
½ teaspoon oregano
¼ teaspoon rosemary
⅛ teaspoon savory
pepper
⅛ teaspoon meat tenderizer
½ teaspoon salt

8 mushroom caps
1 green pepper, cut into
   8 wedges
1 Bermuda onion, peeled and
   cut into 8 wedges
1 firm beefsteak tomato, peeled
   and cut into 8 wedges
French dressing

Place the meat cubes in a shallow baking dish and sprinkle with garlic. Mix well together. Crush the oregano, rosemary, savory, and pepper together and mix with the meat tenderizer and salt. Sprinkle evenly over the meat. Let stand at room temperature for 1 hour, stirring from time to time.

Dip the mushroom caps and vegetables in the French dressing. To assemble the kebabs, skewer the meat, mushrooms, green pepper, onion, and tomato wedges alternately on 4 long skewers.

Broil for 4–5 minutes under the flame, turning as they brown, and broil for 10–12 minutes in all.

LAMB CURRY
SERVES 6–8

Whole books have been written on the subject of curries, and their varieties are virtually limitless. Curry can be hot, bland, sweet, or spicy, and can be made with practically everything— eggs, fruit, meat, fish, or vegetables.

This is a simple curry, takes only about an hour to prepare, and is made with an inexpensive cut of lamb. This makes it an excellent dish to have in your culinary repertoire when you want to cook up something special in a hurry.

2 pounds lamb shoulder, boned
2 tablespoons shortening
1 large onion, chopped

1 clove garlic, chopped
½ green pepper, chopped
salt

dash cayenne pepper   1 tablespoon grated coconut
  (¼ teaspoon chili pepper)   1 tablespoon (or more) curry
2 cups beef broth   powder

Remove the fat and cut the meat into bite-sized pieces. Brown in shortening in a skillet, then add the chopped onion, garlic, green pepper, and a little salt. Cook until the onion is soft, stirring constantly. Add the rest of the ingredients and cover. Cook, stirring occasionally, until the meat is tender, about 1 hour. Serve very hot with fluffy rice.

The amount of curry powder you need depends on the kind you use and how strong a curry flavor you like. After you've added the curry powder, let the mixture cook for about 15 minutes and then taste to see if you want to add more curry.

ROAST VENISON

If I can put rabbit in the poultry and game bird chapter, can anyone give me three good reasons why a venison recipe shouldn't go here? Just because I have yet to cook Whale Gulyás or Elephant à la Mode and can't devote a whole chapter to game animals, do I *have* to leave out perfectly scrumptious dishes? Certainly not!

Either you go hunting, or you have friends who do. And because you know how to cook, you wind up facing a beautiful piece of meat and wondering what to do with it. Venison is supposed to have a "gamy" taste, but this is only true of animals which have been over-exerted. If the meat has been properly selected and hung, it can be served just as beef is—it just has a little extra flavor. The most expert hunter I know, a man who has been supplying his family's table with meat and birds for sixty years, won't even waste his ammunition on an animal that he thinks might have been running for more than a city block. But if you or your hunting friends are less expert than that, marinating your venison roast will remove the possibility of a "gamy" taste and give you a dinner you and your friends will long remember.

Marinade:

1 cup red wine
2 tablespoons tarragon vinegar
½ teaspoon dill
1 bay leaf
10 peppercorns
¼ teaspoon salt
1 small onion, sliced
1 clove garlic, minced

½ cup chili sauce
1 green pepper, sliced
1 bunch parsley
1 carrot
1 parsnip
2–3 stalks celery
1 5-pound roast of venison
3 tablespoons oil or shortening

Gravy:

1 tablespoon flour
3 tablespoons sour cream
1 tablespoon mustard

dash each of ginger and
    cayenne pepper

Combine all the ingredients listed for the marinade and boil until the vegetables are tender. When cool, pour over the meat and let stand in the refrigerator for a day or two, turning occasionally so that it will be thoroughly marinated.

When ready to cook, take the meat from the marinade and wipe it carefully. Strain and reserve the marinade.

Heat the oil or shortening in a skillet and sear the meat well on all sides. Transfer to a baking pan, spoon the hot fat over it, and then pour a cup of the marinade over. Bake in a 375° oven, basting frequently, for 3 hours, or until the meat is tender. Transfer the meat to a hot platter and keep warm.

Make a gravy by adding the flour to the drippings and brown for a minute. Dilute the sour cream with 1 cup of the reserved marinade and pour into the baking pan. Simmer until the liquid is reduced to about 2 cups. Mix the mustard and a dash each of ginger and cayenne pepper and add to the sauce. Serve the sauce separately with the carved roast.

8

DELIGHTS WITH A DIFFERENCE

Variety Meats

Tzotzkiles, roughly translated from the Hungarian, means "knickknacks and novelties"—the little extras that add interest and dispel monotony in living. I consider the variety meats a marvelous example of this. Unfortunately, many Americans are prejudiced against them, although they eat liver because they know it's good for them. But tender little kidneys and succulent sweetbreads are so easy to prepare and so utterly delicious that it's a shame they are not prized here as they are in Europe. So as I've said before, try these recipes and *taste* them, please, just *taste* them.

CALF'S LIVER ITALIAN STYLE
SERVES 4–6

I love Italy and I love the Italians, a sunny, friendly people whose beautiful country is reflected in their music and their wonderful savory food. If you think that Italian food is always one form of pasta or another, then this recipe will show you what they can do to turn a prosaic meat into a gourmet's delight.

2 pounds calf's liver	3 tablespoons chopped parsley
¼ cup butter	1 tablespoon flour
2 slices prosciutto ham, finely chopped	1 cup chicken broth
	½ cup dry Marsala
1 tablespoon finely chopped onion	salt, pepper, cayenne pepper
	lemon wedges for garnish
⅛ teaspoon sage	

Skin the liver and remove the veins, if the butcher has not done so. Wash, dry and carve into thin slices. Sauté the liver, on both sides, for 1–2 minutes in the butter. Remove to a hot platter and keep warm in the oven.

To the butter in the skillet, add the prosciutto ham, onion, sage, and parsley. Sauté, stirring, until the onion is tender but not browned. Stir in the flour and cook a moment, then add the chicken broth and Marsala. Add the seasonings to taste and simmer until thickened. Add the liver to the sauce and reheat. Serve at once garnished with lemon wedges.

CALF'S LIVER PAPRIKASH *(Hungarian)*
SERVES 4–6

We Hungarians have our own way with liver, too, as you'll discover when you try this delicious way of cooking it.

2 pounds calf's liver
1 medium onion, sliced thin
½ green pepper, chopped
1 tomato, peeled and chopped

2–3 tablespoons butter
1 tablespoon paprika
salt

Skin and remove the veins from the liver and slice it thin. Sauté the vegetables in the butter until tender but not browned. Add the liver and sauté for 5–7 minutes longer. Remove from the heat, add the paprika and a little salt. Return to the heat, cover and cook for 2 minutes more. Serve very hot.

BREADED LIVER
SERVES 6

6 thin slices liver
white pepper, paprika
flour for dredging
1 egg
1 tablespoon cream

fine bread crumbs
fat for deep frying
salt
minced fresh parsley for
   garnish

Rinse the liver slices lightly and dry with paper towels. Season with white pepper and paprika (but no salt) and dredge in flour.

Beat the egg with the cream and dip the slices into this, then into fine bread crumbs.

Heat the fat and fry the liver slices in it until brown and golden on each side, then remove to absorbent paper to drain. Salt them now and sprinkle with minced parsley before serving.

BREADED LIVER SAUTÉED
SERVES 6

Prepare the liver as in Breaded Liver above, but sauté in butter in a skillet instead of frying in deep fat. This is very good but not as crisp as the deep fried liver.

FRENCH FRIED LIVER
SERVES 6

6 slices liver	1 tablespoon flour
pepper, paprika	dash salt
1 egg	deep fat or butter
1 tablespoon cream	

Season the liver slices with pepper and paprika. Make a batter of the egg, cream, flour, and salt. Coat the slices and deep fry or sauté in butter.

BAKED CALF'S LIVER
SERVES 6-8

2 to 3 pounds liver, in one piece	3 drops Worcestershire sauce
1–2 cloves garlic	flour
¼ teaspoon pepper	3 tablespoons shortening
¼ teaspoon paprika	½ onion
¼ teaspoon salt	½ green pepper
dash each cayenne pepper, ginger	1 cup water

Skin and trim the liver, if the butcher hasn't already done so, and wash it well. Dry with paper towels. Mash the garlic and seasonings together and mix thoroughly. Make a few slits in the bottom of the liver with a sharp knife and fill them with the seasoning mixture.

Sprinkle the liver lightly with flour and put in a shallow baking pan. Heat the shortening and pour it over the liver. Add the onion and green pepper. Bake, uncovered, in a 450° oven for 15 minutes, then reduce the oven heat to 375° and continue baking until tender and cooked through. To test, prick with a fork. It is done when no pink juice shows after pricking.

Remove the liver to a warm platter and make a pan gravy by adding 1 cup water to the drippings and boil for 5 minutes on top of the stove. Taste for seasoning and serve separately in a gravy boat with the sliced liver.

This is delicious served with the Hungarian Potato Casserole (see page 199).

VEAL KIDNEYS FLAMBÉ
SERVES 6–8

This is a classic French way of cooking the tender veal kidney, and it is one of the best dishes I know to serve to a slightly home-sick French actor or actress—or to that more familiar figure, the person who really loves good food. I first tasted this dish in a little country inn in France. Since my French wasn't up to culinary terms in those days (and I'm not so sure if it is even now), the waiter brought me a tray with the ingredients on it and the chef came out and showed me in pantomime how to make it. Good food makes for such good memories!

4 veal kidneys
1 stick butter
1 wineglass cognac
juice of ½ lemon
½ teaspoon dry mustard
4–6 capers, minced fine

salt, pepper, cayenne pepper
1 teaspoon Worcestershire
  sauce
1 tablespoon tomato paste
4 tablespoons heavy cream

Remove the fat and the thin outside skin from the kidneys. Cut each in half lengthwise and remove the white core and veins with scissors.

Melt the butter in a skillet and sauté the kidneys quickly. (Old cookbooks say they must be "seized" over a bright flame to keep them tender.) Then reduce the fire and cover. Cook slowly for 30 minutes, turning them occasionally.

Remove from the heat. Add the cognac and let it warm

through. Then set it aflame and shake the pan until the flames subside. Remove the kidneys to a heated dish and keep them warm.

Add the rest of the ingredients to the pan and mix well, then replace the kidneys and simmer for 10–15 minutes longer, but do not boil. Taste for seasoning before serving. To serve *flambé*, add a little more cognac at the last minute and as soon as it is warmed, light it and serve at once while the blue flames flicker.

LAMB KIDNEYS
SERVES 4–6

1 pound lamb kidneys
3 tablespoons butter
½ onion, minced
salt, pepper, cayenne pepper

2 jiggers cognac
1 tablespoon tomato paste
½ cup heavy cream

Remove the fat, membrane, and white cores from the kidneys. Slice them thin and sauté quickly in the butter. Remove and keep warm while you sauté the onion until transparent. Return the kidneys, add the seasonings and the cognac. When the cognac is heated, set it aflame and shake the pan until the flames subside. Add the tomato paste and cream and heat through, stirring. Serve very hot, on white toast.

VEAL LUNG HASH
SERVES 4

1 carrot
2–4 stalks celery
½ parsnip
½ onion
few sprigs parsley
10 peppercorns
½ inch slice fresh ginger
1 bay leaf
1 tablespoon salt
2 slices lemon with the rind
1 clove garlic

4 quarts water
½ veal lung
1 dinner roll or 1 slice
    white bread
3 tablespoons shortening
1 tablespoon flour
white and black pepper
vinegar or lemon juice
    (optional)
lemon wedges for garnish

Put the vegetables and seasonings into 4 quarts of water and simmer for 30 minutes.

Soak and wash the lung. Add it to the vegetables and continue cooking for about 1 hour, or until tender. Now remove the meat and strain the broth, reserving it. Grind the meat. Separately, grind the roll or bread and set aside.

Melt the shortening and stir in the flour. Then add the ground meat, bread, and a little liquid and simmer slowly. Add the pepper and taste for seasoning. Add more liquid so that the hash becomes the texture of mashed potatoes. If it seems too bland, add a touch of vinegar or lemon juice to sharpen the flavor.

Serve, garnished with lemon wedges, as a first course.

SWEET AND SOUR LUNG

SERVES 6–8

1 2- to 3-pound lung
2 tablespoons shortening
2 tablespoons flour
1 teaspoon sugar
1 bay leaf
8–10 peppercorns
1 small onion

½ green pepper
few sprigs parsley
2 tablespoons cider vinegar
1 cup water
3–4 tablespoons sweet or sour
   cream (optional)

Slice the lung in long thin strips. Make a roux from the shortening and flour, then add all the other ingredients, except the cream, and let simmer for 20–30 minutes. Taste for seasoning, then strain into a clean saucepan. Now add the strips of lung and cover. Simmer for at least 30 minutes longer. Stir in the cream, if you want it, just before serving.

CALF'S BRAINS

SERVES 2

1 pair brains
2 quarts water
salt, lemon juice, parsley
Parmesan cheese

paprika
4 tablespoons bread crumbs
2 tablespoons butter

Wash the brains under cold running water and remove the veins and membrane. They are clean when the blood vessels are no longer visible. Bring 2 quarts water to a boil with salt, lemon juice, and parsley and simmer the brains in this for 6–8 minutes. Remove them carefully with a slotted spoon and transfer to a buttered casserole.

Sprinkle with grated Parmesan cheese, paprika, bread crumbs and then dot them with butter. Bake in a 350° oven for 15 minutes. Serve hot as a first course.

FRIED CALF'S BRAIN

SERVES 2

1 pair brains	1 egg, beaten
2 quarts water	fine bread crumbs
salt, lemon juice, parsley	deep fat or butter for sautéing
pepper	lemon wedges for garnish
flour	

Clean and prepare the brains as in the above recipe. After simmering, slice them, season with salt and pepper, and coat in flour. Dip in the beaten egg and then in bread crumbs. Fry in deep fat or sauté in butter, being sure to get a crisp coating. Garnish with lemon wedges and serve with Tartare Sauce (see page 267).

SWEETBREADS IN PATTY SHELLS

SERVES 6–8

3 pairs sweetbreads	1 cup milk
2 quarts water	salt, white pepper, cayenne
2 tablespoons vinegar	pepper, nutmeg
1 teaspoon salt	3 egg yolks
½ pound mushrooms, sliced	½ cup sour cream
3 tablespoons flour	patty shells or toast
3 tablespoons butter	

Soak the sweetbreads in ice water for 20 minutes. Boil 2 quarts of water with 2 tablespoons vinegar and 1 teaspoon salt. Add the sweetbreads and cook for 5 minutes. Remove the sweetbreads with a slotted spoon and plunge again into ice water. Let them cool in the water.

While the meat cools, simmer the sliced mushrooms in a little water until tender. Brown the flour in the butter, add the milk and the seasonings and simmer, stirring, until quite thick.

Beat the egg yolks with the sour cream and add to the sauce. Continue cooking gently for 5 minutes, stirring constantly. Remove from the heat.

Slice the sweetbreads and add to the sauce. Return to the heat, add the mushrooms, and correct the seasoning. Heat through but do not boil. When heated, serve at once spooned into patty shells (buy them at a bakery, use the frozen ones, or make Miniature Shells, page 283) or onto toast.

Note: In Europe, the sweetbreads or kidneys are often left right on the roast, and cooked as part of it. Ask your butcher for a veal roast with either left on, and serve them as part of the roast, for a really delicious novelty.

BEEF OR VEAL TONGUE

SERVES 6–8

1 tongue (fresh, not pickled)	1 tomato
1 onion	parsley, thyme, marjoram
1 green pepper	10 peppercorns

Put the tongue into a large kettle with the rest of the ingredients and cover with water. Simmer gently for 2–3 hours until it is tender—and only a fork will tell you that.

Remove it from the broth and skin it, taking off the fat and bones as well. Replace in the broth and let stand overnight. Dry with paper towels and serve, thinly sliced, with Horse-radish Sauce (see page 262) or a good bottled horse-radish sauce on the side.

TRIPE

All over Europe tripe is a very popular luncheon dish. It is savory and delicious and has a further advantage—the basic preparation can—indeed, should—be undertaken the day before.

INITIAL PREPARATION

This is the part you can do the day before.

2–3 pounds tripe	1 large onion
2 quarts water	1 clove garlic
1 small veal shank	1 green pepper
2 carrots	1 bay leaf
1 leek	8–10 peppercorns
1 parsnip	1 small piece ginger
1 small bunch parsley	½ tablespoon salt

Trim, wash, and soak the tripe in salted water, then drain. Put it into a large 3- to 4-quart kettle with 2 quarts water and the other ingredients. Simmer for 2–3 hours, or until the tripe is tender, allowing plenty of time.

When the tripe is tender, remove from the stock and cool, then proceed with either of the following:

PAPRIKASH TRIPE

SERVES 6–8

1 onion, chopped	1 cup water
½ green pepper, chopped	1 tablespoon paprika
1 tomato, peeled and chopped	dash cayenne pepper
2 tablespoons shortening	1 tablespoon tomato paste
2–3 pounds cooked tripe, cut into 1-inch squares	

Sauté the chopped onion, green pepper, and tomato in the shortening until limp. Then add the tripe and sauté a few minutes more. Remove the pan from the stove and add the water, and the rest of the ingredients. Return to the stove and bring to a simmer. Taste for seasoning, then transfer to a double boiler to keep hot until serving. Mashed potatoes or rice go well with this dish.

TRIPE À LA MODE

SERVES 6–8

2–3 pounds cooked tripe	2 tablespoons shortening
2 cups cooking liquid from the tripe	2 tablespoons flour
	2 cloves garlic, minced

¼ teaspoon white pepper
dash thyme
dash rosemary
dash cayenne pepper

2 tablespoons minced parsley
salt
1 cup dry white wine

After cooking the tripe, cut it into long thin strips and reserve 2 cups of strained liquid from the cooking kettle. Make a roux from the shortening and flour. Add the rest of the ingredients and the tripe strips. Let it simmer for about 1 hour, covered, and taste for seasoning before serving. This is best with plain boiled potatoes.

9

THE DISH
THAT HAS
EVERYTHING

Casseroles

The same delightful woman who always urged me to "Take, take, eat more than you want" had another phrase I loved. If you appeared at her door, unexpectedly, her first thought was to feed you—a thought much appreciated by the young and hungry man I was in those days. "What would you like, dolling?" she'd ask. "I'll bake you, I'll cook you, I'll fry you. . . ."

When my telephone rings today and a voice calls me "dolling" it is often a ravishingly beautiful Hungarian actress calling to invite me (I keep telling you I love America—such opportunities it has given me!) to her home for the evening. And she's going to pay for the evening, too!

"Okay, Zsa Zsa," I tell her, "I'll come and cook for your party. You send a thousand Care packages, yes?" I'm proud to say that I hire out as a cook! I will go anywhere and cook for charity, and all my friends know it and love it, because I make them the kind of food they can't buy anywhere else.

Casseroles fall into the "bake, cook or fry" category because sometimes you use all three processes in making them. And anybody who wants to get a reputation as a cook will find that casserole dishes such as these in this chapter can become very reliable specialties. Most of them you make the day ahead, and that's a real convenience when you are cooking for a crowd. There are many quick casseroles, too, which are perfect to prepare when you want to bring just one person home for a really impressive "pot luck" dinner.

When I was working with Esther Williams, I invited her to dinner very often. The poor girl was in and out of the water, in and out of the water, for days on end, and the least I could do was to feed her some of her favorite dishes to keep her energy up. Sometimes I'd think to take her home without having prepared anything in advance. Then I'd go home a little early and whip up one of my special casseroles—hearty, nourishing, unusual, and quick to prepare.

BAKED BEANS HUNGARIAN STYLE (*Scholet*)
SERVES 6-8

2 pounds beef brisket
2 pounds pastrami
1 ham hock (optional)
2 marrow bones
1 large onion
1 green pepper
2 cloves garlic
1 tomato, peeled

2 cups uncooked navy beans, soaked
½ cup large barley
2 tablespoons shortening
2 tablespoons flour
1 tablespoon paprika
1 teaspoon salt
¼ teaspoon pepper
4 cups water, at least

Wash and clean the meats and bones, being sure that all the skin and pepper coating is removed from the pastrami. Mince the onion, green pepper, and garlic. Chop the tomato.

Next, wash the beans and barley and dry on absorbent paper. In a large roasting pan, mix the shortening, flour, paprika, salt, and pepper. Add the beans, barley, and vegetables and mix, then add the 4 cups water and mix again.

Put the marrow bones and the ham hock between two layers of the bean mixture and top with the other meats. Bake, covered, in a 375° oven for 2 hours.

Now stir with a wooden spoon, being very careful not to crush or mash the beans. If the liquid has boiled away, add more hot water. Replace the cover and cook until the meat and beans are thoroughly done. Turn off the heat, but leave the dish in the oven.

Next day, 1 or 2 hours before serving, stir the beans again carefully. You can add another cup of heated water if they look dry. Cook again in a 300° oven and serve very hot.

Serve the beans in a large casserole. Slice the meats very thinly and serve separately on a large platter, with some of the sauce from the beans poured over them. Pickles and a crisp salad are nice side dishes for this casserole.

HUNGARIAN STUFFED CABBAGE
(*Töltött Káposzta*)
SERVES 6-8

1 cabbage
salted water

1 pound ham hock or smoked sausages

6 peppercorns
1 teaspoon caraway seeds
1 onion
2 cloves garlic
¾ teaspoon pepper
2 pounds ground beef
1 pound ground pork
3 tablespoons cooked rice
1 egg yolk

4 tablespoons shortening
2 tablespoons minced parsley
salt to taste
2 teaspoons paprika
2 tablespoons sour cream
2 1-pound cans sauerkraut
1 tablespoon flour
½ cup water

Boil the whole cabbage in salted water for 5 minutes. Drain thoroughly and remove the leaves, one by one. Cut out and discard the core of the cabbage.

Boil the ham hock or sausages in water to cover with the peppercorns, caraway seeds, half the onion, 1 clove of the garlic, and ¼ teaspoon of the pepper. Cook until tender. Strain and reserve both the liquid and the meat.

Next comes the stuffing: Mix the ground beef, pork, cooked rice, egg yolk, 2 tablespoons of the shortening, the other half of the onion, minced, the other clove of garlic, minced, the remaining ½ teaspoon pepper, minced parsley, salt to taste, and 1 teaspoon of the paprika. Add the sour cream last and blend well.

On each cabbage leaf, place a large tablespoon of the filling. Fold one end of the leaf over the filling, then turn the two sides of the leaf over and roll tightly to make a neat package that won't come undone when cooking.

Wash and drain the sauerkraut. Place half of sauerkraut in a big casserole, add the cabbage rolls, and cover with the remaining sauerkraut. Over it pour the strained liquid from the meat and cook gently until the rolls are done, about 1½–2 hours.

Remove the little rolls to a plate. In a saucepan, make a roux of 2 tablespoons shortening and the flour. Brown it lightly, then dilute with ½ cup water. Mix into the sauerkraut and simmer slowly. When the fat rises to the top, add the remaining 1 teaspoon paprika.

Now, in a large casserole place a layer of the cabbage rolls. Top with sauerkraut and continue alternating layers until the casserole is almost full. Slice the ham (or smoked sausages) around the casserole. Bake, covered, for at least 30 minutes longer, in a 350° oven, to heat through. Serve with a dish of sour cream on the side.

HUNGARIAN GOULASH CASSEROLE
(*Székely Gulyás*)
SERVES 4-6

When I cook I concentrate completely, and I don't mind admitting it makes me nervous to have people watching, especially when I'm preparing a specialty from my native Hungary. But Lana Turner loves this Hungarian *gulyás*, and she loves to watch me cook it. She'll give almost anything to come into the kitchen and watch, and she'll say, "Joe, I'll give you a kiss . . ." So I stifle my temperament and let Lana watch. A kiss from Lana Turner is *worth* getting nervous about.

2 pounds pork leg or shoulder	1 green pepper, chopped
1 tablespoon flour	1 tomato, peeled and chopped
1 teaspoon salt	2 tablespoons shortening
½ teaspoon paprika	4-5 tablespoons water, at least
¼ teaspoon cayenne pepper	1-pound can sauerkraut
1 medium onion, minced	1 pint sour cream
1 clove garlic, minced	dash caraway seeds

Cut the meat into small dice. Mix the flour, salt, paprika, and cayenne pepper together in a paper bag. Shake the meat in this to coat well on all sides. Then sauté the meat with the onion, garlic, green pepper, and tomato in the shortening until golden. Add 4-5 tablespoons water, cover, and simmer until the meat is tender. Add a little more water if necessary.

Drain and rinse the sauerkraut, then rinse again. Mix into the meat. Add the sour cream, caraway seeds, and a little water and stir well. Place in a casserole and cook for 30 minutes in a 350° oven. Taste and correct the seasoning before serving.

IMPERIAL SAUERKRAUT
(*Kolozsvári Rakott Káposzta*)
SERVES 6-8

2 1-pound cans sauerkraut	1 green pepper, minced
1 pound ham	½ onion, minced
1 pound ground pork	1 clove garlic, minced

salt, pepper
1 cup cooked rice
4 fresh mushrooms, minced
3 tablespoons minced parsley

flour, paprika, cayenne pepper
8 thin pork chops
2 tablespoons shortening
1 pint sour cream

Wash and drain the sauerkraut. Grind the ham and pork and mix with the green pepper, onion, and garlic. Season to taste with salt and pepper. In another bowl, mix the rice, mushrooms, and parsley and season this to taste, too.

In an oblong baking dish (8 x 10 inches) alternate layers of sauerkraut, meat, and rice, ending with a layer of sauerkraut.

Mix together a little flour, salt, pepper, paprika, and cayenne pepper and dust the pork chops with the mixture. Sauté them in the shortening until lightly browned on both sides. Do not drain them, but arrange neatly on top of the casserole. Pour the sour cream, thinned a little with water if it is very thick, over everything. Sprinkle with paprika and cover with foil or a lid. Bake for 1–1½ hours in a 350° oven.

STUFFED GRAPE LEAVES

SERVES 6–8

Today, even supermarkets have imported Greek grape leaves in jars, and they're wonderful when stuffed with a savory stuffing and steamed gently.

1 pound round steak
1 pound pork loin
¼ cup rice, cooked and drained
1 onion, minced
½ teaspoon paprika
½ teaspoon white pepper

1 jar grape leaves
juice of 1 lemon
1 onion, thinly sliced
minced or dried dill
1 cup sour cream
1 can chicken broth

To make the stuffing, grind together the round steak and pork. Add the cooked rice and minced onion, season with paprika and white pepper, and mix well. Let the mixture sit to blend while you carefully spread out the grape leaves and sprinkle them with lemon juice. Place a small spoonful of stuffing on each leaf and roll as you would cabbage leaves.

In the bottom of an 8 x 10-inch baking dish place a thinly sliced onion. Lay the stuffed leaves side by side on the onion and sprinkle with dill. Add a second layer of leaves if you have enough and sprinkle again with dill.

If there are grape leaves left over after you've used up the filling, shred them and add them to the dish before baking.

Mix the sour cream with the chicken broth and pour over the leaves, adding another sprinkling of dill. Bake in a 375° oven for 1–1½ hours. Before serving, sprinkle with paprika.

HUNGARIAN STUFFED PEPPERS IN TOMATO SAUCE (*Töltött Paprika*)

SERVES 6–8

6–8 large green peppers
1 pound ground beef
1 pound ground pork
2 tablespoons rice, boiled and drained
½ medium onion, minced
1 clove garlic, minced
salt

1 teaspoon pepper
½ teaspoon paprika
2 tablespoons shortening
2 tablespoons flour
1 1-quart, 14-ounce can tomato juice
2 8-ounce cans tomato sauce
2 tablespoons sugar

Cut the stems from the green peppers, remove the seeds and ribs carefully, and boil for 5 minutes in water to cover. Drain.

Make a stuffing of the meat, rice, onion, garlic, salt, pepper, and paprika. Taste to be sure it is well seasoned, since a well-seasoned mixture is very important to good stuffed peppers. They can be very dull and taste like a school-lunch cafeteria dish, than which few things can be more *blah* (I've raised three sons and I know!), if you don't taste and make sure the mixture has a flavor to it. Stuff the peppers with this mixture.

Make a roux of the shortening and flour. Let it brown slightly, then stir in the tomato juice and tomato sauce. Let the sauce come to a simmer and add the sugar and a little salt. Place the stuffed peppers upright, one next to the other, in a pan that can be covered, and pour the sauce over. Cover and cook over low heat on top of the stove for 1½–2 hours. Arrange the peppers on a serving platter and pour the sauce over them, then serve hot.

STUFFED CABBAGE ROLLS WITH CORNED BEEF

SERVES 6

2 cups ground corned beef
1 cup soft bread crumbs
2 tablespoons finely minced
   onion
¼ plus ⅛ teaspoon pepper
1¼ teaspoons salt
¼ cup butter

6 large cabbage leaves
¼ cup diced green pepper
¼ cup chopped onion
2 cups diced, fresh tomatoes
4 cups water or bouillon
¾ teaspoon ground oregano

Combine the ground corned beef with the bread crumbs, minced onion, ¼ teaspoon pepper, 1 teaspoon of the salt, and butter and set aside.

Simmer the cabbage leaves in salted water until tender. Remove from the heat, drain, and cut off the tough ends, cores, and hard veins. Place a spoonful of filling on each leaf, fold over and roll, turning in the ends to make sure the stuffing won't leak out.

Arrange the stuffed leaves in a large shallow baking dish. Combine the remaining ingredients and bring to a boil. Simmer for 2 minutes and pour over the rolls. Cover with foil and bake in a 350° oven for 30–40 minutes, basting 3 or 4 times with the sauce.

STUFFED CABBAGE ROLLS IN TOMATO SAUCE

SERVES 6-8

1 medium cabbage
2–3 tablespoons shortening,
   at least
¾ cup chopped onion
¼ cup chopped celery
1 #2 can tomatoes, mashed
½ teaspoon sugar
salt, pepper, cayenne pepper
   to taste
¼ teaspoon sweet basil
1 pound ground beef

1 pound ground pork
½ pound ground ham
1 clove garlic, minced
1 egg, beaten
2 tablespoons grated Parmesan
   cheese
½ teaspoon salt
½ teaspoon pepper
dash sweet basil
1 teaspoon minced parsley

Wash the cabbage, remove the core, and boil in salted water for about 5 minutes, or until tender. Remove, drain, separate the leaves, rinse off, and dry.

Heat the shortening in a skillet. Add ¼ cup of the chopped onion and the ¼ cup chopped celery. Cook for 5 minutes, then add the tomatoes, sugar, salt, pepper, cayenne pepper, and sweet basil. Let simmer.

For the stuffing, mix well the remaining ingredients. Lay each cabbage leaf flat and place about 2 tablespoons of stuffing on each. Roll, turning in the sides, to make neat little packages. Heat some shortening in a skillet and brown the rolls lightly then place in a casserole and pour the simmering sauce over. Cook gently on top of the stove about 1 hour, or until tender and done.

STEAK AND KIDNEY PIE

SERVES 6–8

1½ pounds round steak
4–6 veal kidneys
½ small onion, chopped fine
4 tablespoons butter
2 tablespoons white wine or
   sherry
2 tablespoons cognac
3 tablespoons flour

½ tablespoon tomato paste
1 tablespoon Worcestershire
   sauce
1½ cups water, soup stock, or
   bouillon
salt, pepper, cayenne pepper
   to taste

Trim the fat from the round steak and cut the meat into 1-inch cubes. Remove the outer membrane from the kidneys, cut them in half lengthwise, and cut out the white cores. In a heavy skillet brown the steak pieces and chopped onion in 1 tablespoon of the butter. Remove the browned steak, add 1 more tablespoon of the butter and brown the kidneys over a hot fire. Add the wine and cognac and swirl around, then remove the kidneys.

Add the remaining 2 tablespoons butter to the skillet and let it melt. Then take the pan from the fire and blend in the flour, tomato paste, Worcestershire sauce, and 1½ cups water, soup stock, or bouillon. Mix well, then return to the fire. Bring to a boil, stirring constantly, and season highly. Add the steak and kidneys and simmer, covered, for 1 hour, or until the meats are tender. Refrigerate to chill thoroughly.

While this cooks, make the pastry:

PASTRY FOR STEAK AND KIDNEY PIE

2 cups flour	½ cup ice water
1½ sticks of butter	1 egg, beaten
1 teaspoon salt	

Place the flour on a board. Make a well in the center, and in it place the butter, salt, and ½ cup ice water. Work until this becomes a smooth paste, kneading with your hands lightly but thoroughly. Form into a ball, wrap in waxed paper, and chill for at least 1 hour.

When cooled, divide the dough into two halves and roll them thin. Brush the edges of a deep pie dish with beaten egg to prevent the dough from shrinking. Fit half of the rolled pastry into the dish as you would for any other pie.

Fill with the cooled meat mixture and cover with the other half of the dough, sealing the edges and making an upstanding fluted rim. Make a few slits in the top crust to allow steam to escape and brush with the remaining beaten egg to make a nice glaze.

Chill for at least ½ hour before baking. Place the dish on a cookie sheet and bake in a 400° oven for 30 minutes, or until golden brown. Serve hot.

HUNGARIAN HOT DOG GOULASH (*Lecsó*)

SERVES 4

The first time I served *lecsó* to Van Johnson he looked at it and said, "Hot dogs and tomatoes and green peppers! I don't even like those when they're *not* mixed up together!" So as usual I said, "Taste it, taste it, just taste it. . . ."

Now, I play very bad tennis and Van Johnson plays very good tennis. But after he had eaten the *lecsó*, we made a deal. Every time I make it for him, he plays tennis with me for an hour. I think that's a pretty good deal, too, because I get to do *two* things I like, play tennis and cook, and he only gets to eat. (This is a good example of Hungarian logic.)

2–3 onions, chopped	dash pepper
2 green peppers, diced	5–6 potatoes, peeled and diced
2 tomatoes, chopped	2 cups water
2–3 tablespoons shortening	1 pound hot dogs
1 tablespoon paprika	cayenne pepper
½ teaspoon salt	green pepper rings for garnish

In a 2-quart pan, sauté the onions, green peppers, and tomatoes in the shortening until limp. Take the pan from the stove, sprinkle with paprika, salt, and pepper and stir. Return to the fire. Add the potatoes and the 2 cups water.

Let this mixture simmer gently until the potatoes are done, about 20 minutes. Skin and slice the hot dogs in ½-inch rounds and add them to the pan. Let cook, covered 10–15 minutes more. Taste for seasoning and sprinkle with cayenne pepper. Serve, garnished with green pepper rings, with a crisp green salad.

WALNUT-SHRIMP CASSEROLE ANTIBES

SERVES 4–6

Once, in the scented night of Singapore, I sat and gorged on shrimp that had been deep fried with a batter of ground walnuts. *That* was a recipe I couldn't get! But a few years later, watching the white yachts bobbing gaily in the sparkling waters at Antibes, I found a similar combination of flavors and a recipe for creating it that I'm very happy to give you, so that you may share my delight in a lovely dish.

2 pounds fresh shrimp	¼ cup catsup
salted water	1 tablespoon Worcestershire
2 slices lemon	sauce
½ bunch parsley	4 tablespoons ground walnuts
½ cup butter, plus butter for	salt, pepper, cayenne pepper
browning	½ pound mushrooms, thinly
2 tablespoons flour	sliced
1 cup milk	½ cup fine bread crumbs
1 cup cream	

Shell and devein the shrimp. Cook for 5 minutes in simmering salted water with the lemon and parsley, then drain.

Melt the ½ cup butter in a saucepan, blend in the flour and cook until it bubbles, stirring constantly. Remove from the heat and add the milk and cream while stirring. Return to the fire and bring to a simmer. Let cook a few minutes, stirring constantly. Again remove from the heat and season with the catsup, Worcestershire sauce, ground walnuts, salt, pepper, and cayenne pepper.

Sauté the thinly sliced mushrooms in a little butter and add to the shrimp. Then pour the sauce over and mix well. Put the mixture in a buttered casserole and sprinkle it with the bread crumbs, lightly browned in a little more butter. Bake in a 350° oven for 20–30 minutes, or until thoroughly heated.

BEEF AND ONION CASSEROLE
SERVES 6-8

2–3 pounds round or sirloin steak	1 6-ounce can sliced mushrooms
1 package onion soup mix	1 cup hot water
1 cup dry red wine	

Remove some of the fat from the meat and melt it in a skillet. Brown the meat slowly on both sides and transfer to a casserole.

In the same skillet, mix the other ingredients and bring to a simmer, stirring to pick up any browned bits from the meat. Pour over the steak. Cover and bake in a 350° oven for 1 hour, then uncover and bake 15 minutes longer, or until the steak is tender.

HAM SOUFFLÉ
SERVES 4

6 tablespoons quick-cooking tapioca	¾ cup milk
¼ teaspoon salt	¾ cup chicken broth
dash pepper	2 tablespoons minced parsley
dash ginger	3 eggs, separated
2 tablespoons grated onion	1 cup ground cooked ham

Combine the tapioca, salt, pepper, ginger, onion, and milk in a saucepan. Add the chicken broth and bring to a boil, stirring constantly. Remove from the heat, add parsley, and allow to cool while beating the eggs separately.

Beat the whites until stiff. Beat the yolks until thick and lemon colored. Add the tapioca mixture and the ham to the yolks and blend well. Fold the egg whites in lightly. Carefully turn into a 2-quart greased baking dish. Place the dish in a pan of hot water and bake in a 350° oven for 1 hour, or until firm. Serve immediately.

HAM AND NOODLE CASSEROLE

SERVES 4-6

1 package egg noodles	2 tablespoons chopped parsley
3 tablespoons butter	1 cup chopped ham
4 eggs, separated	1 cup sour cream
2 green onions, white part only	salt, pepper

Boil the egg noodles in salted water until tender. Rinse, drain, and mix with the butter. Beat the egg yolks until thick. Add the beaten egg yolks, onions, parsley, ham, sour cream, and seasonings to the noodles. Mix well. Beat the egg whites until stiff and fold them into the noodle mixture. Turn into a greased 2-quart baking dish and bake in a 350° oven for 1 hour.

JAMBALAYA

SERVES 4-6

1½ cups rice	½ green pepper, minced
3 quarts salted water	2 stalks celery, chopped
3–4 cups diced, cooked meat (chicken, turkey, veal, or lamb)	½ cup skinned fresh tomatoes
	3–4 tablespoons butter
2 tablespoons chopped onion	1 10½-ounce can chicken broth
1 clove garlic	½ cup sherry

Cook the rice in the 3 quarts salted water with a dab of butter until tender. Drain, rinse, and keep in the strainer.

Sauté the meat with the onion, garlic, green pepper, celery, and tomatoes in 3–4 tablespoons butter until tender. Add the chicken broth and sherry. Mix with the rice, place in a heatproof dish and bake in a 375° oven for 15–20 minutes.

BAKED CRAB

SERVES 4

3 tablespoons butter	1 teaspoon onion juice
3 tablespoons flour	dash Tabasco
1 cup heavy cream	dash Worcestershire sauce
4 hard-boiled eggs, chopped	salt, pepper
1 pound cooked crab	patty shells (optional)
1 tablespoon lemon juice	grated Parmesan cheese

Melt the butter, stir in the flour, and cook gently for a few minutes. Then add the cream and let heat through. Add the rest of the ingredients, except the cheese, and taste for seasoning. Place in a casserole or in individual shells (buy them in a bakery, use the frozen ones, or make Miniature Shells, page 283). Sprinkle with grated Parmesan cheese and bake in a 375° oven for 30 minutes, or until golden.

HUNGARIAN POTATO CASSEROLE
(*Rakott Burgonya*)

SERVES 6–8

6–8 thin Idaho potatoes	¼ pound butter
6 eggs	2 tablespoons grated
salt, pepper, cayenne pepper	Parmesan cheese
1 pint sour cream	paprika
½ pound ground ham	

Boil the potatoes in their skins, and hard-boil the eggs. Cool and peel both, then cut into thin round slices.

Butter a casserole. Arrange a layer of potatoes on the bottom, then a layer of egg slices. Sprinkle with salt, pepper, and a dash of cayenne pepper, then spread with some of the sour cream. Add some of the ground ham and dot with pieces of butter. Continue alternating the layers, ending with a layer of potatoes. Top with the remaining sour cream and sprinkle with the Parmesan cheese. Season, sprinkle with paprika and bake in a 375° oven for 30 minutes.

Note: You may vary this casserole by leaving out the ham and adding layers of fresh sliced tomatoes.

SCALLOPED POTATOES AND HAM
SERVES 4–6

1 medium onion, chopped
3 tablespoons butter
3 tablespoons flour
1 teaspoon salt
black pepper
dry mustard

½ cup grated sharp Cheddar
cheese
4 medium potatoes, boiled
and sliced
2 cups diced ham
1½ cups milk

Make a sauce by sautéing the onion in butter until tender. Stir in the flour, salt, a dash of black pepper, and a dash of dry mustard. Add the milk gradually, and stir constantly until the sauce thickens. Add the grated cheese and continue stirring until the cheese melts and the sauce is blended.

In a 2½-quart casserole alternate layers of sliced potatoes and diced ham. On each layer pour some of the sauce, then pour the remaining sauce over the top. Bake, covered, in a 350° oven for 30 minutes, then uncover and continue baking until the top is light brown.

MUSHROOM PANCAKE CASSEROLE
SERVES 4–6

1 stick butter, plus butter
for sautéing
2 tablespoons flour

¼ cup milk
3 egg yolks
salt, pepper

3 egg whites, beaten	1 teaspoon minced parsley
½ pound fresh mushrooms, sliced	paprika
1 tablespoon minced onion	2–3 tablespoons sour cream
	grated Parmesan cheese

Make a light roux with the butter and flour. Add the milk and mix until very smooth. Cool, then add the egg yolks, salt, and pepper, and fold in the beaten egg whites.

From the batter, make 4 pancakes. Bake each in a skillet, over medium heat, until golden on each side.

While the pancakes are baking, sauté the mushrooms, onion, and parsley in a little butter and season with salt, pepper, and paprika.

Butter a casserole and place one pancake on the bottom. Spread it with some of the sautéed mushrooms and place another pancake on top, then more mushrooms, then another pancake, and so on, make sure the last layer is a pancake. Spread the top pancake with the sour cream, sprinkle with Parmesan cheese and bake, uncovered, in a 375° oven for 30 minutes. Serve very hot.

EGGPLANT PARMIGLIA

SERVES 4–6

1 large eggplant	½ pound fresh mushrooms,
½ cup cooking oil	sliced and sautéed in butter
½ pound mozzarella cheese, thinly sliced	1 can spaghetti sauce
½ teaspoon salt	grated Parmesan cheese

Peel the eggplant and slice crosswise in ½-inch slices. Sauté in oil, turning once, until tender. Drain the slices on absorbent paper and place a layer of them in an ungreased baking dish. Top with a layer of thin mozzarella slices and season with salt. Repeat until all the eggplant is used. Then add the mushrooms on top of the final layer. Pour the spaghetti sauce over and sprinkle with Parmesan cheese. Bake in a 350° oven for 25 minutes, or until browned.

10

THE MYSTERIOUS EAST AND POINTS WEST

Pasta and Rice

An Italian without his pasta? An Oriental without his rice? Unthinkable! But an American without his potato (baked, mashed, or French fried)—well, let's give it some thought. Think of Mushroom Rice, for example. Or Macaroni au Gratin. Or Hungarian Dumplings (*spatzle*). Better still, try some of the following recipes and discover for yourself the joys of varying your menus with unusual side dishes.

Like every other food, potatoes are wonderful in moderation— and if you present them imaginatively (I'll give you some pointers on that in the next chapter). But with *three* marvelous basic starches to choose from every meal can be an adventure for you and for your guests.

Just to show you what incredible things you can do with pasta, I'll start off with three main-course pasta dishes, lasagnes par excellence. I'll follow these with a variety of pasta side dishes, a fried rice main dish, and my favorite savory rice recipes. I can safely predict that they'll liven up your menus so much that even the most dogmatic meat-and-potatoes man on your guest list will be telling his wife to get the recipes.

Pasta

LASAGNE

The Italians always cook their lasagne and noodles and pastas *al dente*, which does not mean "hard as a tooth." (It means still slightly firm, with a little bite left to it.) And that's the way I always cooked lasagne for the late Mario Lanza, during his brilliant, too-short career.

How that boy loved to eat! And one of his most famous songs was born at my house one night after a dinner of Chicken Paprika and Stuffed Lasagne. Mario came out of the dining room, flung his arms around me and said, "Joe, if you could be a girl I'd marry you! *Be my love!*" Nicky Brodsky and Sammy Cahn, who were there, too, just looked at each other and said, "That's it." Mario had given them the title for the new song they were working on. And that's how a beautiful song can come from a good dinner.

LASAGNE AU GRATIN
SERVES 6–8

1 pound ground round steak
½ pound mushrooms, chopped
2 cloves garlic, chopped
½ small onion, chopped
½ green pepper, chopped
1 stalk celery, chopped
2 tablespoons cooking oil
1 8-ounce can Italian tomato
   sauce
1-pound can whole Italian
   tomatoes
¼ teaspoon oregano

½ teaspoon salt
pepper
1 bay leaf
¼ teaspoon paprika
dash cayenne pepper
1 pound wide lasagne noodles
1 mozzarella cheese, sliced
½ pound ricotta (Italian
   cottage cheese)
¼ cup grated Parmesan
   cheese
butter

First, start the sauce: Sauté the ground round steak, chopped mushrooms, garlic, onion, green pepper, and celery in the oil until lightly browned. Transfer to a saucepan and pour in the tomato sauce and the tomatoes. Season with oregano, salt, pepper to taste, the bay leaf, paprika, and cayenne pepper. Cover and cook for 2 hours over low heat.

When the sauce is almost done, boil the lasagne noodles in plenty of salted water until tender but still firm. Drain.

Line the bottom of an oiled square baking dish with a layer of noodles, then a layer of the sliced mozzarella cheese, then a layer of meat sauce. Now add another layer of noodles, then one of the mozzarella, one of sauce and another of noodles. Now add a layer of ricotta cheese, a layer of meat sauce, and last, a layer of noodles topped with the grated Parmesan cheese. Dot with butter and bake in a 375° oven for 30 minutes.

STUFFED LASAGNE
SERVES 6-8

If you want to make a true Italian Stuffed Lasagne, cook the noodles and make the meat sauce for Lasagne au Gratin. Then finish the dish like this:

1 10-ounce package frozen leaf spinach	salt, pepper
	1 mozzarella cheese, cubed
1 4-ounce container ricotta cheese	¼ cup grated Parmesan cheese

Cook the spinach and drain. Grind fine and mix with the ricotta cheese. Season with salt and pepper.

Cut each lasagne noodle in half crosswise. Place on each section a large spoonful of the spinach-cheese mixture and roll up. Place the stuffed noodles in an oiled baking dish and cover with the sauce. Top with the cubed mozzarella. Add another layer of plain noodles and cover with the Parmesan cheese. Bake in a 375° oven for 45 minutes, or until nicely browned.

LASAGNE III
SERVES 4-6

This is a simpler version of the authentic lasagne, and can be made with almost any pasta you happen to have in the cupboard.

½ pound noodles, macaroni, or lasagne	1 1-pound can tomatoes
salted water	1 8-ounce can tomato sauce
1 pound ground beef	½ cup plus 2 tablespoons grated Parmesan cheese
butter	1 mozzarella cheese, cubed
1 teaspoon salt	1 4-ounce container ricotta cheese
2 cloves garlic, minced	
½ teaspoon pepper	

Boil the noodles in salted water until tender. Drain and rinse. Sauté the ground beef in the butter with the salt, garlic, and pepper until lightly browned. Add the can of tomatoes, the can of tomato sauce, and the ½ cup grated Parmesan cheese.

Line the bottom of a greased casserole with a layer of noodles. Cover with cubed mozzarella. Add a light layer of ricotta, then add a layer of the meat mixture. Continue alternating layers in this order until the casserole is full, ending with a layer of noodles. Sprinkle with 2 tablespoons grated Parmesan cheese and bake in a 350° oven for 20–25 minutes.

SPAGHETTI PIE

SERVES 4–6

½ pound spaghetti, cooked
    and rinsed
4 tablespoons butter
½ cup plus 4 tablespoons grated
    Parmesan cheese
1 tablespoon minced parsley

½ cup heavy cream
1 unbaked pie shell
    (see page 282)
salt, pepper
2–3 tomatoes, peeled and sliced

Mix the spaghetti with the butter, the ½ cup Parmesan cheese, parsley, and cream. Fill the pie shell and season with salt and pepper. Cover with the peeled, sliced tomatoes. Dot with more butter and sprinkle generously with 4 tablespoons Parmesan cheese. Bake in a 350° oven for 20–30 minutes, or until nicely browned.

NOODLE BAKE

SERVES 6–8

1 1-pound package fine noodles
salted water
3 eggs, beaten
2 cups milk

1 teaspoon salt
¼ teaspoon pepper
3 tablespoons butter

Cook the noodles in salted water until tender. Rinse and shake in a colander to prevent them from sticking together, then put in a 2-quart casserole.

Combine the beaten eggs, milk, and seasonings and pour over the noodles. Dot with the butter. Place the casserole in a pan of hot water. Cover and bake in a moderate 350° oven for 1 hour, or until firm and golden.

MACARONI AU GRATIN

SERVES 4-6

1 pound plain or elbow
macaroni
salted water
1 stick butter
½ pint sour cream

1 cup grated Parmesan cheese
salt, white pepper to taste
1 cup cream
2 eggs, separated

Boil the macaroni in salted water until tender. Drain and rinse.

Melt the butter in a saucepan and mix it with the macaroni, sour cream, grated Parmesan cheese, and salt and white pepper to taste. Add the cream and blend. Beat the egg yolks and whites separately. Stir in the beaten egg yolks and then fold in the beaten egg whites. Turn into a casserole. Top with grated Parmesan cheese and bake in a 350° oven until nicely browned.

If you want to vary this casserole, you can add ground boiled or baked ham as well. But even plain, this Continental version of "macaroni and cheese" is new and delicious. And when you can make macaroni and cheese interesting, you're really cooking!

FETTUCCINE

When a restaurant can build a worldwide reputation on a simple dish of noodles, there has to be a reason. And Alfredo, in Rome, has done just that with his fettuccine. But to make this dish truly superb, you must have real fettuccine noodles (available in Italian stores), the best butter you can find, heavy cream, and *freshly* grated Parmesan cheese.

1 1-pound package fettuccine
noodles
3 tablespoons butter
per serving
2 tablespoons heavy cream
per serving

¼ cup freshly grated Parmesan
cheese per serving
coarsely ground black pepper

Boil the noodles in plenty of salted water until tender, then drain. Pour them onto a heated serving platter. Toss one portion at a time adding butter, cream, and cheese. Toss with two forks, being careful not to tear the noodles, and serve at once with freshly ground pepper and additional grated Parmesan cheese on the side.

HUNGARIAN DUMPLINGS (*Spatzle*)
SERVES 4–6

A friend of mine was once courting a girl who worked very long and arduous hours in a department store in New York. Utterly exhausted, she usually fell asleep over her dinner, no matter where he took her, until he hit upon the idea of taking her to a delightful Hungarian restaurant complete with gypsy violins, and ordering for her a chicken *paprikash* with *spatzle*. She loved the decor and the music, but it was her first experience with our wonderful food that caused her to sit up, wide awake. So from then on, whenever he really wanted to talk to her, that was where he took her and that was what he fed her. The story has a happy ending: they were married. Soon she learned how to make *spatzle* with a *paprikash* for him when *he* came home tired and *she* wanted to talk.

2 cups flour	salt
2 eggs	3 quarts water
½ cup milk (to make a medium dough)	½ teaspoon baking powder
	4 ounces butter

Mix the flour with the eggs, milk, salt, and baking powder. Beat until light and bubbly. Set aside.

Bring 3 quarts water to a boil with 1 tablespoon salt. Drop the dough into the boiling water a teaspoonful at a time. When the dumplings rise to the surface, taste one to make sure they're done. When they are done, remove them with a slotted spoon and rinse lightly with cold water.

Melt the butter in the top of a double boiler. Add the drained dumplings and mix well with two forks. Keep them warm over hot water and serve separately with stew or *paprikash*.

BREAD DUMPLINGS (*Zsemlye Gombóc*)

SERVES 6–8

3 hard dinner rolls	1 teaspoon baking powder
butter	salt
2 cups flour	milk
2 eggs	3–4 quarts water

Cut the rolls into small dice and sauté in butter until crisp but not browned.

Mix the flour, eggs, butter, baking powder, salt, and enough milk to make a medium dough. Blend together thoroughly. Fold in the sautéed, diced rolls.

Bring 3–4 quarts water to a boil and add 1 tablespoon salt. Drop the dumplings into the boiling water a tablespoonful at a time. When they come to the surface, taste one. If done, remove the dumplings from the water with a slotted spoon. Dot with melted butter and place in a warm oven to heat through. If you want them crisp, turn the oven to 400° and let them brown slightly, but do not let them dry out.

CHEESE DUMPLINGS (*Túros Gombóc*)

SERVES 6–8

1 pound hoop cheese	½ pound flour
6 egg yolks	2 tablespoons bread crumbs
4 tablespoons butter	6 egg whites, stiffly beaten
pinch salt	¼ cup bread crumbs, browned
pinch sugar	in butter
1 teaspoon baking powder	4 quarts water

Drain the liquid from the hoop cheese and put through a fine sieve. Mix it with the egg yolks, butter, salt, sugar, baking powder, flour, and bread crumbs. Blend well, then fold in the stiffly beaten egg whites.

Bring 4 quarts of water to a boil with 1 tablespoon salt. Wet your hands and form the dumpling dough into small balls, using about 1 tablespoon for each. Drop the balls into the boiling water. When they come to the surface they should be done, but taste one to make sure. Remove them from the water with a slotted spoon.

Have the browned bread crumbs ready in a heatproof dish. Roll the dumplings in the dish to coat them thoroughly with crumbs, and keep warm. Serve with a side dish of sour cream, or as a dessert with sour cream, sugar, and cinnamon.

MATZO BALLS   (*To Serve with Meat*)

SERVES 4–6

2 eggs, separated
½ tablespoon shortening
dash white pepper
dash ginger
¼ teaspoon plus
   1 tablespoon salt

1 teaspoon baking powder
1 cup matzo meal
butter
3 quarts water
minced parsley or red paprika
   for garnish

Mix the egg yolks with the shortening. Add the white pepper, ginger, ¼ teaspoon salt, baking powder, and the matzo meal. Blend well. Beat the egg whites until stiff and fold them lightly into the mixture.

Bring 3 quarts water with 1 tablespoon salt to a boil. Make small round balls from the dough and drop them into the salted water. They should cook from 12–15 minutes. Be careful not to overcook them.

When they are done, remove from the water, rinse, and butter them lightly. To serve, arrange them around meat on a hot platter. Pour gravy over the meat and sprinkle the dumplings with minced parsley or red paprika.

EGG BARLEY

SERVES 4-6

1 cup egg barley
2 tablespoons shortening
2 cups boiling water, at least

¼ teaspoon salt
pepper to taste

Sauté the egg barley in the shortening until golden. Add 2 cups boiling water with ¼ teaspoon salt and continue cooking for 10 minutes, adding a little more water if necessry. Turn into a heatproof dish and cover. Bake in a 350° oven for 30 minutes. Taste for seasoning and add pepper to taste. Serve with *paprikash* or any stew.

Rice

The world over—from Nepal to Novgorod, from Nagasaki to Norwalk, Conn.—everybody loves rice. Instead of potatoes, in puddings or custards, in pilafs or casseroles, rice appears in as many roles as you choose to cast it. You can't ask more of a food than that.

BASIC METHOD FOR PREPARING RICE

SERVES 6-8

1 cup raw rice
3 quarts boiling water
2 tablespoons salt

¼ stick butter
juice of ½ lemon

Add the rice to the seasoned boiling water. Use a wooden fork to stir lightly. After 12–15 minutes of cooking, taste the rice to see if it is done.

When it's done, rinse and place in a warm but not hot oven to dry, so that the grains remain separated.

You should always stir rice lightly with a wooden fork, or

with two forks. If you use a spoon you will mash and break the grains, and it will be gummy.

This makes 3 cups of cooked rice.

FRIED RICE
SERVES 4–6

3 cups hot cooked rice
3 tablespoons minced onion
1 cup bean sprouts
1–2 cups cooked roast pork,
    shrimp, or lobster

3 tablespoons butter
1 tablespoon soy sauce

This is a noble way to serve rice as a main dish or with a roast. Keep the cooked rice warm over steam. Sauté the onion, bean sprouts, and meat in 1 tablespoon of the butter until the onions are soft. Now add the steamed rice. Toss in the soy sauce and 2 more tablespoons butter. Mix well so that the soy sauce colors the rice. Stir over low heat until heated through.

HERBED RICE
SERVES 4–6

1 medium onion, finely minced
½ stick butter
1 cup raw rice
1 teaspoon finely minced
    parsley

pinch each dried tarragon and
    thyme
1 10½-ounce can chicken broth

Sauté the finely minced onion in the butter until pale gold. While it cooks, wash the rice and dry on paper towels. Stir the rice into the onion and sauté gently until the rice begins to turn pale brown. Add the herbs and stir thoroughly. Stir in small amounts of chicken broth, 1 tablespoon at a time, allowing the rice to absorb all the broth each time before adding more. Keep stirring with a wooden fork until all the broth is absorbed and the rice tender.

WILD RICE

SERVES 8–12

Would you like to know why wild rice is so expensive? It is a special grass, not really a rice at all, that grows on tall stalks only in certain marshes. It must be gathered by hand, by Indians who are skilled enough to stand in flat-bottomed boats as they are navigated through the swamps. Truly a "wild" grain, it grows without cultivation and resists all man's efforts to tame it.

Wild rice's unique flavor is worth its price, though, when you really want to offer something special.

1 pound wild rice	1½ quarts chicken broth
1 onion	1 stalk celery
½ pound fresh mushrooms	salt, pepper, sage, thyme
2 tablespoons butter	

Thoroughly wash the wild rice. Chop the onion and mushrooms very fine. Brown the onion and mushrooms in the butter, then add the rice and stir lightly with a fork until the rice has absorbed the moisture. Add the chicken broth. Bring to a boil and add the stalk of celery. Place, covered, in a 400° oven and let cook undisturbed for 20 minutes. Remove the celery and season with salt, pepper, sage, and thyme.

RICE WITH NUTS

SERVES 6–8

4 cups hot cooked rice	½–2 cups chopped pecans,
¼ cup melted butter	walnuts, filberts, or almonds

Combine the rice with the melted butter and chopped nuts and heat through in a warm oven. Serve this with any kind of fowl.

HAWAIIAN RICE

SERVES 6–8

2 tablespoons butter	¼ teaspoon salt
1 cup raw rice	1 teaspoon curry powder

1 cup pineapple juice   ½ cup raisins
1 cup chicken broth   ½ cup chopped nuts
½ cup diced pineapple

Melt the butter. Add the rice, salt, and curry powder and stir until well mixed. Add the rest of the ingredients, stir lightly to mix, and cover. Bake in a 350° oven for about 18–20 minutes.

GREEN RICE
SERVES 12–14

3 cups raw rice   1½ cups minced parsley
2 teaspoons salt   3–4 tablespoons butter
5½ cups boiling water

Add the rice and salt to the 5½ cups boiling water. Reduce the heat and cook, covered, over low heat for 20–25 minutes. Remove the cover and let stand in a warm oven for 5 minutes. Add the parsley and butter and toss lightly to mix.

PARMESAN RICE
SERVES 4–6

1⅓ cups hot cooked rice 3 tablespoons butter
3 tablespoons freshly grated 2 tablespoons coarsely chopped
 Parmesan cheese   pimiento

Toss the rice with the other ingredients and serve immediately.

BAKED SAFFRON RICE
SERVES 4–6

1 cup raw rice   2 green onions, minced
3 cups salted water 1 clove garlic
butter   pinch saffron

Boil the rice in 3 cups salted water with about 1 teaspoon butter for 15–20 minutes, or until done. Rinse.

While the rice cooks, sauté the green onions and garlic in a little more butter. When the onions are limp and tender, discard the garlic. Add the saffron. Mix the onions, with their butter, with the rice, being careful not to break the grains. Put the rice in a buttered casserole and bake in a 375° oven for 10 minutes.

MUSHROOM RICE
SERVES 4–6

1 cup raw rice	1 teaspoon minced onion
salted water	3 tablespoons butter
butter	salt, pepper, cayenne pepper
¼–½ cup minced fresh mushrooms	2 tablespoons minced parsley

Cook the raw rice in salted water with about 1 teaspoon butter for 15–20 minutes. Rinse when done. In the meantime, sauté the mushrooms and onion in 3 tablespoons butter until tender. Season with salt, pepper, and cayenne pepper, add the minced parsley, and mix carefully with the cooked rice. Cover and bake in a 250° oven for 10 minutes.

RICE RING FOR BEEF STEW
SERVES 4–6

1 cup raw rice	2 tablespoons butter
3 cups beef bouillon	parsley

Cook the rice, using beef bouillon instead of water. When the rice is tender, stir in the butter. Then pack it into a 1-quart buttered ring mold. Let stand for 5 minutes. Unmold onto a hot platter and fill the center with a beef stew. Sprinkle with parsley and serve.

SPANISH RICE AU GRATIN
SERVES 4–6

1 cup raw rice
2 cups water
1 teaspoon salt
3 tablespoons butter
1 cup chopped onion
1 cup chopped celery
½ cup chopped green pepper
2 cups canned tomatoes

½ teaspoon Worcestershire
   sauce
1 teaspoon sugar
1 teaspoon monosodium
   glutamate
1½ teaspoons chili powder
1–2 cups grated Cheddar cheese

Cook the rice in 2 cups water with 1 teaspoon salt for 14 minutes.

In the meantime, heat the butter in a skillet, add the chopped vegetables, and sauté until they are tender, stirring with a wooden spoon. Add the rice, tomatoes, and the rest of the ingredients except the cheese. Cook over low heat until the rice has absorbed the liquid. Turn into a buttered casserole and top evenly with the grated cheese. Place under the broiler until the cheese is melted and nicely browned.

RICE-CHEESE RING
SERVES 4–6

4 cups shredded Cheddar cheese
salt
1⅓ cups milk
½ cup finely chopped green
   pepper
½ cup finely chopped celery
1 tablespoon minced onion

1 cup mushrooms, chopped
¼ cup chopped pimientos
2 tablespoons butter
6 hard-boiled eggs, coarsely
   chopped
1½–2 cups hot cooked rice

Combine the cheese, salt, and milk in the top of a double boiler and cook over hot water until blended, stirring occasionally.

Sauté the chopped vegetables in the butter, and when tender, add the coarsely chopped eggs. Stir into the cheese sauce.

Pack the hot rice into a buttered 1½- or 2-quart ring mold and let sit a few minutes. Unmold onto a large heated platter and fill the center with the hot egg and cheese sauce.

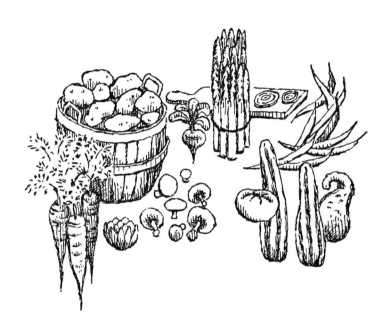

11

DOWN THE GARDEN PATH

Vegetables of Distinction

When I grew up in Europe, fresh vegetables were never to be had before spring. Here in America we can enjoy asparagus, green peas, baby string beans, artichokes, or corn any time of the year.

Furthermore, every good supermarket today carries almost everything that is grown in the whole wide world. If it isn't fresh it's frozen, and if it isn't frozen it's in a can. But it is available to you. Nowhere else in the world has the cook the choice that you have.

Maybe that's one of the reasons Americans find vegetables boring. In Europe, *les primeurs* (the firsts) are looked forward to with real anticipation. They are served as a separate course—and they are expensive. You may take the lovely fresh and frozen vegetables for granted. You're supposed to have vegetables, so you have vegetables, but somehow they always taste the same.

I will give you some ideas about how to serve vegetables differently. Then, I think, you'll understand why Europeans find them so exciting. You know the commonplace methods, I'm sure. You know that you cook most vegetables in salted water, as little as possible, for as little time as possible. And you know that you can dress up your vegetables with cheese, sour cream, toasted almonds, and other garnishes to make them more interesting. My recipes for vegetables take a little more time, a little more patience, and a little more love on your part. But they also make the vegetables just that much more exciting to eat.

ARTICHOKES
½–1 PER SERVING

Trim the bottoms of the artichokes and cut off the tips of the leaves. Soak in salted water, drain, and then cook in plenty of boiling salted water for 30–40 minutes, or until a quick pull easily loosens an outside leaf. (In Italy, a dollop of olive oil, a dash of vinegar, and a clove of garlic are added to the water to intensify the flavor.)

Drain thoroughly and serve warm with melted butter for dipping, or Hollandaise Sauce (see page 261), or Vinaigrette Dressing (see page 251).

Note: For a more formal service, spread the leaves apart, remove the purple choke (a French ball cutter is a real help here), and fill with the sauce.

ASPARAGUS PARISIENNE

SERVES 6–8

2 pounds fresh asparagus
salted water
¼ pound grated Parmesan
   cheese
1 pint sour cream

pepper or cayenne pepper
2 tablespoons bread crumbs
½ stick butter
paprika

Clean the asparagus, cutting off the hard ends. Boil in salted water until tender, and drain. Place a layer of asparagus on the bottom of a buttered baking dish. Sprinkle with grated Parmesan cheese. Add another layer of asparagus, then of cheese, and continue layering, ending with a layer of asparagus. Season the sour cream with pepper or cayenne pepper and pour over the dish. Sprinkle with bread crumbs, dot with butter, and sprinkle with paprika. Bake in a 375° oven for 30 minutes, or until nicely browned.

SCALLOPED ASPARAGUS

SERVES 4

1 pound fresh asparagus
salted water
dash sugar
6 tablespoons butter
3 tablespoons flour
1 tablespoon minced onion

2 cups milk
½–1 clove garlic, minced
½ cup sliced American cheese
3 hard-boiled eggs, diced
¼ cup buttered bread crumbs

Wash and peel the asparagus, breaking off the tough ends. Cut the stalks into 1-inch lengths. Cook until tender in salted water with a dash sugar. Drain.

Melt the butter and stir in the flour and onion. Add the milk and garlic and cook over low heat until thick and smooth. Stir in half the cheese. Combine the cooked asparagus with the sauce. On the bottom of a casserole, put a layer of asparagus, then one of diced hard-boiled eggs, then one of asparagus, then one of eggs and finally one of asparagus. Top with bread crumbs and the remaining cheese. Bake in a 350° oven for about 15 minutes.

CREAMED BRUSSELS SPROUTS OR BROCCOLI
SERVES 4

2 10-ounce packages frozen Brussels sprouts or broccoli	1 cup chicken broth
	1 cup light cream
¼ cup butter	dash cayenne pepper
¼ cup flour	salt, pepper

Cook the vegetable according to package directions, then rinse and drain. Melt the butter and blend in the flour to make a light brown roux. Remove from the heat and add the broth and cream. Stir until smooth. Return to the heat and bring to a boil, after adding seasonings. Remove from the heat and pour over the vegetable in a serving dish.

CARROTS WITH COGNAC
SERVES 4–6

Poor old carrots, always considered such a dull vegetable! They need not be, if you'll try them this way. I admit they aren't very glamorous served plain, but you should see some of the stars *au naturel*, too. A little fixing up helps almost everything, including the carrot.

1 bunch carrots	1 teaspoon sugar
½ stick butter	1 jigger cognac
salt, pepper	2–3 tablespoons water

Scrape the carrots and cut into thin slices or sticks. Heat the butter in a saucepan, add the carrots, salt, pepper, and sugar. Cover and braise for about 15 minutes, then add the cognac and 2–3 tablespoons water and taste for seasoning. Cover and continue to cook over low heat. When all the liquid is absorbed they are ready to serve with fowl or pork.

CAULIFLOWER AU GRATIN
SERVES 4–6

1 head cauliflower	1 pint sour cream
salted water	2 egg yolks
drop of vinegar or	1 cup milk
1 slice bread	salt, white pepper
½ stick butter	½ cup grated Parmesan cheese
1 tablespoon flour	paprika

Clean and trim a nice firm head of cauliflower. Boil in salted water until tender, adding a drop of vinegar or a slice of bread to absorb the odor. Drain.

While it cooks, melt the butter in a skillet with the flour and make a light brown roux. Remove from the heat. Blend in the sour cream, egg yolks, and milk. Season with salt and white pepper. Place the cauliflower in a heatproof dish that you can use at the table. Pour the sauce over, and sprinkle with grated Parmesan cheese and paprika. Dot with more butter and bake in a 350° oven for 30 minutes.

CAULIFLOWER PUDDING
SERVES 4–6

1 head cauliflower	grated Parmesan cheese
2 eggs	butter
2 tablespoons sour cream	bread crumbs
salt, pepper	paprika
4 ounces ground ham	

Boil the cauliflower until tender, then drain. Remove the stems and core and place the florets in a buttered casserole.

Combine the whole eggs with the sour cream, salt, pepper, and ham. Add to the casserole. Top with grated Parmesan cheese, dot with butter, and sprinkle with bread crumbs and paprika. Bake in a 350° oven for 20–25 minutes.

BUTTERED CELERY

SERVES 2–4

8 stalks of celery	dash white pepper
beef stock	1 tablespoon grated Parmesan
½ teaspoon salt	cheese
2 tablespoons butter	parsley for garnish

Wash the celery, remove the tops and strings, and cut each stalk into 3 pieces. Place in a saucepan with enough beef stock to prevent burning, and cover. Cook gently for 10–12 minutes, or until tender. Remove the cover and reduce the flame as low as possible. Add the salt, butter, and pepper and shake the pan. When the butter is melted, transfer to a serving dish. Sprinkle with Parmesan cheese and garnish with fresh parsley.

BAKED STUFFED MUSHROOMS

SERVES 4–6

Mushrooms richly deserve their popularity. In addition to tasting wonderful by themselves, they add great flavor to other dishes. And they have another virtue—almost no calories! If your guests are weight conscious (as so many of my stars have to be) you will find this and the following mushroom recipes very popular. They taste so good that non-dieters love them, too.

12 large mushrooms	2 tablespoons minced nuts
1 small clove garlic, minced	½ cup bread crumbs
3 tablespoons butter	pimiento strips for garnish
2 tablespoons minced parsley	

Carefully remove the stems from the mushroom caps. Mince the stems very fine and sauté them with the garlic in butter for about 5 minutes. Then mix in the parsley, nuts, and bread crumbs. Stuff the caps with this mixture. Place a dot of butter on each cap and bake in a buttered pan in a 350° oven for 15 minutes. Just before serving, garnish each cap with a little strip of pimiento.

BROILED STUFFED MUSHROOMS
SERVES 4-6

12 large mushrooms	2 tablespoons chopped almonds
½ pound ground beef steak	2 tablespoons bread crumbs
½ onion	1 tablespoon tarragon vinegar
¼ green pepper	1 egg
salt, pepper	2 tablespoons butter
1 teaspoon Worcestershire sauce	

Remove the stems from the mushrooms. Put the stems, ground meat, onion, and green pepper through a grinder twice. Mix with the seasonings, almonds, bread crumbs, vinegar, and egg.

Sauté the mushroom caps lightly in butter on both sides, then place on a baking sheet. Mix the butter remaining in the pan with the stuffing and fill the caps with this mixture. Put a dot of butter on each. Broil for 5 minutes, 3 inches below the flame. Serve hot.

MUSHROOMS À LA RITZ
SERVES 4-6

1 pound mushrooms	2 tablespoons minced parsley
1 onion, minced	1 cup milk or ½ cup milk and
1 green pepper, minced	½ cup light cream
3 tablespoons butter	1 tablespoon flour
salt, pepper	½ tablespoon paprika

Wash and slice the mushrooms. Sauté them with the onion and green pepper in the butter. When the onion is limp, add salt, pepper, finely minced parsley, and ½ cup milk or light cream. Cover and simmer until the liquid is almost cooked away.

Dust with the flour and stir to brown the flour lightly. Remove from the fire. Add the paprika and ½ cup milk and simmer a few minutes longer. Serve with scrambled, fried, or poached eggs and hashed brown potatoes, with a green salad on the side.

GREEN PEAS
SERVES 2–3

1 10-ounce package frozen peas	¼ cup butter
dash sugar	½ teaspoon lemon juice
dash salt	powdered rosemary, salt, white pepper

Cook the peas in a little water with a dash of sugar and salt. Drain thoroughly. Place in a saucepan and heat with the butter and seasonings. The rosemary adds a subtle flavor that is wonderful with chicken or veal.

POTATO PUFFS
SERVES 4–6

Pity the potato! To me, he is like an actor of infinite talent and skill, versatile and clever and capable of playing a great variety of roles. But the potato is usually limited to only four roles—baked, boiled, French fried, or mashed. Now I ask you—is that limited repertoire any scope for a real talent?

Nobody's going to deny the virtues of those roles. Yet how dull to go on in them day after day, meal after meal! I can assure you that this potato recipe and the ones that follow will call on more of his talents than that!

½ cup sifted flour	2 eggs, lightly beaten
1 teaspoon baking powder	2 cups unseasoned mashed potatoes
1 teaspoon salt	1 cup shortening
dash white pepper	
1 teaspoon minced onion	

Combine the flour, baking powder, salt, pepper, onion, eggs, and mashed potatoes and mix well. Melt the shortening in a skillet. When it is hot, drop the batter in a small spoonful at a time and fry until golden brown.

STUFFED POTATOES

SERVES 6

6 large baking potatoes
1 medium onion, diced
1 medium green pepper, diced
½ cup butter
1–2 tablespoons cream

1 teaspoon salt
½ teaspoon ground pepper
½ teaspoon ground rosemary
paprika for garnish

Scrub the potatoes. Dry them and bake in a 400° oven for 1 hour.

While they bake, sauté the onion and green pepper in the butter until limp. When the potatoes are tender, scoop out and mash the centers, leaving the shells intact. Add the vegetables, cream, and seasonings to the mashed potatoes and mix well. Fill the shells with this mixture and dot with butter. Bake in a 400° oven for 20 minutes. Sprinkle with paprika and serve at once.

TOASTED POTATOES

1 PER SERVING

potatoes
melted butter

fine bread crumbs
salt, pepper

Peel and slice the potatoes in large wedges. Dip them in melted butter, then in fine bread crumbs. Season with salt and pepper and line them in a row in a greased pan. Dot with butter. Bake in a 400° oven for 35–40 minutes, or until golden brown.

GERMAN POTATOES

SERVES 4–6

4 medium potatoes
salt, pepper

¼ cup shortening

Grate the potatoes. Season with salt and pepper. Sauté in the shortening until golden brown. Turn like a pancake to brown both sides.

POTATO PATTIES

SERVES 4

2 cups seasoned mashed
    potatoes
1 egg, well beaten
2 tablespoons minced onion
¼ teaspoon salt

¼ teaspoon white pepper
¼ cup grated cheese
4 tomato slices
¼ cup bread crumbs
melted butter

Combine the potatoes, egg, onion, salt, and pepper and mix well. Shape into four patties and place on a greased baking sheet. Make a depression in the center of each and fill with grated cheese. Cover with a tomato slice. Place a small mound of bread crumbs on each tomato slice. Sprinkle with melted butter. Bake in a moderate oven, 350°, for about 30 minutes.

POTATOES FONDANT

SERVES 6–8

10 medium-sized Idaho
    potatoes
1 stick butter

1 teaspoon salt
¼ teaspoon white pepper
2 cups chicken broth

Peel the potatoes and place in a shallow baking dish with a small amount of the butter. Melt the rest of the butter and pour over them. Bake for 10 minutes in a 375° oven. Combine the salt and pepper with the broth and pour over. Bake 10–20 minutes longer, basting frequently.

POTATO-CHEESE PUDDING

SERVES 6–8

6 potatoes
4 eggs, separated
1 stick butter
1 cup sour cream

salt, pepper
½ cup grated Parmesan cheese
3 tablespoons bread crumbs
1 package frozen peas

Boil and mash the potatoes. Mix them with the egg yolks, butter, sour cream, salt, pepper, cheese, and bread crumbs. Beat the egg whites and fold them in.

Pour this mixture into a pudding dish. Place in a pan of water and bake in a 400° oven for 30 minutes. Serve with the buttered peas cooked according to package directions. If you have a ring mold, bake the pudding in it and serve with the peas in the center.

POTATO PANCAKES
SERVES 6–8

3 cups grated or ground raw potatoes
3 eggs

3 tablespoons flour
salt, pepper
fat for deep frying

Mix the ground potatoes with the eggs, flour, salt, and pepper. Drop a spoonful at a time into about 1 inch of hot fat in a skillet. Brown one side, turn and brown the other. Drain on absorbent paper and serve hot and crisp.

PAPRIKA POTATOES (*Hungarian*)
SERVES 8–10

8–10 potatoes
1 medium onion, minced
3 tablespoons butter

salt, paprika, pepper
1 cup water, at least
1 cup sour cream

Peel and dice the potatoes. Sauté the onion in the butter until limp. Add the potatoes, seasonings, and the 1 cup water. Continue cooking until the potatoes are tender, adding a little more water if necessary. When done, add the sour cream. Don't stir, just shake the pan and heat the cream through.

HUNGARIAN CREAMED SPINACH
SERVES 6–8

2 10-ounce packages frozen leaf spinach

1 clove garlic
3 tablespoons butter

1 tablespoon flour
1 cup cream
salt and pepper to taste

2 hard-boiled eggs and
8 slices bacon for garnish

Cook the spinach, with the garlic, according to package directions. Strain, rinse, and drain. Put through a grinder, using the finest blade.

Melt the butter, add the flour, and brown. Add the finely ground spinach and stir. Add the cream and seasonings and keep hot over hot water. When ready to serve, garnish with quartered hard-boiled eggs and bacon, cooked until crisp and diced.

SPINACH SOUFFLÉ
SERVES 6-8

¼ cup butter
¼ cup flour
¼ teaspoon salt
¼ teaspoon nutmeg

1 cup milk
5 eggs, separated
1 cup cooked, chopped,
  well-drained spinach

Melt the butter and blend in the flour, salt, and nutmeg. Add the milk and cook until the mixture thickens, stirring constantly. Remove from the heat and stir in the beaten egg yolks carefully so that they do not curdle. Cool. Fold in the finely chopped spinach. Beat the egg whites until stiff and fold in carefully. Rinse a 1½- to 2-quart casserole in cold water, but do not grease. Carefully turn the mixture into the dish. Bake in a 350° oven for 45 minutes and serve immediately.

SPINACH SOUFFLÉ
SERVES 2-3

1 10-ounce package frozen
  leaf spinach
2 eggs, beaten
1 cup cottage cheese
2 tablespoons flour
2 tablespoons cooking oil

½ onion, grated
2 tablespoons shredded
  Parmesan cheese
salt, pepper
fat for deep frying

Cook the spinach, rinse, and put through a fine grinder. Mix in the beaten eggs. Add the other ingredients and mix well.

Drop one tablespoon at a time into the hot fat. Fry until crisp and remove to absorbent paper to drain. Serve hot.

SPINACH AU GRATIN
SERVES 4

1 10-ounce package frozen leaf spinach	3 eggs
	1 tablespoon flour
6 slices white bread	3 tablespoons milk or broth
3 tablespoons butter	salt, pepper
1 tablespoon minced onion	grated Parmesan cheese

Cook the spinach, rinse, and put through a fine grinder. Trim the crusts from the bread and cut into small dice. Toast them in 1 tablespoon of the butter until golden. Mix the spinach, bread, onion, and eggs.

Make a roux of the remaining 2 tablespoons butter and the flour, and dilute with the milk or broth. Add to the spinach mixture and season. Place in a baking dish and sprinkle with cheese. Bake in a 375° oven for 30–45 minutes.

SPINACH ROULADE
SERVES 4–6

This is one of those unclassifiable specialties. Since it's built around a vegetable, it's here. But it's really a main course dish.

1 cup flour	2 small green onions
½ cup butter	1 cup finely ground cooked
½ cup light cream	meat (chicken, ham, brains)
4 eggs, separated	salt, pepper, cayenne pepper,
1 package frozen spinach	Tabasco
2 tablespoons grated Parmesan cheese	¼ cup heavy cream or sour cream
salt, pepper	

Brown the flour slightly in 2 tablespoons of the butter. Dilute with light cream to make a thick paste. Remove from the fire and beat in the egg yolks, one by one.

Cook the spinach. Rinse and drain to remove all liquid. Chop finely or grind. Add to the egg yolk mixture. Season to taste with the cheese, salt, and pepper, then fold in the beaten egg whites.

Grease a baking sheet. Pour the mixture onto it and bake in a 325° oven for 45 minutes.

While it bakes, prepare the filling. Mince the onions and sauté in the remaining butter until tender. Add the finely ground meat and season well. Add the heavy cream or sour cream to make a paste, and keep hot over boiling water.

When the spinach mixture is cooked, remove from the oven and place on a clean towel. Roll up like a jelly roll and let sit a few moments. Unroll and spread filling on it with a spatula. Reroll and place on a heated platter. Sprinkle with a little more grated Parmesan cheese and serve hot with Mushroom Sauce (see page 264) on the side.

STRING BEANS SUPREME

SERVES 4–6

1 pound string beans	thyme
½ stick butter	½ pint sour cream
2 tablespoons flour	1 tablespoon water
½ cup light cream	bread crumbs or crumbled
salt, pepper	crisp bacon
chervil	paprika
onion powder	

Wash the beans and cut off the ends. Cook in salted water for 8 minutes, or a little longer if necessary. Drain.

Make a cream sauce by melting the butter, stirring in the flour, and adding the cream and seasonings. Mix the sour cream with the 1 tablespoon water.

Arrange the beans lengthwise in a buttered casserole (from which you'll serve them), then add the sour cream to the cream sauce and pour it over. Sprinkle with the bread crumbs or crum-

bled bacon bits, dot with a little butter, sprinkle with paprika, and bake in a 325° oven for 30 minutes, or until golden brown.
Note: Broccoli and Brussels sprouts are delicious this way, too.

STUFFED TOMATOES AU GRATIN

SERVES 4–6

6 medium tomatoes	1 tablespoon Marsala
salt, pepper	1 large green onion
12 large mushrooms	½ clove garlic
3 tablespoons butter	heavy cream
dash lemon juice	grated Parmesan cheese

Cut off a slice from the tops of the tomatoes, turn upside down, and squeeze lightly to force out the seeds and juice. Sprinkle lightly inside with salt and pepper and bake on a greased sheet in a 350° oven for 20 minutes, or until tender but still firm.

Slice the mushrooms. Sauté in butter with a dash of lemon juice for a few moments, then add the Marsala, salt, pepper, onion, and garlic. Cover and cook slowly for 10 minutes, then remove the lid and continue cooking to reduce the liquid. Add a few tablespoons heavy cream and continue cooking until the cream is absorbed.

Fill the tomatoes with the mushrooms. Place in a buttered casserole and sprinkle with grated cheese. Bake in a 400° oven until the cheese is golden.

YAMS OR SWEET POTATOES IN ORANGE GLAZE

SERVES 6

6 yams	½ cup orange juice
½ cup brown sugar	dash salt
1 tablespoon cornstarch	5 tablespoons butter
½ cup sugar	orange sections for garnish

Boil the yams in their jackets for 20 minutes. Cool, peel, and cut into thick slices. Place in a shallow buttered baking dish.

Make a sauce by mixing the other ingredients and cooking for 5 minutes. Pour over the yams and garnish with peeled orange sections from which all the membrane has been removed. Bake in a 375° oven for ½ hour. Serve hot.

YAMS FLAMBÉ
1 PER SERVING

whole canned yams in syrup | chopped pecans
butter | cognac or rum
brown sugar

Arrange the yams in a baking dish. Dot with butter, sprinkle with brown sugar and pecans, and bake in a 375° oven for ½ hour. Just before serving, pour warmed cognac or rum over and serve flaming.

YAMS AND CHESTNUTS FLAMBÉ
SERVES 2–4

4 red yams | ½ cup brown sugar
½–1 pound chestnuts | 1 teaspoon cinnamon
¼ cup raisins | grated orange rind (optional)
2 tablespoons butter | rum or cognac

Boil the yams until tender, but do not overcook. Peel and cut them lengthwise into ½-inch thick slices. Arrange side by side on a buttered baking dish that can go to table, laying the slices flat.

Make a little cut in each chestnut with a sharp knife and boil in water for 25 minutes. Peel off the outside shell and inner skin. If they are not tender, cover the shelled nuts with boiling water and cook until tender. On each slice of yam place 2 or 3 chestnuts.

Sauté the raisins in the butter for a few moments and then surround each chestnut with raisins. Dust them with plenty of brown sugar. Sprinkle the dish with cinnamon and grated orange rind. Place under a 400° broiler until the sugar caramelizes. Remove from the broiler and put 1 teaspoon rum or cognac on each slice. Light with a match and serve flaming.

CREAMED ZUCCHINI

SERVES 4-6

8–12 small Italian squash (zucchini)	1 tablespoon butter
vinegar	1 tablespoon flour
1 tablespoon salt	1 tablespoon water
1 slice onion	1 tablespoon minced fresh dill and parsley
1 teaspoon pepper	1 cup sour cream
dash sugar	lemon juice, if necessary

Peel the zucchini and halve lengthwise. Discard the center pulp and seeds with a teaspoon. Slice lengthwise into thin strips. Boil for 8 minutes in a little water with a dash of vinegar, the salt, onion, pepper, and a dash of sugar. Drain.

Make a roux of the butter and flour. In a bowl mix 2 tablespoons vinegar and 1 tablespoon water with the dill and parsley, then blend in the sour cream. Mix into the roux and heat, but do not boil. When hot, add lightly to the squash and keep warm in a double boiler until ready to serve. Correct the seasoning, if necessary, with salt, lemon juice, or a touch more sugar. This is delicious with pork.

VEGETABLE TRAY AMANDINE

ABOUT 12-14 SERVINGS

Here is the *pièce de résistance*, a vegetable dish of such delicious variety that for special occasions it can't be beat, and so good that your family may decide to invent causes for celebration.

1 head cauliflower	1 pound fresh green beans
1 tablespoon vinegar	1 pound whole summer squash
¼ onion	½ pint sour cream
¼ green pepper	butter
sugar	grated Parmesan cheese
1 slice bread	bread crumbs
6 medium carrots	toasted, slivered almonds
1 package frozen peas	for garnish

Cook the cauliflower in well-salted water with the vinegar, onion, green pepper, a dash of sugar, and a slice of bread to absorb the odor. Cook quickly and drain.

Cook the other vegetables separately, each in salted water with a dash of sugar. Drain, season, and keep warm.

When the cauliflower is done, put it in a heatproof dish and pour the sour cream over it. Add a few dots butter, sprinkle with Parmesan cheese and bread crumbs, and bake in a 400° oven for ½ hour.

Place the cooked cauliflower on a large, warm round platter and arrange the other buttered vegetables around it. Sprinkle with toasted, slivered almonds and serve at once.

12

OF GREENS
AND
GASTRONOMY

Salads, Salad Dressings, and Aspics

When you go out to the average "good" restaurant these days, a very depressing phenomenon occurs. Your order is taken and then comes the inevitable question, "Roquefort, French or Thousand Island?" It has boiled down to a kind of verbal shorthand—they don't even add "on your salad" very often—and eight people out of ten seem to answer "Roquefort." That disposes of the salad course, with about as little imagination as it is possible to use. If I thought of movies as simply as that, I'd probably still be washing dishes in the old Paramount studios on Long Island!

Suppose that every time you went to the movies, you saw either the same faces or the same story. Wouldn't that get to be pretty dull? You want variety and so do I, and I feel the same way about salad dressings. I urge you to try some of the different ones that I've collected to add a little more excitement to the food I serve. And I use different kinds of lettuces, too, both for color and flavor interest, when I do make a tossed green salad.

In Europe we made salads with the vegetables and fruits we had, not merely of some lettuce. And one of my newest stars, the beautiful blonde Elke Sommer, who is not too long in this country from Germany, came the other day for lunch. Now I make very good potato salad and the Germans are famous for potato salad. But Elke is a very good cook and when she left, she had my recipe with her because mine was better than hers. That's quite a compliment from a German! So we'll start the recipes for salads with:

HUNGARIAN POTATO SALAD
SERVES 6–10

6 medium potatoes	1 teaspoon salt
4 tablespoons mayonnaise	paprika
6 tablespoons sour cream	3 small green onions
2 teaspoons mustard	½ green pepper, peeled
¼ teaspoon white pepper	¼ red pimiento

½ carrot
4–5 stalks celery
2 teaspoons vinegar
1 tablespoon oil

grated hard-boiled egg yolks
and minced fresh parsley
for garnish

Boil the potatoes in their jackets, then cool, peel, and cut into dice. Mix together the mayonnaise, sour cream, mustard, pepper, salt, and a dash of paprika and blend well.

Mince fine the green onions, green pepper, pimiento, carrot, and celery. Mix these together with a little vinegar and the oil and blend in the mayonnaise mixture. Taste and correct the seasoning. Mix in the diced potatoes with two forks, being very careful not to crush them.

Let stand for a few hours and correct the seasoning again, if necessary. Before serving, sprinkle with grated hard-boiled egg yolks, paprika and minced fresh parsley. (To serve at a buffet, arrange the salad on a large plate of lettuce leaves and garnish with olives and hard-boiled egg quarters.)

CUCUMBER SALAD #1
SERVES 4–6

2–3 cucumbers
1 clove garlic, minced
1 tablespoon minced parsley
1 tablespoon salt
¼ cup white vinegar

⅛ cup salad oil
salt, pepper
dash sugar
paprika and green pepper rings
for garnish

Peel the cucumbers and slice in thin rounds. (Taste the ends to make sure the cucumbers are not bitter.) Place in a bowl with the garlic, parsley, and salt and cover. Let stand for 30 minutes. Then wash the slices in a strainer under cold running water.

Mix the vinegar with the oil and salt and pepper to taste. Add a dash of sugar and the cucumbers and blend thoroughly. Transfer to a salad bowl and garnish with paprika and green pepper rings.

CUCUMBER SALAD #2
SERVES 4-6

2–3 cucumbers	salt and pepper to taste
1 clove garlic, minced	1 tablespoon minced fresh
1 tablespoon salt	dill (or parsley)
1 cup sour cream	dash sugar
1 teaspoon vinegar	paprika and parsley for garnish

Peel and slice the cucumbers and mix with the garlic and salt. Cover and let stand for 30 minutes. Wash in a strainer under cold running water.

Mix the other ingredients to make a dressing and taste for seasoning. Then add the cucumbers and serve sprinkled with paprika and parsley.

CREAMY CABBAGE SLAW
SERVES 6-8

4 cups finely shredded cabbage	1 teaspoon mustard
salt	dash cayenne pepper
½ cup mayonnaise	½ teaspoon sugar
1 pint sour cream	salt, pepper, paprika
2 tablespoons vinegar	lemon juice, if necessary

Place the cabbage in a bowl. Salt lightly, cover, and let stand for 30 minutes. Rinse in a sieve, then chill.

While the cabbage is chilling, make the dressing. Mix all the other ingredients together. Taste and correct the seasoning, adding a touch of lemon juice if you think it necessary.

Toss the chilled cabbage with the dressing and serve very cold.

LETTUCE AND KIDNEY BEAN SALAD
SERVES 4-6

1 tablespoon vinegar	2 tablespoons minced onion
3 tablespoons oil	1 tablespoon mustard
salt and pepper to taste	1–2 tablespoons Worcestershire
1 head romaine	sauce
1 #2 can kidney beans	salt, coarse black pepper

Make a basic dressing of vinegar, oil, salt, and pepper and toss the broken lettuce in it. Arrange in a bowl.

Drain the kidney beans and add the rest of the ingredients, mixing well. Pour into the bowl on top of the lettuce and chill well before serving.

CAESAR SALAD À LA PASTERNAK
SERVES 4–6

2 eggs
1–2 heads romaine
4 anchovies, chopped fine
2 tablespoons Parmesan cheese
1 teaspoon black pepper
½ tablespoon mustard

1 tablespoon Worcestershire
   sauce
½ cup oil-and-vinegar
   French dressing
1 cup of croutons, toasted

Slip the eggs into boiling water for 1 minute. Tear the romaine into a salad bowl, add the coddled eggs and all the other ingredients, except the croutons, and toss well. Chill. Before serving, fold in the croutons.

MEAT OR FISH SALAD
SERVES 2–4

1–2 cups cold leftover meat
   or fish
3 tablespoons vinegar
2 tablespoons oil
1 tablespoon mustard

1 teaspoon Worcestershire
   sauce
paprika, salt
sliced onions and quartered
   tomatoes for garnish

Cut the meat or fish into strips or small dice. Mix the other ingredients to make a dressing and pour over the meat, tossing to distribute the sauce. Arrange on a platter and garnish with thin onion slices and quartered tomatoes. Serve with toasted French bread.

CHICKEN AND FRUIT SALAD

SERVES 2–4

1 head lettuce	1 apple, cubed
1–2 cups cubed cooked chicken, preferably white meat	½ cup finely chopped celery
	½ cup nuts (optional)
1–2 oranges, peeled and sectioned	Lemon French Dressing (see page 247)

Tear the lettuce into bits and mix with the other ingredients, tossing well. Dress with Lemon French Dressing and toss again. Chill before serving.

TUNA SALAD

SERVES 6–8

½ cup sour cream	1 tablespoon minced parsley
¼ cup mayonnaise	1 tablespoon minced chives
2 tablespoons catsup	salt, cayenne pepper, black pepper to taste
1 tablespoon lemon juice	
2 teaspoons horse-radish	2 6½-ounce cans tuna, drained and chilled
1½ tablespoons Worcestershire sauce	1 head lettuce
2 teaspoons minced capers	

Mix all the ingredients except the tuna and lettuce, blend well and chill. Just before serving, shred the lettuce and place in a salad bowl. Top with the chilled tuna and pour the chilled dressing over. Serve very cold.

VEGETABLE SALAD PLATTER

1 cauliflower	parsley
peas	lettuce
carrots	asparagus
green beans	capers
celery	mint
beets	sieved egg
French Dressing (see page 248)	paprika
	minced green onions

This salad greatly depends on how many vegetables you want to use. Start the day before you plan to serve it and cook each of the vegetables separately. I cook the peas with a little mint and the carrots with a lot of minced parsley. Slightly undercook all of the vegetables. Then marinate each separately in French Dressing overnight.

To serve, arrange the cauliflower in the center of a large, lettuce-covered platter and group the vegetables around it in separate, attractive mounds. Sprinkle a little more mint onto the peas, a few capers on the green beans, and minced green onions over the beets. Alternating strips of sieved egg white and egg yolk look very nice on the asparagus. Sprinkle the cauliflower with parsley and paprika. Serve the whole salad very cold with a separate bowl of mayonnaise.

SOUR CREAM DRESSING #1
SERVES 4

1 cup sour cream	½ teaspoon salt
2 tablespoons lemon juice	dash cayenne pepper
1 tablespoon sugar	½ teaspoon finely minced onion

Combine all the ingredients and beat until the mixture thickens. Serve with mixed vegetables or potato salad. To use with fruit salad, omit the cayenne pepper and onion.

SOUR CREAM DRESSING #2
SERVES 4

1 cup sour cream	¼ cup finely chopped celery,
2 tablespoons finely chopped	radishes, and cucumber,
green onion or chives	mixed
1 tablespoon lemon juice	1 clove garlic, whole
	salt and pepper to taste

Blend all the ingredients thoroughly and chill for a few hours. Remove the garlic and serve as is, or strain if you prefer a smooth dressing.

BUTTERMILK SALAD DRESSING

SERVES 4

1 cup buttermilk
2 tablespoons horse-radish
2 teaspoons sugar

1 teaspoon mustard
salt and pepper to taste

Combine all the ingredients and chill thoroughly. Shake well before using.

LEMON FRENCH DRESSING

SERVES 4-6

1 cup oil
¼ cup lemon juice
1 teaspoon vinegar
⅓ cup sugar
1 teaspoon salt
1 teaspoon paprika

1 teaspoon finely chopped
  onion
pinch dried salad herbs
1 teaspoon mustard
1 clove garlic
dash pepper

Put all the ingredients into a screw-top jar and cover tightly. Shake well and let stand, unrefrigerated, for a day. Then chill, and before using, shake again thoroughly.

FRUIT SALAD DRESSING

SERVES 6-10

½ cup sugar
2 tablespoons flour
¼ teaspoon salt
2 eggs, slightly beaten
¼ cup lemon juice

¼ cup orange juice
1 cup pineapple juice
1 cup heavy cream, whipped
  stiff

Mix the sugar, flour, and salt in the top of a double boiler. Add the eggs and mix well. Then add the lemon juice, orange juice, and pineapple juice. Cook over simmering water, stirring constantly, until thickened. Cool. Fold in the stiffly beaten cream just before serving with fresh fruit salad or over canned fruit.

MY SPECIAL SALAD DRESSING
SERVES 6–8

1 cup oil
½ cup mayonnaise
1 tablespoon mustard
½ tablespoon Worcestershire
  sauce

dash lemon juice
dash white vinegar and wine
  vinegar
salt, pepper
dash sugar

Mix all the ingredients together thoroughly and chill. Serve over crisp cold lettuce, romaine, or mixed greens.

FINE FRENCH SALAD DRESSING
SERVES 6–8

1 cup oil
⅓ cup vinegar
⅓ cup mayonnaise
pinch dry mustard
dash each black and cayenne
  pepper

1 clove garlic
1 teaspoon finely chopped
  chives or green onions
1 teaspoon finely chopped
  parsley

Make this ahead of time by mixing all the ingredients and letting it stand. Mix well again and strain just before serving.

SEAFOOD DRESSING
SERVES 4–6

½ cup sour cream
¼ cup catsup
¼ cup chili sauce
2 tablespoons lemon juice

1 teaspoon chopped parsley
1 teaspoon chopped chives
few drops Tabasco

Blend all the ingredients thoroughly and chill. Serve with any seafood.

LENKE'S SALAD DRESSING
SERVES 6–8

Everybody cooks in my family—my kids, my brothers, my sisters. My youngest sister, Lenke, is the best cook in the world. But then, so is my oldest sister. It depends on whose house I'm eating in that night. And this is the favorite salad dressing of all of us.

1½ cups mayonnaise
½ cup oil
½ teaspoon salt
½ teaspoon mustard

few drops lemon juice
1 clove garlic, whole
pepper and paprika to taste

Combine all the ingredients in a jar and shake well. Chill. Remove the garlic before serving.

LEMON HONEY DRESSING
SERVES 6–8

1 teaspoon grated lemon rind
½ cup lemon juice
½ cup honey

½ cup oil
¼ teaspoon salt

Combine all the ingredients in a covered jar. Chill and shake well before serving.

MUSTARD FRENCH DRESSING
SERVES 4–6

½ teaspoon garlic powder
½ teaspoon celery salt
1 teaspoon dry mustard
½ teaspoon sugar
5 tablespoons oil

1 tablespoon tarragon vinegar
1 tablespoon wine vinegar
1 tablespoon white vinegar
1 tablespoon Worcestershire
  sauce

Combine all ingredients in a jar and shake well. Chill and shake again before serving, adding a little water if it seems too thick.

CHILI FRENCH DRESSING

SERVES 6–8

1 small can anchovies
1 clove garlic, minced
2 green onions, minced
1 teaspoon capers, minced
salt, pepper, paprika, cayenne
   pepper
½ cup salad oil

¼ cup tarragon vinegar
1 tablespoon lemon juice
1 teaspoon sugar
¼ cup mayonnaise
1 teaspoon mustard
¼ cup sour cream

Mash and blend the anchovies, garlic, green onions, and capers. Then mix in the other ingredients and blend until smooth. Taste for seasoning, then chill thoroughly and use for any vegetable or fruit salad.

SOUR CREAM ROQUEFORT DRESSING

SERVES 6–8

2 tablespoons, chopped onion
1 clove garlic, crushed
¼ cup chopped parsley
1 cup mayonnaise
1 tablespoon anchovy paste
½ cup sour cream

1 tablespoon lemon juice
¼ cup vinegar
¼ cup crumbled Roquefort
   cheese
salt, pepper, paprika, cayenne
   pepper

Mix all the ingredients thoroughly and chill well before serving.

SPECIAL CHEF'S BLUE CHEESE DRESSING

SERVES 2–4

3 ounces blue cheese
1 teaspoon anchovy paste
juice of ½ lemon
2 tablespoons vinegar
½ cup oil

1 clove garlic, minced
⅛ teaspoon Worcestershire
   sauce
salt and pepper to taste

Crumble the blue cheese with a fork. Then add the rest of the ingredients and mix well. Chill thoroughly before serving.

VINAIGRETTE DRESSING
ONE SERVING

1 tablespoon vinegar
2 tablespoons oil
salt and pepper

chervil and chives
½ hard-boiled egg yolk,
sieved

Mix together the oil and vinegar, adding salt, pepper, chervil, and chives to taste. Serve cold.

Aspics

It has always surprised me that a nation practically raised on gelatin salads and desserts should have neglected the pleasures of the aspic as a garnish to adult food. A sparkling red-wine aspic will dress up even the plainest cold beef. A cold chicken in sparkling clear aspic is a delight on a warm day.

There are many ways to use a clear aspic as a garnish. You can pour the liquid into small molds or into a shallow tray, to be turned out later and sliced or chopped into glistening diamonds. And if there is any secret as to why one aspic will taste better than another, it will lie in the wine, cognac or kind of broth you use. Beef stock makes an aspic for robust dishes; veal stock is used for more delicate ones; and chicken stock makes a versatile one that can be used with most anything. Fish stock, however, can only be used as a garnish for fish dishes.

ALL-PURPOSE ASPIC
SERVES 6–10

4 cups liquid: 2 cups tomato
juice and 2 cups canned or
homemade chicken stock
(see page 46)

4 envelopes unflavored
gelatin

Basic flavoring:
1 teaspoon salt
¼ teaspoon black pepper
¼ teaspoon sugar

1 bay leaf
few sprigs parsley
pinch thyme

To clarify:

2 egg whites, beaten, and the shells, washed and crushed	¼–½ cup sherry, Madeira, or cognac

Measure out the liquid and add the gelatin, stirring well. Add the flavoring, the egg whites and shells and stir over medium heat until it boils up. Remove from the heat immediately and strain through a fine sieve or a piece of flannel wrung out in hot water. Then add the sherry, Madeira, or cognac and pour into molds or a tray. Let set until firm.

This will be a clear aspic, since the gelatin takes the color out of the tomato juice.

WHITE WINE ASPIC

Substitute 1 cup dry white wine for 1 cup of the chicken stock.

RED WINE ASPIC

Substitute 1 cup red wine for 1 cup of the tomato juice. For a pale rose color, add a drop or two of red food coloring to the strained liquid before putting it to set.

BEEF ASPIC

Substitute a strong beef stock (canned or homemade—see page 44) for the chicken stock and add a few slices of onion to the basic flavoring. You can also substitute 1 cup red wine for 1 cup of the tomato juice if the aspic is to go with a robust dish.

TARRAGON ASPIC

Use the basic recipe, adding both tarragon and thyme to the flavoring ingredients.

DELICATE ASPIC

SERVES 6–10

4 stalks celery
1 carrot
1 onion
2 cloves garlic
½ bunch parsley
1 bay leaf
1 teaspoon salt

10 peppercorns
6 cups water
1 egg white, slightly
  beaten
2 envelopes gelatin
½ cup white wine
food coloring (optional)

Put the vegetables and seasonings into the 6 cups water and boil until the liquid is reduced by half. Add the slightly beaten egg white and bring to a boil again, then strain through a fine sieve or a cloth wrung out in hot water. Dissolve the gelatin in the white wine and add to the strained liquid. Bring to a boil again, then cool.

At this point, you can color the aspic if you like. You can pour it into small bowls and color each with a different food coloring before pouring into individual molds. Then refrigerate to set. Use as a garnish for cold meats, salads, or chilled dishes of any kind.

13

A TOUCH
OF SORCERY

An Assortment of Sauces

Now I have made a lot of musicals, as a producer, because I love music and feel that a world without it would be a gray world indeed. But when you make a musical, just as when you make a meal, you have to balance the voices to make good duets. The clear pure soprano of a Jane Powell will balance with the warm rich tones of a Melchior and each adds something to the other. The same is true in the kitchen when you make a sauce to go with a dish.

Sauces are used far more extensively in Continental cooking than in American, where a "creamed" vegetable and a pan gravy are about the extent of the average cook's knowledge. In the classic French cuisine, sauces have been called a religion, which is carrying things a little too far, but there is no doubt about the improvement that a well-chosen sauce can work on what might otherwise be a fairly ordinary dish.

And a sauce is not a gravy. Gravy is the natural product of cooking; sauces are created by the cook. Seasoning is of the greatest importance in sauce making, for the flavor of the sauce should complement the flavor of the dish it accompanies, each making the other taste better. So you always start with small amounts of seasoning, tasting as the sauce progresses, adding more flavor if needed to achieve the right balance.

STANDARD WHITE SAUCE

MAKES 1½–2 CUPS

2 tablespoons butter
2 tablespoons flour

salt, pepper, cayenne pepper
1 cup cream or milk

Melt the butter in a heavy saucepan over very low heat. Blend in the flour with a wooden spoon to make a light roux and add the seasonings. Add the liquid, stirring constantly. Continue cooking until the sauce thickens and is satiny smooth, stirring constantly. (For a thick, or very thick sauce, continue cooking over hot water in a double boiler, stirring constantly.)

BÉCHAMEL SAUCE (*Basic Cream Sauce*)
SERVES 6-8

3 tablespoons butter
3 tablespoons flour
¼ teaspoon white pepper

¼ teaspoon paprika
salt
1 cup heavy cream

Melt the butter and stir in the flour until it bubbles. Add the seasonings and gradually pour in the cream. Blend until smooth and cook, stirring, until thick.

BÉARNAISE SAUCE
SERVES 6-8

2 tablespoons each tarragon
  vinegar and wine vinegar
½ teaspoon sugar
1 tablespoon chopped onion
2 egg yolks

salt, white pepper
2 tablespoons butter, melted
  and cooled
few drops lemon juice

Mix the two vinegars with the sugar and add the chopped onion. Cook until the liquid is reduced by half. Place over simmering water.

Beat the egg yolks, salt, pepper, and butter together thoroughly. Add this mixture drop by drop to the vinegar and onion, stirring constantly, until a mayonnaise consistency is achieved. Add a few drops lemon juice at the very end. This sauce is best served with red meat.

BORDELAISE SAUCE
SERVES 4-6

2 tablespoons butter
2 tablespoons flour
1 tablespoon chopped onion

1 cup red wine
black pepper, paprika, salt
1 cup meat stock or bouillon

Make a roux of butter and flour and let it brown. Then add the onion, red wine, seasonings, and finally, the meat stock or bouillon. Boil until the liquid is reduced by half. Taste and correct the seasoning, and if the sauce is too thick, add a little more red wine.

COCKTAIL SAUCE

SERVES 4–6

2 tablespoons horse-radish
½ cup catsup
3 tablespoons chili sauce
dash Tabasco sauce

2 tablespoons Worcestershire
sauce
2 tablespoons lemon juice
salt and pepper to taste

Mix all the ingredients together and chill. Serve with fish or shellfish.

CUMBERLAND SAUCE #1

SERVES 4–6

2 oranges
1 tablespoon sugar
1 tablespoon horse-radish
½ cup currant jelly

1 tablespoon hot water
2 drops Tabasco sauce
salt and pepper to taste

Grate the rinds of the oranges and squeeze 1 cup of juice. Add all the other ingredients, blending well, then heat and taste for seasoning. This is an excellent sauce for duck or game birds.

CUMBERLAND SAUCE #2

SERVES 4–6

½ cup currant jelly
5 tablespoons orange juice
2 tablespoons lemon juice
dash cayenne pepper

1 teaspoon dry mustard
½ teaspoon powdered ginger
2 tablespoons grated orange
rind

Combine all the ingredients in a saucepan and cook over hot water until the jelly melts, stirring from time to time. Serve with cold ham, sliced roast veal or pork roast.

CURRY SAUCE

SERVES 4-6

1 stick butter
2 tablespoons flour
1 tablespoon curry powder
pinch of powdered saffron

½ teaspoon salt
dash white pepper
1 cup chicken or
   fish stock

Use this sauce for either chicken or fish and use the kind of stock that matches your entree.

Cream the butter with the dry ingredients, then add the stock and stir until blended. Put the sauce in the top of a double boiler over hot water and cook slowly, until thickened, about 10–12 minutes. Let heat through for ten minutes more, stirring from time to time, and serve the sauce hot.

DILL SAUCE

SERVES 6-8

1 tablespoon shortening
2 tablespoons flour
1–2 tablespoons fresh finely
   chopped dill
1 teaspoon sugar
salt and paprika to taste

1 tablespoon lemon juice
1 tablespoon vinegar
1 cup water
1 egg yolk
1 cup sour cream

Melt the shortening and add the flour, stirring over medium heat until golden. Add the dill, sugar, seasonings, lemon juice, vinegar, and water and bring to a boil. Taste and correct the seasoning and reduce the heat.

Beat the egg yolk with the sour cream and stir it into the mixture, off the heat, then bring back to a warm temperature but do not allow to boil. Sprinkle with paprika and serve with boiled beef or fish.

EGG SAUCE

SERVES 6-8

2 egg yolks
3 tablespoons butter
1½ tablespoons flour

1 cup chicken, fish, or shellfish
   stock or bouillon
½ teaspoon salt

¼ teaspoon dry mustard
dash cayenne pepper

1 cup cream
2 tablespoons lemon juice

You should plan to serve this sauce with chicken, fish, or sea-food, and you should make it with a stock or bouillon of the same flavor as your entree.

Cream the two egg yolks with the butter and flour until smooth, then add the rest of the ingredients, except the lemon juice, beating constantly, until smooth again. Pour the sauce into the top of a double boiler set *over*, not *in*, simmering water and beat with an electric beater for 10–12 minutes, or until it thickens.

Remove from the heat, add the lemon juice and taste for seasoning. Chill before serving.

GREEN SAUCE

SERVES 8–10

½ cup spinach leaves or
    watercress leaves

salt
½–1 cup mayonnaise

Blanch the green leaves in hot water with a little salt for a few minutes, drain thoroughly, and press dry in a clean cloth. Pass through a fine sieve and add to the mayonnaise.

HOLLANDAISE SAUCE

SERVES 6–8

1 stick butter
2 egg yolks
dash salt

few drops vinegar
juice of 1 lemon

Place the butter, egg yolks, salt, and vinegar in the top of a double boiler over hot water and stir until the butter melts. Add the lemon juice, still stirring, and let heat until thickened. If it gets too thick, you can add a little hot water, or if you are serving this sauce with fish, a little fish stock.

HORSE-RADISH SAUCE
SERVES 6–10

½ small 4-ounce bottle
  prepared horse-radish
1 teaspoon mustard
pinch sugar

2 tablespoons grated almonds
lemon juice
½ pint heavy cream,
  whipped

Mix all the ingredients except the cream and blend thoroughly, then fold in the cream. This sauce is very good for either a hot or a cold buffet, since it looks beautiful and tastes even better. Try it with roast beef, too.

LEMON BUTTER SAUCE
SERVES 6–8

butter
mustard
minced parsley

minced green onions or chives
salt, pepper
lemon or lime juice

Melt as much butter as you think you will need to serve with fish. Add ¼ teaspoon mustard, 1 teaspoon minced parsley, 1 teaspoon minced green onion or chives for each ¼ pound of butter. Add salt and pepper to taste, and 1 tablespoon lemon or lime juice for each ¼ pound of butter. Taste again and increase any of the seasonings as you like.

MADEIRA SAUCE
SERVES 6–8

2 tablespoons butter
2 tablespoons flour
1 cup meat stock or bouillon

1 tablespoon chopped parsley
1 bay leaf
1 tablespoon Madeira

Melt the butter, stir in the flour, and cook until light brown. Slowly add the meat stock or bouillon, stirring constantly, then add the seasonings and Madeira and cook until thickened. This can be served with any meat.

MAYONNAISE SAUCE

SERVES 6-8

In Provence, France, there is a charming custom. When a young man is getting serious about a girl, the girl's mother invites him to a little party one evening, and together the young couple make a mayonnaise, he pouring the oil as she beats the egg yolks. If he pours too fast, if she beats too slowly, or if for any other reason the mayonnaise curdles, any further thoughts of marriage are out! It would never work if they couldn't make a simple sauce together.

2 egg yolks	1 teaspoon vinegar or lemon
pinch mustard	juice
dash white pepper and salt	1 cup olive oil

Beat the egg yolks and seasonings with the vinegar or lemon juice until well blended. Use a rotary beater and add the olive oil, drop by drop, beating constantly until thick. Taste and correct the seasoning.

You can vary this basic sauce by adding a little tomato puree, a good caviar, chopped green onions, or more mustard for a sharper flavor. Also, as a rule I add a few grains of sugar.

MOUSSELINE SAUCE

SERVES 6-10

Mousseline is a variation of Hollandaise and is made in exactly the same way, except that at the last minute you carefully fold in about ½ cup stiffly beaten cream. I serve this with vegetables.

MUSHROOM SAUCE #1

SERVES 6-8

½ pound fresh mushrooms	salt, pepper, cayenne pepper
½ green pepper	1 cup water, stock, or milk
2-3 green onions	minced parsley
½ stick butter	heavy cream (optional)
1 tablespoon flour	

Slice the mushrooms and chop the green pepper and the white tops of the onions. Sauté in the butter until tender, then add the flour and seasonings and brown slightly. Slowly stir in the liquid and bring to a boil. Let thicken, stirring, then sprinkle with minced parsley and serve. If you want a heavier sauce, add a little heavy cream as well.

MUSHROOM SAUCE #2

SERVES 4–6

1 tablespoon butter
1 tablespoon flour
½ pound mushrooms, chopped

½ cup chicken broth or water
salt and pepper to taste
2–3 tablespoons sour cream

Make a roux of the butter and flour and in it sauté the chopped mushrooms. When they are tender, add the chicken broth or water and simmer for a few moments, stirring. Taste for seasoning. Just before serving, stir in the sour cream and heat through. This is excellent with fish, shellfish, or chicken dishes.

MUSTARD SAUCE

SERVES 4–6

1 tablespoon mustard
½ pint sour cream
½ cup mayonnaise
3 hard-boiled egg yolks, grated

1 tablespoon tarragon vinegar
1 teaspoon lemon juice
salt and pepper to taste

Mix together the mustard, sour cream, and mayonnaise. Then add the rest of the ingredients and blend well. Taste for seasoning and serve at room temperature.

ORANGE SAUCE #1

SERVES 4–6

2 tablespoons butter
2 tablespoons flour

½ cup water
½ teaspoon mustard

¼ cup currant jelly
1 cup dry red wine
salt, paprika

juice and chopped rind of
1 orange
1 tablespoon butter

Melt the butter and add the flour. Stir a moment or two, then add the rest of the ingredients except the butter. Bring to a simmer and let thicken. When cooked, strain and stir in the butter. Serve with any game or fowl.

ORANGE SAUCE #2
SERVES 4-6

juice and grated rind of
2 oranges
½ cup sherry or Madeira

2 tablespoons sugar
¼ cup apricot jam
salt, cayenne pepper

Mix all the ingredients well together and chill. Serve cold as a sauce for cold roast meat.

PARSLEY SAUCE
SERVES 4-6

3 tablespoons butter
1 tablespoon flour or
cornstarch

1 teaspoon lemon juice
2 tablespoons minced parsley
½–1 cup heavy cream

Melt the butter and stir in the flour or cornstarch to cook for a minute or two. Add the lemon juice and parsley and blend, then gradually add the cream. Heat, but do not boil, and taste for seasoning. Serve with fish.

PINK SAUCE
SERVES 4-6

1 cup mayonnaise
½ cup sour cream
¼ cup catsup
1 tablespoon lemon juice

salt, cayenne pepper
chopped chives or chopped dill
½ teaspoon curry powder
(optional)

Combine all the ingredients and mix well. Add curry powder to taste, if you like it, and chill thoroughly. Serve with fish or shellfish.

RÉMOULADE SAUCE
SERVES 4–6

5 stalks celery
1 teaspoon salt
juice and rind of ½ lemon
1 cup mayonnaise
¼ teaspoon dry mustard
1 teaspoon minced onion
1 tablespoon minced pimiento

1 tablespoon minced pickle
1 teaspoon minced parsley
¼ teaspoon minced capers
⅛ teaspoon anchovy paste
pinch dried tarragon
pinch cayenne pepper
1 tablespoon lemon juice

Scrape the celery to remove the strings and cut into very thin slices. Pour ice water into a bowl, add the teaspoon salt, and the juice of half a lemon. Then add the half lemon for the taste of its rind, and finally, the celery.

Let the celery soak while you mix all the other ingredients into the cup of mayonnaise. Let them blend into the mayonnaise for about 30 minutes, then drain the celery and add it last. Taste for seasoning.

This sauce does not need chilling, but it can sit until serving time in the refrigerator. Serve with cold fish or shellfish.

SAUCE À L'HUILLE
SERVES 6–8

2 tablespoons wine vinegar
few drops lemon juice
½ teaspoon dry mustard

1 teaspoon salt
fresh ground pepper
8–10 tablespoons oil

This is a basic oil salad dressing. Combine everything but the oil and whip thoroughly, then add the oil drop by drop. This is for salads and vegetables.

SAUCE ANDALUSIA
SERVES 6-8

2 cups mayonnaise
2 tablespoons finely chopped
   green pepper

2 tablespoons tomato puree

Mix all the ingredients together and serve cold on eggs or fish.

SPECIAL SAUCE FOR COLD MEATS
SERVES 6-8

3 hard-boiled egg yolks
1 cup mayonnaise
½ cup ground blanched
   almonds
1 teaspoon minced onion

2 tablespoons chopped celery
salt, pepper, cayenne pepper
2 cups whipped cream
lemon juice (optional)

Mash the egg yolks and mix with all the other ingredients except the whipped cream and the optional lemon juice. Taste for seasoning, then fold in the whipped cream and a dash of lemon juice if you want a slightly sharper flavor. Serve with any cold meat or fish.

TARTARE SAUCE (*A Genuine French Sauce*)
SERVES 6-8

4 hard-boiled egg yolks
2 raw egg yolks
2 tablespoons mustard
2 tablespoons vinegar

¼ cup heavy cream
salt, pepper
dash of sugar
3 tablespoons oil

Mix all the ingredients except the oil and blend very thoroughly. Then add the oil, drop by drop, beating constantly. Taste and correct the seasoning. This sauce keeps well in the refrigerator and is wonderful with any seafood.

TOMATO SAUCE
SERVES 6–8

1 tablespoon shortening
1 tablespoon flour
1 8-ounce can tomato sauce
½ small onion, minced
½ green pepper, finely
  chopped

3–4 sprigs parsley
1 tablespoon sugar
salt and pepper to taste
1 tablespoon butter

Melt the shortening and stir in the flour. Let it cook a minute, then add the other ingredients and bring to a boil. Let simmer for 15–20 minutes, stirring occasionally to thicken, then strain and serve hot.

14

LET THEM EAT KUGELHOPF

Yeast Cakes, Pastries, and Cookies

I'll never forget the warm, wonderful smell of good things baking in my childhood home in Hungary. Nothing in the world smells better in a house than a yeast bread or cake, and whenever I make a Sunday morning coffeecake to serve warm from the oven, I am trying to recreate some of my memories for my family and friends. You could build a reputation as a chef on Sunday brunches alone, if you served hot, homemade coffeecakes along with your scrambled eggs!

Cakes and pastry figure in the memories of my young manhood, too. Vienna and Budapest, when I knew them, were almost built around life in the coffee shops. You met your friends there to exchange news and gossip, and to drink innumerable cups of coffee. The coffee had to be accompanied by one or two or three delectable cakes or pastries. The afternoon saw the ritual of the *Jause*—more coffee and more conversation. We'd drink large cups of coffee (always with a goodly dollop of whipped cream floating on top) and sample more of the artistic creations of the pastry chef. One might (if, heaven forbid, such a thing should happen) go without breakfast or lunch, but never without the *Jause!*

So here are the recipes for some of the confections that helped not only to make our little house a real home in Hungary, but also to make the *Jause* one of the institutions that established Vienna as a gastronomic paradise. Preferences among fine foods can change with the times, but these old favorites will never lose their popularity. Could it be that girls like Angie Dickenson and Connie Francis diet when I'm not looking? I *know* they are eating when they come to my house and I give them Hungary's famous coffeecake, Kugelhopf.

Note: Some of the lists of ingredients in the recipes in this and the next chapter call for measurements in ounces. On the Continent we used a little kitchen scale instead of measuring cups, but standard measuring cups are also marked in ounces. For instance, 5 ounces will be halfway between the ½ and the ¾ mark on your cup.

Yeast Cakes

KUGELHOPF

SERVES 6–8

2 cakes yeast, crumbled, or 2
   packages active dry yeast
3 cups sifted flour
4 tablespoons sugar
1 cup lukewarm milk

1 stick butter
4 egg yolks
2 tablespoons sour cream
¼ teaspoon salt

Mix together the crumbled yeast, 2 tablespoons of the flour, 1 teaspoon of the sugar, and the lukewarm milk. Cover with a clean towel, and set aside to rise in a warm place.

In the meantime, cream the butter and remaining sugar for 30 minutes, by hand or in an electric mixer. Then add the egg yolks, one by one, and continue mixing until the batter is thick and yellow.

Place the remaining flour in a large bowl. Make a hole in the center and put the yeast sponge into it, along with the egg batter and the sour cream. Sprinkle with the salt and beat the dough with a large wooden spoon until it comes loose from the sides and bottom of the bowl. Cover again with a cloth and set aside in a warm place to rise until doubled in bulk, about 1 hour.

While it rises, prepare the filling. Mix together the following:

2 tablespoons melted butter
3–4 tablespoons sugar
2 ounces white raisins,
   cleaned and washed

1 tablespoon cinnamon
1 teaspoon each vanilla,
   orange, and lemon extract

Set aside:

1 egg

vanilla powdered sugar*

When the dough has risen, place it on a floured board and knead it well with your hands. Roll it out, spread the filling mixture on it and then roll it up, around the filling, like a jelly roll.

* Vanilla sugar, either powdered or granulated, is made by placing the sugar in a jar with a vanilla bean, covering tightly, and allowing to stand.

Transfer it to a greased 9-inch tube pan—it should not fill more than three-fourths of the mold—and let it rise again.

Beat an egg and brush over the top of the cake. Bake in a 450° oven for 15 minutes, then cover with a piece of brown paper and bake at 350° for about 1 hour longer. When done, sprinkle with vanilla powdered sugar and serve warm.

This is very good with a ground walnut or ground chocolate filling. Just substitute walnuts or chocolate for the cinnamon in the filling. And you can frost it with Chocolate Icing (see page 321), if you like.

HUNGARIAN COFFEE CREAM CAKE

SERVES 6–8

2 cakes yeast or 2 packages	pinch salt
active dry yeast	1 cup lukewarm cream
4 cups sifted flour	2 ounces raisins
6 tablespoons sugar	1 tablespoon cinnamon
1 cup lukewarm milk	1 egg, beaten
½ pound butter	vanilla powdered sugar
6 eggs, separated	(see preceding recipe)

Mix the yeast with 1 cup of the flour, 1 teaspoon of the sugar, and the lukewarm milk. Beat the mixture until it bubbles, then cover with a cloth and put in a warm place to rise.

While it rises, cream the butter with the egg yolks and the remaining sugar for about 20 minutes. Add the salt alternately with the remaining flour and the cream while continuing to mix. Finally, add the yeast mixture and beat with a wooden spoon until it leaves the bowl clean. Beat the egg whites separately and fold them carefully into the batter.

Mix together the raisins and cinnamon.

Pour one-third of the batter into a large greased and floured cake pan. Sprinkle with half of the cinnamon-raisin mixture. Pour in one-third more of the batter, sprinkle with the remaining cinnamon mix, then add the last of the batter. Cover with a cloth and let rise in a warm place for 30 minutes. Brush with beaten egg and bake in a 450° oven for 15 minutes. Cover with brown paper and bake at 350° for 1 hour more. The cake is done when it leaves the sides of the pan and is nicely brown.

Remove from the pan, sprinkle with vanilla powdered sugar, and serve warm or cool.

HUNGARIAN TWIST
SERVES 6–8

4 cups sifted flour	pinch sugar
pinch salt	2 egg yolks
1 cake yeast or 1 package	1 stick melted sweet butter
active dry yeast	1 egg, beaten
1–2 cups milk	

Put the flour and salt in a mixing bowl. Add the yeast dissolved in a little milk with a pinch of sugar. Add enough additional milk to make a soft, not too firm dough, and knead it well. Add the egg yolks, one by one, and continue kneading until smooth. Add the melted butter last, and continue kneading until bubbles form on the surface of the dough. Cover and set aside in a warm place to rise for about 1 hour.

Transfer to a well-floured board and knead again until the dough is smooth and elastic. Divide into four parts to make two twists, or two parts to make one large twist. Shape the dough into long rolls and twist together, then place in a buttered baking pan. Let rise for about 1 hour, until double in size. Brush with beaten egg and bake in a 375° oven for 1 hour.

VIENNESE COFFEECAKE
SERVES 6–8

2 cakes yeast, or 2 packages	4 eggs
active dry yeast	½ teaspoon salt
2 cups lukewarm milk	½ pint sour cream
1 cup plus 1 tablespoon sugar	1 tablespoon cinnamon
4½ sifted cups flour	1 tablespoon melted butter
1 stick butter	powdered sugar

Dissolve the yeast in 1 cup of the lukewarm milk with 1 teaspoon of the sugar and ½ cup of the flour. Mix well, cover, and let rise in a warm place.

While it rises, cream the butter with the remaining sugar for at least 30 minutes. Then add the eggs, one by one, beating after each addition. Next add the salt, sour cream, 1 cup of the flour, the second cup of milk, and the yeast mixture. Now add the remaining 3 cups flour and beat well. The dough should not be too soft. If it seems so, add a little more flour. Cover and let rise in a warm place until double in bulk, about 2 hours.

Grease and flour a cake pan. Spread the bottom with half of the batter. Mix the cinnamon, the 1 tablespoon sugar, and melted butter together and pour over the batter. Put the remaining batter on top, cover, and let rise again for 1 hour. Bake in a 350° oven for 1½ hours, or until golden brown. Remove from oven. Cool and sprinkle with powdered sugar.

Variation:

Omit the cinnamon, sugar, and butter mixture. Instead, divide the batter into three parts and place one in the bottom of the pan. Into the second mix 3–4 tablespoons of ground chocolate or cocoa, then place in the pan and top with the remaining batter. Brush with beaten egg and bake as above.

SPECIAL CAKES TO SERVE WITH TEA OR COFFEE
SERVES 6–8

1 heaping cup sifted flour	1 teaspoon lemon juice or
1 cup sweet butter	vinegar
1 egg yolk	water and vinegar
½ cup sour cream	jam
dash salt	vanilla powdered sugar
	(see page 272)

Work 1 tablespoon of the flour into the butter and make a square of it. Wrap in waxed paper and refrigerate.

Knead together the remaining flour, the egg yolk, sour cream, salt, and lemon juice or vinegar. Keep kneading until shiny and smooth.

Roll the dough out on a floured board. Place the chilled butter on it and fold the four sides of the dough over the butter. Roll it out again and give the dough a quarter turn on your board. Fold again in the same way you did before, roll out and turn again. Repeat until you have done this six times. After the last folding, place in the refrigerator and let stand overnight.

Next day, roll and fold the dough as before, three times. Return to the refrigerator for 30 minutes, then roll very thin. Sprinkle the dough with water to which you have added a few drops of vinegar.

Using a hot knife, cut the dough into three strips and spread the strips with your favorite jam. Put the strips together and lay in a baking pan. Bake in a 400° oven for about 30 minutes. Take from the oven, sprinkle with vanilla powdered sugar, and cut into thin slices. Serve hot or cold.

HUNGARIAN DOUGHNUTS (*Fánk*)

1½–2 DOZEN

2 cakes yeast or 2 packages
   active dry yeast
2 tablespoons plus a dash sugar
2 cups sifted flour
1½ cups milk
½ stick butter
6 egg yolks
½ teaspoon salt

½ cup sour cream
grated rind of 1 lemon
1 tablespoon vanilla
2 tablespoons rum
3 pounds shortening
vanilla powdered sugar
   (see page 272)
jam

Dissolve the yeast with a dash of sugar in 3 tablespoons of the flour and ½ cup of the milk to make a paste. Cover and let rise in a warm place for 30 minutes.

Put the rest of the flour in a large bowl. Make a hole in the center, and pour in, all at once, the yeast mixture and all but the last three ingredients. Beat with a large wooden spoon until smooth and shiny and the dough leaves the sides of the bowl. Remove the spoon and flour the top of the dough lightly. Cover and keep in a warm place until it doubles in size, 1–2 hours.

Place the dough on a floured board and knead it, then roll out about 1 inch thick. Cut small round circles. Cover them with a cloth and let rise again.

Heat the shortening in a wide pan with a cover until a cube of bread dropped in will brown. Then start frying the doughnuts, a few at a time. Drop them in, top side down, being careful not to overcrowd, and cover. Cook until they rise to the top of the fat, then uncover and turn with a slotted spatula. Cook *uncovered* until the second side is done. Transfer to paper towels with your spatula and keep warm while frying the rest.

Before serving, sprinkle with vanilla powdered sugar. Heat the jam in a small saucepan and serve it in a separate dish.

Pastry

SNOWBALLS AND STRIPS (*Csörege*)
SERVES 6–8

2 cups sifted flour	1 quart cooking oil or
4 egg yolks	3 pounds shortening
pinch salt	vanilla powdered sugar
pinch sugar	(see page 272)
1 stick butter	jam
2 tablespoons white wine	

Mix together the flour, egg yolks, salt, sugar, butter, and wine. Using your hands, work the dough very well on a floured board. Roll it very thin and divide into three parts.

Cut the first part of the dough into small squares and slit them, being sure not to cut them quite through.

Cut the second part into strips 1 inch wide and 5 inches long. Either knot these strips or wind them around your finger in loops.

The third part will make "roses." Using a wineglass as a cutter, make small rounds. Cut four small slits around the outside of each round, then place three of these together and pinch the middle. This will make a "rose" effect when you fry them.

Heat the cooking oil or shortening as directed for Hungarian Doughnuts. (These cakes need very deep fat.)

Fry the cakes a few at a time, being sure to drop the "roses" in with the rose side down. Fry until crisp and remove to paper towels. Serve hot, sprinkled with vanilla powdered sugar, and accompany them with warmed jam in a separate dish.

SOUR MILK DOUGHNUTS

SERVES 8–10

4½ cups sifted flour
1½ teaspoons baking soda
1½ teaspoons cream of tartar
½ teaspoon salt
¼ teaspoon nutmeg
3 eggs
1 cup sugar

3 tablespoons melted butter
1 cup buttermilk
fat for deep frying
vanilla sugar (see page 272)
   sugar and cinnamon, or
   Lemon Icing (see page 323)

Sift together the flour, baking soda, cream of tartar, salt, and nutmeg. Beat the eggs with the sugar until yellow and smooth, about 30 minutes. Add the melted butter and buttermilk and blend, then add the flour mixture and mix well.

Roll the dough out on a floured board to a ¼-inch thickness and cut with a doughnut cutter. Fry in deep fat, turning once, until brown. Serve sprinkled with vanilla powdered sugar, or sugar mixed with cinnamon, or frost with Lemon Icing.

BASIC PUFF PASTE

There are, I suppose, as many recipes for puff paste as there are cook books, and nobody seems to agree much on anything except the basic principles. These are my family recipes, handed on through the years, and they are the ones that I now use with great success.

The basic principles are few, and very simple. Everything must be kept as cold as possible at all times. Refrigerate your rolling pin and your board if possible during the periods when the dough is being chilled, and work in a cool place. Finally, keep your board and rolling pin well floured so that the dough won't stick and let the butter break through.

I always keep puff paste on hand. I make it in large amounts, since it will keep for weeks under refrigeration. You can always whip up a spectacular dessert from it to brighten an otherwise last-minute or emergency dinner, or surprise drop-in cocktail guests with delicate little hors d'oeuvres made in about the time it takes to mix up a round of drinks.

1 pound sweet butter	½ teaspoon salt
4 cups sifted all-purpose flour	1 tablespoon vinegar
	a *little* ice water

With two knives or a pastry blender, cut the butter into one cup of the flour until it forms a smooth ball. Wrap in waxed paper and put in the refrigerator.

Mix the remaining flour in a bowl with the salt, vinegar, and just barely enough ice water to make a stiff dough. Work it until it produces bubbles.

With a floured rolling pin, roll this dough out to a square shape on a floured board, making the dough about ½ inch thick. Put the prepared butter from the refrigerator in the center of the dough and fold the four sides of the dough over to completely cover and encase the butter. Now roll the dough out again to ½ inch thickness, and repeat the folding. Roll and fold again three more times. Then put the dough back in the refrigerator to chill and rest for 30 minutes. Take it out and repeat the rolling and folding three more times. Now let it stay in the refrigerator overnight.

The next day, repeat the rolling and folding three more times. Then roll out the amount you want to use and put the rest of the dough back in the refrigerator, wrapped in waxed paper, for future use.

FOR NAPOLEONS:

Roll out three very thin, rectangular sheets and bake in a preheated 425° oven for 20–25 minutes, or until golden brown. Layer with Vanilla Cream (see page 323) between the sheets and cut into rectangles.

FOR PIES:

Roll out the dough into two thin circles like ordinary pie crust, one to fit into the pie pan and the other to place on top, after you have filled the bottom crust. Cut a few slits in the top crust and bake in a pre-heated 375° oven for about 30 minutes, or until golden. While still warm, brush the top crust with sour cream.

FOR HORS D'OEUVRES:

Roll out your dough about ¼ inch thick and cut small circles from it with a cookie cutter. Brush the rounds with beaten egg and bake in a pre-heated 400° oven for 10–15 minutes, or until golden. Take them from the oven and cut a small circle in the top of each. Remove the center, being careful not to break through the bottom. Fill with creamed ham, chicken, or seafood and serve warm.

Note: This crust also makes a delicious chicken pie. Roll the dough thin and line a deep pie plate with it. Fill with creamed chicken. (To make "creamed" anything, cube or chop your basic ingredient and add to Basic White Sauce [see page 257] or Béchamel Sauce [see page 257], adding a little more seasoning to taste. Minced pimientos, green peppers, and a very little finely minced green onion add to the flavor, as do mushrooms and green peas, if you have them cooked and on hand.) Cut a heart, star, or circle from thin dough left over from lining the pan and place on top of the pie. Brush with beaten egg and sprinkle with grated Parmesan cheese. Bake in a pre-heated 375° oven for 30 minutes, or until golden brown.

ELABORATE PUFF PASTE

1 pound sweet butter	2 tablespoons sugar
4 cups sifted flour	juice and grated rind of
2 egg yolks	½ lemon
¼ teaspoon salt	a *little* ice water

Make a paste of the butter and 1 cup of the flour. Flatten it into a round shape and place in the refrigerator.

Make a dough from the remaining ingredients using just barely enough ice water to hold the dough together. Knead it well with your hands until it is smooth and shiny. Divide it into two parts and roll each part out, making them slightly larger than the butter paste. Put the chilled butter paste between the two sheets of dough and roll very thin into a square. Fold the four sides of the dough to meet in the middle, but *not* so they overlap. Roll out thin again and repeat the folding. Roll out and fold again, repeating this process five or six times. After the final folding, replace the dough, wrapped in waxed paper, in the refrigerator and leave overnight.

The next morning, roll out again very thin. Then fold and roll again three times. Fold once more and return to the refrigerator to chill for an hour. Now roll it to the size and thickness you want (for pastries, napoleons, pies, or hors d'oeuvres) and cut it to the shape you want with a hot knife. Wrap any leftover dough in waxed paper and return to the refrigerator, where it will keep as long as two weeks. Refrigerate your cut paste again for ½ hour and then, before baking, prick with a fork in several places to prevent bubbling.

Bake in a very hot oven, pre-heated to 500°, for 10 minutes. Then turn the pan around in the oven and lower the oven to 375°. Bake until puffed and golden, undisturbed (you can peek at it, but don't pull it out of the oven to look).

BALANCED BATTER (*Gleichgewicht*)

2 cups sifted flour	½ tablespoon vinegar
½ pound butter	1 teaspoon baking powder
½ pound cream cheese	2–3 tablespoons ice water

Work all the ingredients well with your hands to make a smooth, shiny dough. Roll it out and use for hors d'oeuvres, cookies, or turnovers.

For Hors d'Oeuvres:
MAKES 2–3 DOZEN

Add ½ teaspoon salt while kneading. Cut squares or circles and use a filling of minced ham or chicken, liver pâté, seafood, or cheese. Fold over and crimp the edges together with a fork. Bake at 375° until golden, about 30 minutes.

For Cookies:
MAKES 2–3 DOZEN

Add 1 tablespoon sugar to the dough while kneading and use a filling of jam or nuts mixed with raisins, a little sugar and cinnamon, and a drop of cream. Bake as above.

For Fruit Turnovers:
MAKES 1–1½ DOZEN

Peel, core, and slice the fruit and mix with a little sugar, cinnamon, raisins, and a drop of cream. Fill and bake as above.

For Cottage Cheese:
MAKES 1–1½ DOZEN

Sieve the cottage cheese and add 1–2 egg yolks, sugar to taste, a dash of cinnamon, raisins, and a little sour cream. Fill and bake as above.

Note: All of the above will be a prettier color if brushed with a beaten egg before baking.

PIES AND PASTRIES

There are a few basic rules to remember when handling pie crust or pastry dough. The ingredients should always be very cold in order to achieve a tender, flaky crust, and the dough should be handled as little as possible.

To set the crust, place the pie first in a hot oven, 450°–500°, for 10 minutes. Then reduce the oven temperature to 350° or 375° and continue baking. Bake only long enough to cook the filling—do not dry it out.

An empty pastry shell is best baked in an oven-glass pie plate, so you can see when it is brown enough. Use a quick 450° oven the whole time.

For a nice color, brush the upper crust of a two-crust pie with beaten yolk, milk, or cream.

PLAIN PIE PASTRY
MAKES 2 8- OR 9-INCH CRUSTS

2 cups sifted flour	1 stick butter
¼ teaspoon salt	a *little* ice water

Sift the flour and salt together and cut in the butter with two knives or a pastry blender until the mixture makes small balls the size of barley. Add 1 tablespoon ice water and stir with a fork to start the dough, and add another tablespoon ice water to make the dough form a ball (or even a third tablespoon ice water if necessary). Flour a board and put the ball of dough on it, flattening it out. Divide into two parts, making two balls, and refrigerate for at least 1 hour, but preferably overnight. Use one ball for a one-crust pie and roll thin, fitting into the pie tin—use the second ball for a two-crust pie.

FLAKY PASTRY DOUGH
MAKES 2 8- OR 9-INCH CRUSTS

Place Plain Pastry dough on a floured board and roll thin. Spread with very thinly shaved sweet butter. Fold the four edges to meet in the middle and roll out again. Repeat with the shaved butter. Roll and fold again and repeat four times, using about 1 stick sweet butter in all. Place the dough in the refrigerator overnight.

The next morning, roll it out and fold it—but this time *without* the butter—two or three times. Use a cold board and rolling pin and work fast, for the dough melts easily. Fold and chill again, and then roll to use.

MINIATURE SHELLS
4 DOZEN

3 cups sifted flour	1 cup butter
½ teaspoon salt	a *little* ice water

Sift the flour and salt together. Cut in the butter with two knives or a pastry blender until the mixture forms small balls the size of peas. Sprinkle in 1 tablespoon ice water and work with a fork, adding a little more ice water if necessary to make a firm dough.

Roll very thin on a floured board. Cut into two-inch rounds and fit into small muffin pans. Prick the bottoms with a fork and bake in a 450° over for 10–12 minutes, or until golden.

This recipe will make about four dozen small shells. Fill them with creamed ham, meat, cheese, or shrimp for hors d'oeuvres, or with pie filling or fruit and cream for dessert.

One shudders to contemplate just how many different pies you could make in a lifetime if you like to cook and entertain. The mind reels. It would have to be, as Eliza Doolittle says, "Hundrids and thousings. . . ." But everybody who cooks has their favorite recipes for fillings, and so no matter how many times I make these, they're still the most popular in my collection, and I still enjoy making (and eating) them. So do my friends. So will yours.

LEMON CREAM PIE
SERVES 6–8

2 tablespoons butter	1 cup half and half
1 cup sugar	3 tablespoons flour
2 egg yolks	2 egg whites, stiffly beaten
juice and grated rind of	1 unbaked 8- or 9-inch
1 lemon (or orange)	pie shell

Cream the butter with the sugar and add the egg yolks, juice, and grated rind of 1 lemon or orange. Blend well, then add the half and half and flour and mix thoroughly. Finally, fold in the stiffly beaten egg whites.

Pour the mixture into the unbaked pie shell and bake 10 minutes in a 450° oven. Reduce the oven heat to 375° and continue to bake for 30 minutes, or until the filling is set and browned.

CREAM CHEESE PIE
SERVES 6–8

3 ounces cream cheese	grated rind of 1 orange
¾ cup cream	dash salt
¾ cup sugar	4 tablespoons flour
3 egg yolks	3 egg whites, stiffly beaten
½ teaspoon vanilla	1 unbaked 8- or 9-inch pie shell

Blend all the ingredients except the egg whites and mix thoroughly. Then carefully fold in the egg whites. Pour into the unbaked pie shell and bake in a 450° oven for 10 minutes. Reduce the oven temperature to 375° and continue baking for 30 minutes, or until the mixture sets and the shell is nicely browned.

CHOCOLATE PIE

SERVES 6–8

2½ cups milk
4 squares semisweet chocolate
4 tablespoons flour
1 cup sugar
dash salt

4 egg yolks
2 tablespoons sweet butter
1 tablespoon vanilla
1 9-inch plain pastry shell,
  half-baked

Put the milk in the top of a double boiler and shave the chocolate into it. When the chocolate is melted, remove from the heat and beat the mixture with an egg beater.

Combine the rest of the ingredients except the butter and vanilla, and beat well to make a batter. Then pour the chocolate mixture gradually into the batter, stirring. Return this mixture to the double boiler and cook, stirring constantly, until thick. Remove from the heat and add the butter and vanilla.

Pour into a half-baked pie shell and bake in a pre-heated 350° oven for 12 minutes, or until delicately browned. Refrigerate and serve cold.

EGGNOG PIE

SERVES 6–8

4 egg yolks
dash salt
½ cup sugar
½ cup hot water (freshly
  heated, not from the tap)
2 tablespoons flour
1 tablespoon unflavored
  gelatin

¼ cup cold water
3 tablespoons rum
4 egg whites, stiffly beaten
1 baked 8- or 9-inch pie shell
whipped cream and cinnamon
  for garnish

In the top of a double boiler, combine the egg yolks with the salt, sugar, hot water, and flour. Stir over hot water until the mixture becomes a custard. Add the gelatin, which has been soaked in ¼ cup cold water. When the gelatin has dissolved, add the rum and beat well. Remove from the heat and cool. When the mixture begins to set, fold in the stiffly beaten egg whites carefully and pour into the baked pie shell. Chill in the refrigerator, and just before serving, garnish with whipped cream sprinkled with cinnamon.

LEMON CHIFFON PIE

SERVES 6–8

4 eggs, separated
⅔ cup plus ¼ cup sugar
½ cup lemon juice
grated rind of 1 lemon
1 teaspoon flour

dash salt
1 envelope gelatin
¼ cup cold water
1 baked 8- or 9-inch pie shell
whipped cream for garnish

Cream the egg yolks with ⅔ cup sugar, the lemon juice, grated lemon rind, flour, and salt. Transfer to a double boiler and cook until smooth and thick, stirring constantly. Add the gelatin, which has been dissolved in ¼ cup cold water, and continue to stir until it thickens. Remove from the heat and cool until it begins to set. Beat the egg whites until stiff, beating the ¼ cup sugar into them, then fold into the custard. Pour into the baked pie shell and chill. Before serving, garnish with slightly sweetened whipped cream.

CREAM PUFFS

1 DOZEN LARGE

1 cup cake flour
¼ teaspoon salt
½ cup shortening

1 cup water
4 eggs

Sift the flour, then measure and sift again with the salt. Put the shortening in a saucepan with the 1 cup water and bring to a boil. Remove from the heat and add the flour all at once. Beat until the mixture forms a smooth ball and leaves the sides of the pan. Cool until tepid and add the eggs, one at a time, beating vigorously until you have a smooth, shiny, velvety dough.

Place a spoonful at a time on a lightly greased baking sheet, allowing room to swell and spread. Use a tablespoon if you are planning these for dessert, a teaspoon if you are going to use them for hors d'oeuvres.

Bake the larger puffs in a hot oven (425°) for 15–20 minutes. Then reduce the heat to 350° and continue to bake for 20 minute longer, or until golden brown and dry. The smaller puffs will take less time. Allow to cool, out of a draft, on a cake rack. Slit the bottom, side or top to fill.

For hors d'oeuvres, slit the top and fill with cream cheese, ham, or seafood.

For dessert, slit the side or bottom and fill with soft ice cream, whipped cream, custard, fruit, or berries and top with chocolate sauce, whipped cream, or a frosting.

ÉCLAIRS

1 DOZEN LARGE

Use the Cream Puff dough and make longish strips, about 4 inches by 1 inch. Bake as above and cool, then fill with Vanilla Cream Filling (see page 323), Mocha Cream Filling (see page 323), or whipped cream. Frost with the following:

Coffee Icing for Éclairs:

2 cups powdered sugar   ½ cup very strong coffee

Mix together until creamy, then brush on the éclairs and let dry.

STRUDEL DOUGH

12–16 SLICES

2 cups sifted flour   a little tepid water
1 egg   melted butter
1 tablespoon shortening   sugar
1 tablespoon vinegar

Mix together the flour, egg, shortening, vinegar, and enough tepid water to make a soft dough. Knead it on a floured board until it becomes bubbly and comes clean off your hands. Let it stand for 1 hour on the board, covered with a cloth and a warm pan.

Spread a cloth over a large table and sprinkle it with flour. Put the dough on the cloth and brush with a little melted butter, then begin to pull the dough out, working from the sides and using the tips of your fingers to stretch it gently. Be careful not to tear the dough—work gently! Pull it out paper thin, letting the ends hang over the table. (You can make a second strudel from the ends, after cutting them off.)

Let the dough rest while you make your filling. Then sprinkle the whole sheet of dough with melted butter and dust with sugar. Place your filling on half the sheet and begin to roll from the filled side, using the cloth to help lift the dough evenly as you begin to roll.

Place the filled roll on a baking sheet and brush with more melted butter. Bake in a 350° oven for about 1 hour, or until the filling is cooked and the dough is richly brown. Cut into serving pieces and serve hot or warm.

FILLINGS FOR STRUDEL

APPLE FILLING:

4 apples	1 teaspoon cinnamon
4 ounces walnuts	½ stick melted butter
2 ounces white raisins	vanilla powdered sugar
½ cup sugar	(see page 272)

Peel, core, and slice the apples. Mix together the walnuts, raisins, sugar, cinnamon. Sprinkle the dough with melted butter. Spread the mixture over half the dough, then cover with the apple slices. Roll as directed.

Brush the top of the roll with butter and bake in a 350° oven for about 1 hour. Serve hot or warm sprinkled with vanilla powdered sugar.

FRUIT FILLING:

You can use any kind of fruit to fill your strudel, merely following the apple recipe and substituting a different fruit. But taste for sweetness before you spread the filling, for some fruits require more or less sugar.

CHEESE FILLING:

1 pound hoop cheese
2 eggs, separated
1 cup sugar
2 tablespoons sour cream
1 stick melted butter
2 ounces blanched, grated
    almonds

1 teaspoon cinnamon
2 ounces white raisins
additional melted butter
vanilla powdered sugar
    (see page 272)

Cream the cheese with the egg yolks and ½ cup of the sugar. Add the sour cream. Beat the egg whites stiff and fold them in.

Mix together the butter, almonds, the remaining ½ cup sugar, cinnamon, and raisins, and spread over half the dough. Then spread the cheese mixture over this very carefully with a spatula. Sprinkle with a little more melted butter and roll. Bake at 375° for 45–60 minutes, or until crisp and golden brown. Cut into serving pieces and sprinkle with vanilla powdered sugar. Serve cold or warm.

HUNGARIAN NAPOLEONS (*Crèmes Lepeny*)

16–20 SQUARES

2 cups sifted cake flour
1 egg
1 teaspoon butter
pinch salt
melted butter

lukewarm water
sugar
Vanilla Cream Filling
    (see page 323)
vanilla powdered sugar

Mix the cake flour, egg, butter, and salt, adding enough lukewarm water to make a dough that is not too soft. Knead on a floured board until it bubbles and becomes very shiny and smooth. Cover with a towel and place a warm pan over it. Let sit for 30 minutes to 1 hour.

Pull the dough out as directed for Strudel Dough (see page 287). Sprinkle with melted butter and granulated sugar, then fold it over and over, four to six times. Bake in a 350° oven until it is a nice yellow, but be careful not to burn it.

Split and fill the Napoleons with Vanilla Cream Filling, cut into squares or long pieces, and serve sprinkled with vanilla powdered sugar.

CREAM STRUDEL

SERVES 6–8

1 recipe Elaborate Puff Paste
  (see page 280)
Vanilla Cream Filling
  (see page 323)

whipped cream (optional)
fresh strawberries or
  raspberries (optional)

Make the puff paste and roll the dough ¼ inch thick. Cut into strips 2–3 inches wide and bake. Cool and pile up the strips with Vanilla Cream Filling in between. You can also use whipped cream, or use one layer of Vanilla Cream Filling and one layer of fresh strawberries or raspberries.

Cookies

LINZER COOKIES

ABOUT 2 DOZEN

3 hard-boiled egg yolks
1 stick butter
4 ounces ground almonds
½ cup sugar
1 cup sifted flour
dash salt

1 tablespoon baking powder
1 teaspoon each orange and
  vanilla extract
2–3 tablespoons sour cream
beaten egg
coarsely chopped nuts

Put the egg yolks through a ricer and cream with the rest of the ingredients except the beaten egg and nuts. Knead on a floured board until you have a smooth dough, then roll out and cut with a cookie cutter. Place on a greased and floured cookie sheet, brush with beaten egg and sprinkle with coarsely chopped nuts. Bake in a 375° oven for about 20 minutes, or until golden.

ISCHLI FANK

1½–2 DOZEN

1 cup butter
1 cup sugar
½ cup grated nuts
1 cup sifted flour
juice and grated rind of
  1 lemon

jam
Chocolate Icing (optional)
  (see page 321)

Cream the butter, sugar, nuts, flour, lemon juice, and rind. Knead well on a floured board and roll out very thin. Cut rounds with a wineglass or cookie cutter. Bake in a 375° oven for 10–12 minutes, or until light brown. Remove from the oven and cool. Spread half the cookies with jam and top with the other half. If you like, you can frost them with Chocolate Icing.

ALMOND COOKIES I

2 DOZEN

10 ounces grated almonds
5 tablespoons sugar

2 egg whites
Lemon Icing (see page 323)

Cream the almonds, sugar and egg whites together and knead well on a floured board. Roll to a ¼-inch thickness and cut little sticks from the dough. Bake in a 300° oven for about 5 minutes, or until set. Remove from the oven and cool, then frost with Lemon Icing.

ALMOND COOKIES II

1 DOZEN

½ cup butter
¾ cup sugar
3 egg yolks

1 teaspoon orange extract
¾ cup grated almonds
1 cup flour

Cream the butter and sugar, then add the egg yolks and continue to cream. Add the rest of the ingredients and mix well. Drop a teaspoonful at a time on a buttered, floured baking sheet and bake at 375° for 10–12 minutes, or until delicately brown.

NUT STICKS

1½–2 DOZEN

½ pound sugar
½ pound grated walnuts
1 egg

1 teaspoon vanilla
Lemon or Chocolate Icing
(see pages 321, 323)

Mix the ingredients and knead into a dough on a floured board. Roll out and cut into little sticks and place on a baking sheet in a very slow oven (250°). The nut sticks really require drying for about 30 minutes rather than baking. Remove and cool when done, and frost with either Lemon or Chocolate Icing.

LADYFINGERS

2 DOZEN

5 tablespoons powdered sugar
3 egg whites
2 egg yolks
½ tablespoon vanilla
⅓ cup sifted flour

dash salt
additional powdered sugar
vanilla powdered sugar
(see page 272)

Fold the sugar into the egg whites and beat until stiff. Beat the egg yolks separately until very thick. Fold them and the vanilla into the whites. Sift the flour with the salt and fold carefully into the batter.

Line an ungreased cookie sheet with waxed paper. Force the batter through a pastry bag onto the paper in strips 4 inches long and 1 inch wide. Sprinkle with powdered sugar and bake in a slow oven (325°) for 10 minutes. They should be just golden, not brown. Remove from the oven and cool, then sprinkle with vanilla powdered sugar.

CHOCOLATE MUSHROOMS

1 DOZEN

4 ounces butter
3 teaspoons sugar
2 egg yolks
1 teaspoon rum

6 ounces grated semisweet
   chocolate
grated almonds or chocolate

Cream the butter with the sugar, then add the rest of the ingredients and mix well. Make little balls and roll in grated almonds or grated chocolate.

NUT BALLS

2 DOZEN

juice and grated rind of
   1 orange
6 ounces grated walnuts
3 tablespoons honey

pinch salt
2 tablespoons sugar
grated nuts or chocolate

Mix the orange juice and rind with the walnuts and honey. Boil until thick. Remove from the heat, cool, then add the salt and sugar. Make little balls and roll in grated nuts or chocolate.

VANILLA CROISSANTS

3 DOZEN

1 cup sweet butter
½ cup sugar
pinch salt
5 ounces grated nuts

1 cup plus 2 tablespoons
   sifted flour
vanilla powdered sugar
   (see page 272)

Cream the butter with the sugar, then add the salt, nuts, and flour and knead well on a floured board. Shape small crescents from the dough and place on a buttered and floured baking sheet. Bake in a 375° oven for 15–18 minutes, or until golden brown. While still warm, roll in vanilla powdered sugar.

HAZELNUT BARS
2 DOZEN

1 cup sugar
1 cup ground hazelnuts
1 egg yolk
grated rind of 1 lemon

1 egg white
1 cup powdered sugar
1 tablespoon lemon juice

Knead the sugar, nuts, egg yolk, and lemon rind on a floured board to make a dough. Cut into little bars 2 inches long and ½ inch wide. Bake in a 350° oven for 10 minutes, then remove and cool. Make an icing by mixing the egg white, powdered sugar, and lemon juice and beat until thick. Frost the bars and return to a tepid oven to dry—*not* to bake.

15

SWEETNESS AND LIGHTNESS

Cakes and Tortes, Fillings, and Frostings

The art of making cakes and pastries goes as far back as recorded history, and by 1270 was considered important enough for a trade union of pastry makers to be formed in Paris. By the sixteenth century these "Master Pastrymakers" were enjoying important privileges under the law, and by the eighteenth century all serious diners regarded *les entremets* as the glorious finale to any proper meal.

Of course, in those days the chefs were in the employ of great aristocrats and could afford to spend hours, if not days, whipping up their luscious concoctions. And the amounts of expensive butter, sugar, eggs, and nuts they used were of no consequence. The European cook, too, would think nothing of beating by hand for an hour, which is hardly something you can dash home from the office to do. But you can use an electric mixer, at a slow to medium speed, to beat the mixture to a smooth and fluffy texture. As for the expensive ingredients, these are what make the desserts delicious. But they also make them very rich, and small portions are quite satisfying, thereby balancing out the cost.

Note: You can bake most of these cakes and tortes in your ordinary pans. But where the recipe specifies "torte pan," it means a special pan, with springform sides and a removable bottom. They are essential to the success of these confections; you can buy them in the housewares department of any large store.

Cakes

WHITE CAKE
SERVES 6-8

2 cups sifted cake flour
2 teaspoons baking powder
1 stick butter
1 cup sugar

½ cup milk
1 teaspoon vanilla
4 egg whites

Sift the flour with the baking powder. Cream the butter and sugar for 30 minutes, or beat in a mixer until thick. While beating, slowly add the milk and vanilla, then add half the flour.

Beat the egg whites stiff and fold carefully into the batter, then fold in the remaining flour. Bake in two, three, or four 8- or 9-inch layers in a 375° oven for 30–35 minutes. Cool and fill or frost. (See Frostings and Fillings at the end of the chapter.)

MARBLE CAKE
SERVES 8–10

½ stick butter
½ pound sugar
1 teaspoon baking powder
1 teaspoon vanilla

6 eggs, separated
4½ cups sifted cake flour
1 cup milk
2 tablespoons cocoa

Mix the butter with the sugar, baking powder, and vanilla. Add the egg yolks, one by one, creaming after each addition, and beat until thick and yellow. Add the flour and milk and beat again. Beat the egg whites until stiff and fold carefully into the batter.

Remove one-third of the batter and fold the cocoa into it. Pour one-third of the yellow batter into a buttered and floured 8- or 9-inch cake pan. Pour the cocoa batter over, and follow with the remaining yellow batter.

Bake in a 350° oven for about 30 minutes, or until a toothpick inserted in the center comes out clean. Cool and serve in very thin slices.

ANGEL FOOD CAKE #1
SERVES 6–8

1¼ cups sifted cake flour
½ cup sugar
1½ cups egg whites
   (about 12 eggs)
dash salt

1¼ teaspoons cream of tartar
1 teaspoon vanilla
1 teaspoon orange extract
1⅓ cups powdered sugar,
   sifted

Sift the flour and sugar together four times. Combine the egg whites, salt, cream of tartar, vanilla, and orange extract in a large bowl and beat until soft peaks form.

Measure out the sifted powdered sugar and add to the batter in four portions, beating well after each addition. Carefully *fold* in the flour-sugar mixture in four portions, but do *not* beat.

Pour the batter into an ungreased tube pan and bake at 375° for 35–40 minutes. Cool, upside down, on a rack, then loosen the sides with a spatula and remove from the pan.

Serve plain, or fill or frost any way you desire.

ANGEL FOOD CAKE #2
SERVES 4–6

1 cup egg whites
  (about 8 eggs)
1 tablespoon cream of tartar
dash salt
1¼ cups sugar

1 cup sifted cake flour
red raspberry or apricot jam
Coffee, Lemon, or Orange
  Icing
  (see pages 321–3)

Beat the egg whites until stiff with the cream of tartar and salt. Add the sugar in four portions, as in Angel Food Cake #1. Then fold the flour in gradually. Bake, in three or four layers, in 8- or 9-inch cake pans at 325° for 12–20 minutes.

When cool, spread the layers with red raspberry or apricot jam, placing the layers on top of each other. Frost with Coffee, Lemon, or Orange Icing.

PECAN NUTMEG CAKE
SERVES 6–8

2 cups sifted flour
1 teaspoon baking powder
dash salt
1 teaspoon nutmeg
1 cup white raisins
1½ cups finely grated pecans
1 cup sugar

1 cup brown sugar
3 eggs
1 cup butter (2 sticks)
1 teaspoon vanilla
1 tablespoon milk
brandy, rum, or wine

Sift the flour with the baking powder, salt, and nutmeg. Mix the raisins with the pecans, white and brown sugars, and then add to the flour mixture.

Cream the eggs with the butter, vanilla, and milk and mix into the batter. Beat well and turn into a greased and floured loaf pan. Set the cake in a cold oven and set at 300°. Bake about 2 hours, or until a toothpick inserted in the center comes out clean. Remove from the oven and cool in the pan for 20 minutes, then turn the cake onto a rack to finish cooling.

Wrap the cake in a clean cloth soaked in brandy, rum, or wine and let stand in the refrigerator for a week to ten days before serving. Slice very thin to serve.

WALNUT CAKE #1

SERVES 8-12

6 eggs, separated	grated peel of 1 orange or
6 tablespoons sugar	½ lemon
½ teaspoon vanilla extract	1 tablespoon finely ground
12 tablespoons grated walnuts	bread crumbs

Cream the egg yolks with the sugar until very thick. Add the vanilla, the grated peel, and 6 tablespoons of the grated nuts. Beat the egg whites stiff and fold half of them into the mixture, then add the other half of the nuts, the remaining egg whites, and the bread crumbs. Pour into two greased and floured 8- or 9-inch cake tins and bake in a 350° oven for 30 minutes, or until done.

Fill and frost with the following:

MOCHA FILLING

½ cup sugar	1 pint whipping cream,
½ cup strong black coffee	beaten stiff
1 square semisweet chocolate, grated	

Cook the sugar and coffee together to make a syrup of spreading consistency. Cool. Mix the grated chocolate and whipped cream lightly into the syrup. Fill and frost the cake with this mixture. Keep refrigerated until serving time.

Note: You can fill and frost this cake simply with sweetened, vanilla-flavored whipped cream. But the mocha filling is better.

WALNUT CAKE #2 (*Nuss Kuchen*)
SERVES 6–8

6 egg yolks
6 tablespoons sugar
1 teaspoon baking powder
juice and rind of 1 lemon
12 tablespoons grated walnuts

7 tablespoons sifted cake flour
6 egg whites, stiffly beaten
vanilla powdered sugar
  (see page 272) or
  Coffee Icing (see page 322)

Cream the egg yolks with the sugar for 30 minutes, or beat in a mixer until thick. Add the baking powder, lemon juice and rind, grated walnuts, and flour. Mix gently, then fold in the beaten egg whites.

Pour into a tube pan or coffeecake pan and bake at 350° for about 45 minutes. Cool. Serve sprinkled with vanilla powdered sugar or ice with Coffee Icing.

RIGO JANCSI
16–20 SQUARES

All Hungarians love romance, and the name of this cake is a good illustration of that.

Rigo Jancsi was a Hungarian gypsy violinist, by all reports ugly and cross-eyed. But he had a magic power in his music that caused the beautiful Princess of Simay to fall in love with him, renounce her title and her husband, and run away with him. He became so famous and was so sought after that restaurants named all kinds of dishes for him, and bakers vied to make his favorite cakes. This is one of them, rich and delicious. It is made in three parts, which makes it seem complicated the first time. It really isn't. Try it and you'll see that Rigo Jancsi not only knew about music and women, but about food as well.

BATTER

6 egg yolks
6 tablespoons sugar
3 squares semisweet chocolate
2 tablespoons ground blanched
  almonds

6 egg whites, stiffly beaten
2 tablespoons flour

Cream the egg yolks with the sugar for 30 minutes, or until thick. Melt the chocolate in a saucepan over hot water. When melted, add to the egg yolk mixture and then add the blanched almonds. Fold in the stiffly beaten egg whites, and finally, fold in the flour. Bake this batter in two large sheets (use large cake pans so that the batter is about half an inch thick) in a 350° oven for 15–20 minutes.

FILLING

15–20 lumps of sugar
½ cup very strong black coffee
2 squares semisweet chocolate,
  melted

2 squares semisweet chocolate,
  grated
2 cups heavy cream, whipped

Make a syrup by cooking the sugar and coffee until thick. Then add the melted chocolate and continue cooking until the mixture reaches a pouring consistency. Cool, and when cold add the grated chocolate and the whipped cream in alternate portions, blending after each addition.

ICING

15–20 lumps of sugar
½ cup water
3 squares semisweet chocolate,
  melted

2 tablespoons cream
1 teaspoon butter

Cook the sugar in the ½ cup water to a syrup, then add the chocolate and cream and cook until the mixture reaches a pouring consistency. Remove from the heat and add the butter, stirring to mix well. Let cool but do not chill.

TO ASSEMBLE

Frost one sheet of cake with the cooled chocolate icing. Spread the cream filling evenly over the other sheet with a spatula and place the frosted sheet on top of the filled one. Chill in the refrigerator and cut into small squares to serve.

DEER CAKE (*Öz Hát*)

SERVES 8–10

6 eggs, separated
1 cup plus 2 tablespoons sugar
2 squares semisweet chocolate
dash ground cloves
juice and grated rind of
  ½ lemon

½ pound walnuts
1 tablespoon bread crumbs
Chocolate Icing (see page 321)
blanched slivered almonds
  for garnish

Cream the egg yolks with the sugar for 30 minutes, or until thick. Melt the chocolate over hot water and mix into the egg yolks, adding the cloves, lemon juice, and grated lemon rind. Beat the egg whites stiff. Carefully fold the egg whites, walnuts, and bread crumbs in alternate portions into the batter, ending with the egg whites. Pour the batter into a long buttered and floured baking pan. (If you have a long, ribbed mold, bake the cake in that.) Bake at 375° for about 30 minutes, or until done. Remove to a board and cool. Then frost with Chocolate Icing and garnish with the almonds.

CHESTNUT CAKE

SERVES 6–8

¾ cup butter (1½ sticks)
1 cup plus 2 tablespoons sugar
2 cups chestnuts, boiled,
  peeled, and mashed
1 teaspoon baking powder
1 tablespoon rum

4 eggs, separated
1 cup heavy cream, whipped
vanilla
Chocolate Icing (optional)
  (see page 321)

Cream the butter with 1 cup sugar until fluffy, then cream in the mashed chestnuts. Add the baking powder, rum, and the egg yolks, one by one. Beat the egg whites until stiff and fold carefully into the batter. Pour into a buttered, floured 8- or 9-inch baking pan and bake at 350° for 45 minutes.

When the cake is cool, split it. Fill and frost with the whipped cream sweetened with 2 tablespoons sugar and a few drops vanilla. Or fill with whipped cream and ice with Chocolate Icing.

SWEETHEART CAKE

SERVES 6–8

2 cups sifted cake flour	1 cup milk
1½ cups sugar	1 teaspoon vanilla
2 teaspoons baking powder	¼ teaspoon orange extract
½ teaspoon salt	4 eggs
1 stick soft butter	

Set the oven to 350°. Grease and flour two heart-shaped cake pans.

Sift together the flour, sugar, baking powder, and salt and drop in the butter. Pour in ¾ cup of the milk and the flavorings and beat. Add the eggs, one by one, and the remaining ¼ cup milk, beating well either by hand or in an electric mixer for 2 more minutes. Pour into the prepared pans and bake for 20–25 minutes. Cool in the pans for 10–15 minutes, then turn out onto a cake rack.

Frost with the following:

FROSTING

2 egg whites	1 teaspoon vanilla
dash salt	1–2 drops red food coloring
⅓ cup white corn syrup	flaked coconut (optional)
1 teaspoon cream of tartar	

Beat the egg whites with a dash of salt until they are fluffy and form peaks. Bring the corn syrup to a boil in a small pan and add the cream of tartar and vanilla. Pour this into the egg whites in a thin stream, beating all the time. Tint the frosting pink with the food coloring, then fill the layers and swirl on the top and sides. Sprinkle with canned, flaked coconut, if you wish, to make the cake even fancier.

CHOCOLATE SQUARES OR FINGERS
SERVES 6–8

5 eggs, separated	juice and grated rind of ½
1 cup powdered sugar	lemon
5 ounces semisweet chocolate,	vanilla powdered sugar
grated	(optional) (see page 272)
5 ounces ground walnuts	1 pint whipped cream
2 tablespoons instant coffee	

Cream the egg yolks with the sugar until thick and yellow. Continue beating and add alternately the grated chocolate, nuts, coffee, lemon juice, and rind. Beat the egg whites until stiff and fold carefully into the batter. Pour into a buttered and floured baking pan and bake at 375° for 25–30 minutes, or until the toothpick test shows that it's done.

Sprinkle a board with sugar and turn the cake out onto it to cool. To serve, cut into squares or shapes and sprinkle with vanilla powdered sugar, or ice them individually. Serve with the whipped cream.

CHOCOLATE CAKE
SERVES 6–8

12 ounces semisweet chocolate	6 eggs, separated
chips	1½ cups sifted cake flour
1¼ cups butter	raspberry or apricot jam
¾ cup sugar	whipped cream
dash salt	

Melt half the chocolate chips over hot water. Cream ¾ cup of the butter and the sugar together until thick and fluffy, then add the salt and melted chocolate, blending well. Add the egg yolks and continue to beat after each addition.

Beat the egg whites until stiff and fold into the yolk mixture, then fold in the flour. Turn into a buttered and floured torte pan.

Bake at 375° for 35–40 minutes and cool. Remove from the pan and spread the jam over the top and sides.

Melt the remaining chocolate chips over hot water, then add the remaining ½ cup butter and stir until blended. Cool the mixture until it reaches spreading consistency, then spread over the top and sides of the cake with a spatula. Serve with whipped cream.

CHEESECAKE
SERVES 6–8

4 3-ounce packages cream cheese
2 eggs
½ teaspoon plus ½ tablespoon vanilla

½ cup plus 2 tablespoons sugar
1½ cups sour cream

Cream the packages of cream cheese with the eggs, the ½ teaspoon vanilla, and the ½ cup sugar. Mix well and pour into a buttered and floured 8- or 9-inch cake pan. Bake at 375° for 20 minutes.

While it bakes, mix the sour cream, the 2 tablespoons sugar and the ½ tablespoon vanilla. At the end of 20 minutes, spread this mixture over the cake and return to the oven for 5 minutes. Remove from the oven, chill and serve cold.

STRAWBERRY SHORTCAKE
SERVES 6–8

2 cups sifted flour
3 tablespoons sugar
2 teaspoons baking powder
¼ teaspoon salt
½ stick butter

3 egg yolks
½ cup milk
3 boxes strawberries
1 pint heavy cream, sweetened

Sift together the flour, sugar, baking powder, and salt. Cut in the butter to make small lumps the size of peas, then add the egg yolks and milk to make a soft dough. Turn onto a floured board and knead smooth. Divide the dough into two or three parts and shape into rounds of equal size. Place on buttered baking sheets and brush with a little melted butter. Bake in a hot oven at 450° for 12–16 minutes. Remove from the baking sheets and cool.

Wash and dry the strawberries, reserving the nicest with their stems for the garnish and slicing the rest. Sweeten the sliced berries to taste and force through a sieve.

Whip the cream until stiff, sweetening it slightly. Mix half the whipped cream with the sieved berries. Use this as a filling and frosting for the sides of the cake and top with the remaining whipped cream. Decorate with the reserved berries and refrigerate until serving time.

PETITS FOURS (*Basic Recipe*)

2 DOZEN

½ cup butter	1 teaspoon vanilla
1 cup powdered sugar	½ cup milk
2 eggs, separated	jam
1¾ cups sifted flour	Chocolate or Coffee Icing
½ teaspoon salt	(see page 321 or 322)
2 teaspoons baking powder	

Cream the butter with a wooden spoon until fluffy. Add the sugar gradually, creaming it in with the butter. Then add the egg yolks, one by one, blending well. Sift the flour, salt, and baking powder together and add to the batter, beating constantly. Add the vanilla and the milk, beating after each addition. Beat the egg whites until stiff and carefully fold into the batter. Turn the batter into two 8-inch (or one large) greased and floured baking pan. Bake in a 375° oven for 25–30 minutes. Cool and cut into small shapes. Split and fill with jam and frost with Chocolate or Coffee Icing.

NUT PETITS FOURS

2 DOZEN

Follow the basic recipe and add 1 cup finely chopped walnuts or hazelnuts and ½ cup more milk to the batter.

CHOCOLATE PETITS FOURS
2 DOZEN

Follow the basic recipe and add 2 squares of melted semisweet chocolate and ¼ cup more milk to the batter.

MARBLE CAKE
SERVES 6-8

Follow the basic Petits Fours recipe and divide the batter into two equal parts. Add 2 squares of grated chocolate and ½ cup milk to one part. Drop the two batters a spoonful at a time into a greased and floured 8-inch baking pan, alternating a spoonful of plain batter with a spoonful of chocolate batter. Add a second layer, placing a spoonful of plain over a spoonful of chocolate and the chocolate over the plain. Bake in a 375° oven for about 50 minutes. Remove from the oven and cool. Slice very thin to serve, and if you like, serve whipped cream with it.

Tortes

SACHER TORTE
SERVES 8-10

The delicious Sacher Torte, named for its creator, Mrs. Sacher of Vienna, has become justly famous, not only in Vienna and Europe but around the world. There have been many imitations of it, but this is the original recipe. The secret ingredient is the jam that you spread under the icing!

1 cup butter (2 sticks)	2 tablespoons fine bread crumbs
1 cup sugar	or flour
8 eggs, separated	red raspberry or apricot jam
3 ounces finely ground almonds	
6 squares semisweet chocolate, ground	

Cream the butter and sugar for about 30 minutes, or until thick and fluffy. Add the egg yolk, one by one, creaming all the time, then add the almonds and ground chocolate and blend very well. Beat the egg whites until stiff but not dry and fold about one-third of them into the batter, then half the bread crumbs, then another third of the egg whites, then the remaining bread crumbs, and finally the remaining egg whites. Pour the batter into two greased and floured 8- or 9-inch torte pans and bake in a 375° oven for 30 minutes, or until done.

When cool, spread the tops and sides of both layers with the red raspberry or apricot jam and place one on top of the other. Ice with the following:

ICING

15–20 sugar cubes
a *little* water

3–4 squares semisweet
chocolate, grated

Soak the sugar cubes in just enough water to wet them through and cook over direct heat to make a syrup. Add the grated chocolate and cook the mixture until it reaches spreading consistency. Pour slowly over the cake and use a spatula to smooth it on the sides, if possible, without touching the top. This will keep the cake shiny and beautiful.

HAZELNUT TORTE

SERVES 6–8

6 egg whites
1 cup less 2 tablespoons sugar
  (7 ounces)
3 ounces toasted, ground
  hazelnuts

3 ounces toasted, ground
  almonds
2 squares semisweet chocolate,
  grated
apricot jam

Beat the egg whites until stiff and fold in the sugar, ground hazelnuts, ground almonds, and chocolate until lightly mixed. Pour the batter into three buttered and floured 8- or 9-inch baking pans and bake at 375° for 15–20 minutes.

Remove the cakes to a sugared board and spread thinly with the jam.

Fill and frost with the following:

FILLING

1 stick butter
½ cup sugar
4 ounces toasted, grated
    hazelnuts

2 egg yolks
1 square semisweet chocolate,
    grated
1 pint cream, whipped

Note: If you wish, omit the whipped cream from the filling and frost the cake with Lemon Icing (see page 323).

Cream the butter and sugar until fluffy, then add the egg yolks, one by one, the nuts, and the chocolate. Then fold in the whipped cream. Fill and frost the cake with this, unless you want to frost with Lemon Icing.

CHOCOLATE TORTE

SERVES 8–10

1¼ cups butter
1¼ cups sugar
10 eggs, separated
10 1-ounce semisweet
    chocolate squares

Chocolate Icing (see page 321)
3–4 tablespoons strong coffee
1 teaspoon baking powder
2 tablespoons fine bread
    crumbs

Cream the butter and sugar for 30 minutes, or until thick and fluffy. Add the egg yolks, one by one, and cream well. Grate 5 squares of the chocolate, and melt the other 5 in the coffee. (For a stronger coffee flavor, use extra strong coffee.) Slowly add the baking powder and the melted chocolate and coffee to the creamed butter-sugar-egg yolk mixture.

Beat the egg whites until stiff and fold one-third of them, one-third the grated chocolate and 1 teaspoon of the bread crumbs into the batter. Repeat until the egg whites are used up and fold in remaining bread crumbs.

Carefully pour two-thirds of the batter into two buttered and floured 8- or 9-inch torte pans. Bake in a 375° oven for about 30 minutes, then remove from the oven and cool.

Spread the remaining one-third of the batter on one cake. Put the other cake on top of it and frost with Chocolate Icing. Cut into slices or squares to serve. If you like, you can cut the cake into individual servings and ice each separately.

ROCOCO TORTE
SERVES 6–8

5 eggs, separated
5 tablespoons sugar
2 tablespoons fine bread
  crumbs

2 tablespoons grated chocolate
2 tablespoons flour
nut halves for garnish

Cream the egg yolks with the sugar until thick and fluffy and slowly add the bread crumbs and the chocolate. Beat the egg whites until stiff and fold in, alternating with the flour. Bake in two buttered and floured 8- or 9-inch torte pans at 350° for about 30 minutes, or until done.

Fill with the following:

FILLING

½ pound grated nuts
2–3 tablespoons hot cream
  or milk
1 stick butter

3 tablespoons sugar
2 tablespoons rum
few drops vanilla

Scald the nuts with the milk or cream, then blend in the butter, sugar, rum, and vanilla. When smooth and creamy, spread on one of the torte layers and place the other layer on top.

Frost with Chocolate Icing (see page 321) and garnish with nut halves.

LINZER TORTE (*Viennese*)
SERVES 8–10

1¼ cups butter
1¼ cups sugar
8 eggs, separated
1¼ cups blanched, grated
  almonds
1¼ cups sifted flour

jam
vanilla powdered sugar
  (see page 272) or
  Chocolate Frosting
  (see page 321)

Cream the butter with the sugar until thick and fluffy. Add the egg yolks, one by one, and then the almonds. Beat the egg whites until stiff and fold one-third into the batter, then half the flour, then another third of egg whites, the remaining flour, and the remaining egg whites.

Pour into buttered and floured 8- or 9-inch torte pans to make three or four layers and bake in a 375° oven for 30 minutes, or until done. When cooled, spread the layers with your favorite jam. Sprinkle the cake with vanilla powdered sugar or frost with Chocolate Frosting.

GERBEAUD DOBOS TORTE (*Gerbeaud, Budapest*)

SERVES 6–8

4 eggs, separated	3 tablespoons flour
4 tablespoons sugar	

Cream the egg yolks with the sugar for ½ hour. Continue creaming while adding the flour. Beat the egg whites until stiff and fold lightly into the batter.

Grease and flour 8- or 9-inch cake pans to make five or six layers. Pour the batter into them and bake at 350° for 10–12 minutes until a light, pretty brown.

Fill with the following:

FILLING

4 tablespoons sugar	4 tablespoons grated
4 egg yolks	semisweet chocolate
1 tablespoon flour	1 stick butter

Mix all the ingredients except the butter in the top of a double boiler and cook over hot water until thick. Remove from the heat and stir in the butter, continuing to stir until fluffy. Spread over the tops and sides of all but 1 layer, and stack them with the uncovered layer on top, then spread the filling up over the sides of this layer.

Ice with the following:

ICING

15–20 lumps of sugar	2 tablespoons water

Put the sugar lumps and water in a heavy saucepan and cook until it makes a light brown syrup. When it begins to brown, test it by dropping a drop onto a wet saucer. If it hardens, the icing is ready. Pour it carefully on top of the cake. Let it dry, but before it gets too hard, make slicing marks in the icing with a wet knife, being careful not to cut into the cake. Refrigerate the cake until serving time.

MOCHA TORTE
SERVES 6-8

6 eggs, separated	3 tablespoons flour
6 tablespoons sugar	

Cream the egg yolks with the sugar for 30 minutes, then blend in the flour. Beat the egg whites stiff and fold into the mixture. Pour into 8- or 9-inch torte pans to make 6 layers. Bake at 375° for 15 minutes, or until done.

Fill with either of the fillings below.

FILLING #1

5 tablespoons plus 1 cup sugar	½ pound sweet butter
5 egg yolks	
4-5 tablespoons very strong coffee	

Cream the 5 tablespoons sugar with the egg yolks and coffee and then cook in a double boiler until it thickens. Cool.

Cream the butter with the 1 cup sugar until very smooth and yellow, then cream it into the cooled mixture. Fill and frost your layers with this mixture, or fill and stack the layers with this and frost with Chocolate Icing (see page 321). Refrigerate before serving.

FILLING #2

4 egg yolks	1 tablespoon flour
1 cup sugar	½ cup very strong coffee
1 square semisweet chocolate, grated	2 sticks butter

Cream the egg yolks with the sugar for 30 minutes, or until thick. Add the grated chocolate, flour, and coffee. Cook until thick in the top of a double boiler over hot water, then cool. Cream in the butter and use this as both filling and frosting for the six layers. Refrigerate before serving.

SCHAUM TORTE (*Meringue*)

SERVES 6–8

2 cups sugar
6 egg whites, beaten stiff
1 teaspoon vanilla
1 tablespoon vinegar

1 teaspoon cream of tartar
1 pint heavy cream
vanilla ice cream

Beat the sugar into the stiff egg whites, then add the vanilla, vinegar, and cream of tartar. Turn into a buttered and floured baking sheet, or two 8- or 9-inch round torte pans. Bake in a 250° oven for about 20 minutes, or until the torte has risen and set, then increase the oven temperature to 300° and let it brown slightly.

While the layers bake, whip the cream and flavor with vanilla. To assemble the torte, put one layer on a large glass plate. Spread it with vanilla ice cream. Place the other layer on top and frost the whole with the whipped cream. *Variation:* fill it with raspberry ice cream, frost with whipped cream, and garnish with fresh raspberries or strawberries.

ORANGE CREAM TORTE

SERVES 6–8

5 eggs, separated
1 cup sugar
2 tablespoons orange juice
1 teaspoon grated orange rind

½ teaspoon lemon extract
dash salt
1 cup sifted cake flour

Combine the egg yolks with ½ cup of the sugar, the orange juice, orange rind, and lemon extract. Beat until lemon colored.

Beat the egg whites with a dash of salt until frothy. Gradually add the remaining ½ cup sugar, continuing to beat until round peaks are formed. Spread the egg-yolk mixture over the egg whites and gently fold together. Sift and fold in the flour about one-fourth at a time. Turn into two 9-inch cake pans that have been buttered and floured. Bake at 350° for 30–35 minutes. Cool, then remove from the pans.

Fill with the following:

FILLING

½ cup orange juice	2 egg whites
¾ cup powdered sugar	1 pint whipped cream,
1 tablespoon grated orange	sweetened
rind	

Mix together the orange juice, ½ cup of the powdered sugar, and the grated orange rind. Beat the egg whites until frothy and gradually add the remaining ¼ cup powdered sugar, beating well after each addition. Beat until stiff but not dry, and gently fold in the orange mixture.

About an hour before serving, spread one layer of the torte with part of the sweetened whipped cream. Place the second layer on top and put the filling on this. Cover the sides and top with the rest of the whipped cream and chill in the refrigerator for 30 minutes to 1 hour before serving.

APPLE TORTE

SERVES 6–8

5 eggs, separated	2 apples, peeled, cored, and
1 cup sugar	chopped
1 cup sifted flour	½ cup raisins
2 teaspoons baking powder	½ cup chopped walnuts
dash salt	whipped cream or vanilla
1 tablespoon vanilla	ice cream

Cream the egg yolks and sugar. Sift the flour, baking powder, and salt together. Fold this into the egg mixture and add the vanilla. Now fold in the apples, raisins, and walnuts. Beat the egg whites until stiff and fold them in last. Pour into a greased 9-inch square baking pan and bake in a 300° oven for 45 minutes. Serve hot with whipped cream or cold with vanilla ice cream.

APPLESAUCE TORTE

SERVES 6–8

1 stick butter	2 teaspoons baking powder
2 cups sugar	⅓ cup milk
1 teaspoon vanilla	2 cups applesauce
1 teaspoon grated lemon rind	1 teaspoon almond extract
4 eggs, separated	(optional)
1 cup sifted cake flour	1 cup heavy cream
pinch salt	2 tablespoons powdered sugar

Cream the butter, 1¼ cups of the sugar, and the vanilla. Add the grated lemon rind and the egg yolks, one by one, mixing after each addition.

Sift the flour, salt, and baking powder together. Add the flour mixture and the milk alternately in parts to the batter, ending with the last of the flour. Pour into two buttered and floured 8- or 9-inch round torte pans.

Beat the egg whites stiff but not dry with the remaining ¾ cup sugar. Spread lightly over the cake batter and bake at 300° for 1 hour. Remove from the oven and cool.

Beat the heavy cream until stiff, sweetening it with the 2 tablespoons powdered sugar.

Spread one layer with the applesauce, mixed, if you wish, with the almond extract. Put the second layer on top and frost with the whipped cream. Serve chilled.

POPPY SEED CAKE (*Mohn Torte*)

SERVES 6–8

1 stick butter	1 cup sugar
dash each cinnamon, ground cloves, vanilla and lemon extracts	9 eggs, separated
	1 teaspoon baking soda
	½ pound ground poppy seeds

Cream the butter with the sugar until thick and fluffy. Add the cinnamon, cloves, vanilla, and lemon. Add the egg yolks, one by one, continuing to cream, and mix until yellow and bubbly. Mix in the baking soda and half the poppy seeds. Beat the egg whites until stiff and fold half into the batter. Add the remaining poppy seeds and fold in the rest of the egg whites. Bake in a greased and floured 8- or 9-inch torte pan at 400° for 30–35 minutes. Serve with Wine Sauce for Desserts #1 (*Chadeau*) (see page 340).

ORANGE TORTE

SERVES 6–8

4 eggs, separated	1 teaspoon baking powder
½ cup powdered sugar	3 ounces blanched, grated
juice and grated rind of	almonds
1 orange	1 tablespoon flour

Cream the egg yolks with the powdered sugar and the baking powder for 15–20 minutes. Add the juice and grated rind of the orange, then half the almonds. Beat the egg whites until stiff and fold in half of them. Add the remaining almonds, the flour, and finally, the remaining egg whites.

Bake in two greased and floured 8- or 9-inch torte pans at 375° for 30 minutes, or until done.

Fill with the following:

FILLING

juice and grated rind of	15 lumps sugar
1 orange	½ stick butter

Boil the 15 lumps of sugar with the juice and rind of the orange until thick. Let cool, then stir in the butter and blend thoroughly. Spread on one layer of the cooled cake and top with the second layer.

Frost with the following:

FROSTING

½ pint heavy cream	1–2 tablespoons curaçao or
dash vanilla	Cointreau
sugar	

Beat the cream until stiff with a dash of vanilla and a little sugar, adding the curaçao or Cointreau while beating.

Frost the cake with this and refrigerate until serving time.

If you don't want to use whipped cream, you can, of course, fill and frost the cake with the orange cream.

PUNCH TORTE

SERVES 10–12

This sounds complicated, but it really isn't. It is time-consuming, but you make it at least two days ahead. If you follow the recipe carefully, step by step, you will have a very rewarding delicacy to show—and eat—for your efforts.

8 eggs, separated	juice and grated rind of
1½ cups sugar	2 oranges
4 tablespoons flour	green food coloring
1 cup water	red food coloring
1 tablespoon vanilla	orange marmalade
3 tablespoons rum	apricot jam
3 tablespoons curaçao,	2 tablespoons finely minced
Cointreau, or Triple-Sec	candied fruit

To start with, make a sponge cake batter, half of which you will bake in two thin layers (or rounds) and the other half in one thick sheet:

Cream the egg yolks with ½ cup sugar for 30 minutes, or until thick and yellow. Add the flour. Beat the egg whites until stiff and fold in carefully. Pour into three greased and floured 8- or 9-inch torte pans to make two thin layers and one thick one. Bake at 375° for 30–40 minutes, baking the thicker one a little longer, if necessary.

Set the two thin layers aside and cut the thick one, when cooled, into small dice. Divide the dice and put them in four small bowls.

In a small saucepan, boil ½ cup water and ½ cup sugar to make a syrup. Add the vanilla and rum.

In another saucepan, boil the remaining ½ cup water and

½ cup sugar to make a second syrup. Add the curaçao, Cointreau, or Triple-Sec.

Squeeze 2 oranges and grate the rinds, mixing juice and rind together. Pour equal portions into the four bowls of cake dice, turning with a spatula.

Pour half of the rum syrup into the first bowl and mix gently with your spatula. Put one drop of green food coloring into the rest of the rum syrup and mix, then pour into the second bowl and mix gently.

Pour half of the curaçao syrup into the third bowl and mix gently. Add a drop of red food coloring to the rest of the curaçao syrup and mix, then pour into the fourth bowl and mix gently.

Now you've got four bowls of differently colored cake dice. Turn them all into one big bowl carefully and turn over and over with your spatula, taking care not to crush or break them, but making sure that all are moistened.

Next, start building your cake. Put one of the thin layers on a baking sheet. Place half of the mixed dice in an even layer over it and flatten slightly with your spatula. Next, dot with alternating tablespoons of orange marmalade and apricot jam, but do not spread them around. Sprinkle with the very finely minced candied fruit and place the remaining cake dice on top of the fruit. Flatten again gently with your spatula, and finally, top with the second thin layer of cake. Cover the cake with waxed paper and place a plate or flat lid on top to weigh it down. Leaving the weight on, refrigerate the cake for at least two days.

On the day of serving, cover with the following frosting:

PUNCH FROSTING

2¼ cups powdered sugar	1 tablespoon water
1 tablespoon lemon juice	red food coloring
grated rind of 1 lemon	maraschino cherries or blanched
1 tablespoon rum or kirsch	almonds (optional)

Mix together all the ingredients except the red food coloring and the maraschino cherries or blanched almonds and cook, stirring constantly, over low heat until the frosting thickens. Remove from the heat and add 1–2 drops red food coloring, stirring well to blend evenly. Pour over the cake and use a spatula to smooth the sides. Garnish with cherries or blanched almonds, or for a special occasion like a birthday, write on the cake with white icing.

Icings, Frostings, and Fillings

There is a difference between an icing and a frosting, although the same rules apply when you are using an icing instead of a frosting. A frosting is thick and soft, and is often used as a filling as well as a frosting. An icing is thin and gets hard and shiny— it is really a glaze of flavor and color—and is never used as a filling.

Cakes should please the eye as well as the palate, and their appearance depends upon how decoratively the frosting is applied. Here are a few "tricks" professional bakers use:

1. Use warm frostings on cold cakes and cold frostings on warm cakes. Warm frosting will spread easily on a cold cake, and cold frosting will spread easily on a warm cake.

2. Before frosting the sides of a cake, remove all loose crumbs.

3. To discourage dripping, thicken the frosting for the sides of the cake with a little powdered sugar.

4. Frost the cake on a large platter, so that you can save any frosting that does drip down to use on the same cake or at another time.

Note: All of the fillings and frostings below are for one 8- or 9-inch cake.

CARAMEL ICING

1 cup powdered sugar

In a heavy skillet or saucepan, on top of the stove, stir the sugar until melted and golden. Pour it over the cake while still hot, and smooth it quickly with a spatula before it hardens.

CHOCOLATE ICING

¾ cup semisweet chocolate   ½ cup butter
  chips

Melt the chocolate over low heat or over hot water in a double boiler. Add the butter and stir until well blended. Cool until the icing reaches a spreading consistency, then spread over your cake or torte with a spatula, covering top and sides.

LACY SUGAR TOPPING

Place a fancy paper doily on top of the cake, and sift powdered vanilla sugar over it, gently patting the sugar even with a spatula. (Vanilla sugar is made by placing a vanilla bean in a jar of powdered or granulated sugar, covering tightly, and allowing to stand.) Remove the doily carefully, leaving a sugar design on top of the cake.

ORANGE FROSTING

2 tablespoons orange juice and   1 egg white
  grated orange peel   pinch salt
1 drop red food coloring   1½ cups sifted powdered sugar

Mix together all the ingredients except the sugar and then add the sugar gradually, beating until it reaches a spreading consistency.

FONDANT GLAZE

2 cups granulated sugar   1 cup hot water, freshly heated
⅛ teaspoon cream of tartar   confectioners' sugar

Combine the granulated sugar with the cream of tartar and 1 cup freshly heated hot water in a saucepan. Cook over low heat, stirring constantly, until you have a thin syrup. Remove from the heat and cool until lukewarm. Add enough confectioners' sugar, stirring constantly, until thick enough to pour on the cake and spread.

COFFEE ICING FOR PETITS FOURS
1–1½ DOZEN

1 cup plus 3 tablespoons powdered sugar	1 cup very strong coffee
	1 tablespoon butter

Cook the coffee with the 1 cup powdered sugar until well blended. Remove from the heat and stir until cold. Mix in the additional 3 tablespoons powdered sugar and the butter. Stir until creamy and spread on petits fours or cake.

FLUFFY FROSTING

1⅓ cups sugar	½ cup water
½ teaspoon cream of tartar	3 egg whites, stiffly beaten

Combine the sugar, cream of tartar, and ½ cup water. Cook without stirring until a few drops dropped into cold water form a hard ball. Very gradually, pour this syrup into the stiffly beaten egg whites, beating constantly. When all the syrup is incorporated, the frosting should be ready to spread.

BRANDY FRUIT ICING

1½ cups sifted powdered sugar	1–2 tablespoons brandy
3 tablespoons finely minced candied fruit	1–2 tablespoons heavy cream

Blend all the ingredients together to make a thick frosting and use on any plain cake.

LEMON ICING

2½ cups powdered sugar
2 egg whites

juice of ½ lemon
grated rind of 1 lemon

Mix all the ingredients together and use as icing on cookies or cakes.

BUTTERSCOTCH FROSTING

1 cup brown sugar, firmly
   packed
½ cup milk
¼ cup shortening (butter or
   margarine)

dash salt
1½ cups powdered sugar

Blend the brown sugar, milk, and shortening in a saucepan. Bring to a boil and cook for 3 minutes, then cool. Add the salt and the powdered sugar gradually, beating until creamy and ready to spread.

MOCHA CREAM FILLING

3 egg yolks
3 tablespoons sugar
4 tablespoons very strong
   coffee

½ stick butter

Cream the egg yolks with the sugar, then add the coffee. Cook in a double boiler until thick. Remove from the heat and beat in the butter. Use as a filling between cake or torte layers.

VANILLA CREAM FILLING

4 egg yolks
4 tablespoons sugar
1 teaspoon flour
1 cup light cream
1 1-inch piece vanilla bean or
   ½ teaspoon vanilla extract

1 pint heavy cream,
   whipped stiff
1 tablespoon rum or brandy

Cream together the egg yolks, sugar, and flour and then add the cup of light cream, stirring to make a smooth mixture. Transfer to the top of a double boiler over hot water and add the vanilla. Cook, stirring constantly, until thick. Remove from the heat and cool, removing the piece of vanilla bean (if used). Fold in the stiffly beaten heavy cream very carefully, adding the rum or brandy, and use as a filling for Hungarian Napoleons (see page 289), Cream Strudel (see page 290), or Éclairs (see page 287).

NOUGAT CREAM FILLING

4 squares semisweet chocolate
1 stick butter

½ cup toasted, finely grated almonds or hazelnuts

Melt the chocolate over hot water, mix in the butter and nuts, and beat to a fluffy, spreading consistency.

CHOCOLATE CREAM FILLING AND FROSTING

3 squares semisweet chocolate
2 egg yolks
1 cup sugar
½ cup cream

1 stick butter
1–2 cups cream, stiffly beaten
(optional)

Melt the chocolate in the top of a double boiler. Mix in the egg yolks, sugar and cream. Cook until thick. Remove from the heat and beat in the butter. For a fancier filling, fold in stiffly beaten whipped cream at the last.

16

BLAZES
OF GLORY

Desserts, Flaming and Otherwise

No Continental dinner is really complete without a dessert. It doesn't have to be heavy, rich or calorie-laden if you think your guests are going to worry about those things. A delicate sweet omelet, a fluffy soufflé, or even fruit—all served *flambé*— will end your meal with a graceful flourish, satisfying the essential urge for that happy ending which most people instinctively hope to find, whether in a movie theater or at your dinner table. And I have yet to meet the person who doesn't enjoy a flaming dessert. There are few moments more dramatic than the moment when the dining room lights are dimmed and the dessert bursts into spectacular flame.

Flaming desserts must be prepared and presented skillfully to be truly impressive. The following hints will help guide you to success.

You will find that a chafing dish is not only a necessity for most *flambés*, but that using one will also enable your guests to admire the whole process. An electric tray that will keep things warm at the table or sideboard is very helpful, too. For the greatest ease in serving, prepare everything you can in advance and have it ready in the kitchen.

High-proof liqueurs and brandies will flame longer and be prettier if you warm them first and then pour them over one or two cubes of lump sugar before lighting. The alcohol will burn away, but it will leave a subtle flavor and fragrance that is heightened by the burned sugar. There are two ways to flame your liqueur or brandy. Either tilt the pan, so that the flame will jump from the burner to the alcohol fumes, or ladle up a bit of the alcohol and set alight, then lower the ladle back to flame the rest of the liquid.

You can even make flaming desserts without alcohol, by using flavoring extracts instead! Soak one or two lumps of sugar in lemon or orange extract and light them, and they'll burn with a clear bright flame. This is a simple and very handsome way to dress up a dish of ice cream or fruit, if you want something impressive to end a spur-of-the-moment dinner but find the cupboard bare of glamorous staples.

The art of making crêpes is one that I'd suggest you practice a bit in private. If they don't turn out quite right the first time, they are still delicious and you can eat them yourself. In order to produce the perfect, very thin, evenly rounded little pancake, you must master the trick of swirling the pan very quickly— immediately after you add the batter. Then, you can make the crêpes in advance, keep them warm on a hot tray, and bring them into the dining room with the warmed filling, the liqueurs, and the chafing dish. Everything is then ready for the Grand Finale.

FRUIT FLAMBÉ

apples, pears, peaches, or
  bananas
vanilla powdered sugar (see
  page 272) or cinnamon
  and sugar

grated orange rind
1 cup mixed liqueur and
  cognac, brandy, or rum

Peel and slice the fruit, then sprinkle with sugar and grated orange rind and place in a chafing dish. At the table, place the chafing dish over the flame, add the warmed liqueur and cognac, and ignite.

Serve with cookies and coffee.

PEARS FLAMBÉ

SERVES 4–6

1 #2 can pear halves
1 cup syrup drained from
  the pears
½ cup blanched, chopped
  almonds

½ cup sugar
1 cup port or sherry
1 cup brandy or rum

Drain the pears. Mix the measured syrup with the almonds, sugar, and wine. Place the pears in a chafing dish and pour the almond-syrup mix over them. Warm the brandy or rum, pour over, set alight, and serve.

FLAMING CHERRIES

SERVES 4–6

1 #2 can best black cherries
½ cup syrup drained from the
  cherries

1 liqueur glass kirsch or
  curaçao, or both
1 liqueur glass cognac, warmed
  vanilla ice cream

At the table, in a chafing dish, heat the cherries in ½ cup of their own juice. Add the kirsch or curaçao—or both, which is even better—and then the warmed cognac. Flame, and when the flame dies out, serve over vanilla ice cream.

PINEAPPLE IN KIRSCH

SERVES 4–6

1 #2 can sliced pineapple
3 tablespoons sugar
1 stick cinnamon

2 cloves
½ cup kirsch, warmed

Drain the syrup from the pineapple and pour it into a small pan. Add the sugar and spices and simmer for 8–10 minutes. Cool. To serve, put the pineapple and liquid in a chafing dish and heat at the table. Add the warmed kirsch, set aflame, and serve while still flickering.

CRÊPES SUZETTE #1

MAKES 1 DOZEN

1 cup sifted flour
1 egg
1½ cups milk

1 tablespoon melted butter
dash salt

Combine all the ingredients in a bowl and beat until very smooth. Cover and let sit for 30 minutes, when the batter should be the consistency of thick cream. If necessary, add a touch more milk.

Heat a small 6-inch skillet with rounded sides and grease it lightly. Pour about 1 tablespoon of the batter into the skillet and tilt and swirl the pan swiftly to spread the batter evenly. Cook until lightly browned on the bottom, then turn the pancake with a spatula and cook the other side. Stack the pancakes on a warm plate as you cook them, and keep them warm.

Then fill and finish the crêpes, using the following:

4 tablespoons sugar
3 tablespoons ground blanched almonds
¼ stick butter
juice and grated rind of 1 orange

1 liqueur glass Cointreau
2 liqueur glasses cognac or brandy
1 lump sugar

Mix the almonds, butter, sugar, and orange juice and rind to make a thick paste. Put a teaspoon of this paste on each pancake and fold to make a triangle, then place in a chafing dish. Mix 1 liqueur glass of Cointreau with 1 glass of cognac or brandy and pour over the filled pancakes, then put a lump of sugar on the top. Take the dish to the table and pour over 1 more glass of warmed brandy or cognac. Ignite and serve flaming.

CRÊPES SUZETTE #2

1 DOZEN

1 cup sifted flour
pinch salt
1 cup milk

2 tablespoons melted butter
2 eggs, beaten

Sift the flour and salt into a mixing bowl, then add the milk, melted butter, and finally the eggs. Beat with a rotary beater until smooth and let stand for 30 minutes. Cook as directed for Crêpes Suzette #1 and keep warm.

Fill and finish the crêpes with the following:

1 cup apricot jam
powdered sugar
2 tablespoons butter

1 tablespoon cognac or brandy
1 tablespoon Cointreau
1 lump sugar

When ready to serve, place 1 teaspoon jam in each crêpe and roll, then dust with powdered sugar. Heat the butter with the cognac and Cointreau, add the remaining jam, let melt, and pour over the cakes. To flame them, put a lump of sugar in a large spoon and pour more cognac over it. Ignite this, and when flaming, pour slowly over the crêpes.

Note: These same crêpes may be served plain with vanilla ice cream, whipped cream, Chocolate Sauce (see page 339), or Wine Sauce for Desserts #1 or #2 (see page 340). For entrees or hors d'oeuvres they may be filled with creamed meat, chicken, fish, ham, mushrooms, or seafood.

Be sure to try them with the following filling:

CHEESE FILLING FOR CRÊPES

SERVES 8-12

1 cup hoop cheese	2 ounces melted butter
4 ounces white raisins	3 egg whites, stiffly beaten
2 tablespoons sour cream	4 tablespoons sour cream
3 egg yolks	2 tablespoons sugar
3 tablespoons sugar	1 egg
dash cinnamon	1 tablespoon melted butter

Mix all the ingredients except the last four together, fill and roll the pancakes, and place them in an ovenproof dish. Mix the last four ingredients and blend well, then pour over the pancakes. Bake in a 375° oven for 30 minutes and serve hot.

CRÊPES ANJOU

1 DOZEN

2 pears	1 teaspoon cognac
2 tablespoons orange juice	1 cup sugar
2 tablespoons lemon juice	1 dozen small crêpes
1 teaspoon vanilla	butter
1 teaspoon Cointreau	1 cup cognac or brandy

Peel, core, and cut each pear lengthwise into 6 wedges. Mix together the orange juice, lemon juice, vanilla, Cointreau, 1 teaspoon cognac, and sugar and boil to make a light syrup. Add the pear sections and simmer for a few minutes.

Put one pear wedge and a little syrup on each of the crêpes and fold over four times to make a turnover. Put a little butter in a chafing dish and add the crêpes, then pour the remaining syrup over them.

Warm the cup of cognac or brandy and pour over the crêpes at the table. Flame and serve at once.

BABAS AU RHUM
SERVES 6–8

1 package angel food cake mix	1 teaspoon grated orange rind
1 cup sugar	¼ cup apricot jam
2 tablespoons lemon juice	½ cup rum

Prepare the angel food cake mix according to package directions. Spoon the batter into molds or custard cups and bake for 15 minutes in a 375° oven.

Mix the sugar, lemon juice, orange rind, and jam and pour it on the warm cakes. (They can be served either warm or cold.) When serving, warm the rum and pour over the cakes at the table. Light the rum and serve the cakes flaming.

APPLE FRITTERS
SERVES 4–6

2–3 apples	1 teaspoon baking powder
lemon juice	1 teaspoon cream (or more)
rum	cinnamon
1 egg	fat for deep frying
½ cup pancake flour	rum or brandy (optional)

Peel, core, and slice the apples and place in a bowl. Sprinkle with lemon juice and rum.

Make a batter of the egg, pancake flour, baking powder, and a little cream. Drain the apples and sprinkle with cinnamon, then dip in the batter and deep fry in shortening until golden brown.

Drain on absorbent paper and serve hot. If you want to flame them, save the lemon juice and rum from the bowl and add warmed rum or brandy to it at the last minute. Ignite, pour over the fritters, and serve flaming.

PANCAKES HUNGARIAN STYLE
(*Rakott Palacsin ta*)
SERVES 6-8

1 recipe crêpe batter	about 1 cup grated semisweet
about 1 cup grated nuts, sugar,	chocolate
white raisins	about 1 cup jam

Prepare the pancakes as directed for Crêpes Suzette (see page 330). Mix the grated nuts with a little sugar and some white raisins, and melt the chocolate over hot water.

Arrange the pancakes in layers in an ovenproof dish with a different filling between each layer. Use nuts on the first, chocolate on the second, and jam on the third. Top with a last layer of pancakes. Keep hot in the oven, with the door open, until ready to serve. Serve with Wine Sauce for Desserts #1 (*Chadeau*) (see page 340).

PANCAKES JUDY
SERVES 6-8

1 recipe crêpe batter	12 tablespoons hot Chocolate
12 tablespoons vanilla	Sauce (see page 339)
ice cream	grated, blanched almonds
12 tablespoons whipped cream	curaçao or Triple-Sec

Prepare the pancakes as directed for Crêpes Suzette (see page 330) and keep warm. At serving time, place on each 1 tablespoon ice cream and 1 tablespoon whipped cream. Fold or roll each pancake over the filling. Pour on each 1 tablespoon hot Chocolate Sauce and sprinkle with the almonds and a few drops of curaçao or Triple-Sec. Both the pancakes and the sauce should be warm, so a dish warmer or hot tray at the table is a great help.

RUM OMELET
SERVES 4

4 eggs, separated
¼ cup plus 2 tablespoons
   powdered sugar
dash salt

1 tablespoon flour
4 tablespoons rum
1½ tablespoons sweet butter
apricot jam

Beat the egg yolks until very light. Beat in the ¼ cup powdered sugar, the salt, flour, and 2 tablespoons of the rum. Beat the egg whites until stiff and fold into the mixture.

Melt the butter in an omelet pan and cook the omelet until golden on the bottom, loosening the edges with a spatula so that the uncooked egg runs to the bottom. When done, spread a little apricot jam over the top and fold it out onto a warm serving platter. Sprinkle with the 2 tablespoons powdered sugar and warm 2 tablespoons more rum. Pour the rum over the omelet, ignite, and serve.

FRUIT OMELET (*Omelette Confiture*)
SERVES 3–4

3 eggs, separated
dash salt
3 tablespoons sugar
1 tablespoon cake flour
2–3 tablespoons cream

2 tablespoons butter
preserves or jam
vanilla powdered sugar
   (see page 272)

Beat the egg yolks with the salt, sugar, flour, and cream until thick. Beat the whites stiff and fold the two mixtures together carefully.

Heat the butter in a pan and pour in the batter. Bake in a 375°–400° oven about 12 minutes, or until set. Spread with preserves or jam and remove to a platter for serving. Sprinkle with vanilla powdered sugar and serve hot.

TOASTED ALMOND SOUFFLÉ (*Koch*)
SERVES 6–8

The recipe for this delicious soufflé is written in fading ink on a little piece of paper that must be at least eighty-five years old. I cannot imagine how many times it must have been made. And incidentally, if you wonder if it is possible to make a soufflé without egg yolks, I can only say that this recipe is the proof of it.

½ pound almonds 7 egg whites
1 cup sugar 1 tablespoon flour, if needed
½ lemon

Chop the almonds coarsely, mix with the sugar, and toast carefully in a skillet on top of the stove until nicely browned. Then squeeze the juice of half a lemon over and let it stand until cool. Grind the mixture.

Beat the egg whites until stiff and fold the almond mixture in lightly. If the eggs are really very large, fold in a tablespoon of flour. Turn the mixture into a buttered and floured mold and place in a shallow pan. Pour about an inch of water into the shallow pan around the mold and bake in a 375° oven for 40–45 minutes. Serve, *immediately*, with Wine Sauce for Desserts #2 (see page 340).

CREAMED APPLES
SERVES 4–8

4 apples ½ cup flour
3 cups water dash salt
2¾ cups sugar 4 eggs
½ teaspoon vanilla 2 cups cream
juice and rind of ½ orange ½ cup slivered almonds

Peel, core, and slice the apples in half lengthwise. Make a syrup of 3 cups water, 2 cups of the sugar, vanilla, and orange juice and rind. Bring to a boil in a skillet, add the apples and cook for 10 minutes. Remove the apples and place in a buttered baking dish that can go to the table. Let cool.

Mix the flour, the remaining ¾ cup sugar, and salt. Beat the eggs with the cream and fold gradually into the flour-sugar mixture. Transfer to the top of a double boiler and cook over high heat, stirring constantly, until smooth and thick. Pour over the apples and sprinkle with the almonds. Bake in a 375° oven for 20 minutes and serve hot from the baking dish.

MELON BOWLS WITH HONEY DRESSING
SERVES 4

2 honeydew melons
½ cup sour cream
¼ teaspoon dry mustard
2 tablespoons honey
½ teaspoon grated orange rind
dash salt

1 tablespoon orange juice
1 tablespoon lemon juice
fresh raspberries or
    strawberries
grated pistachios
    (or other nuts)

Cut the melons in half and remove the seeds. Combine all the other ingredients except the berries and nuts and beat well. For a fluffy dressing, use an electric mixer.

Fill the melon halves with the berries, top with dressing and sprinkle with grated nuts. Chill thoroughly before serving.

FRUIT DELIGHT
SERVES 6–8

¼ cup chopped orange rind
¼ cup chopped pineapple
⅛ cup chopped citron
¼ cup candied ginger
½ cup candied cherries

½ cup curaçao or Cointreau
¼ cup rum or brandy
1 quart vanilla ice cream
whipped cream for garnish

Mix all the ingredients together well. Rinse a pretty mold in cold water and fill with the mixture, packing it down hard. Freeze for 8 hours or overnight. Unmold onto a cold dish to serve. (If it sticks, cover the mold with a hot towel for a few minutes.) Frost with whipped cream and return to the freezer until ready to serve.

PUREE OF CHESTNUTS
SERVES 6–8

2 pounds chestnuts
2 squares semisweet chocolate
2 cups sugar
1 teaspoon vanilla

2 tablespoons rum or Cointreau
4 ounces finely grated almonds
1 pint heavy cream
maraschino cherries (optional)

Slit the chestnuts on the round side and boil in water until tender, about 20–25 minutes. Shell them and remove the brown inner skin. (*Shortcut*: Buy cooked, canned chestnuts—not creamed or candied—at an Italian grocery store.)

When they are cold, put them through a grinder. Grate the chocolate finely and mix with the chestnuts, sugar, vanilla, rum or Cointreau, and almonds. Blend this mixture well, then put lightly through a potato ricer and into an attractive glass serving dish. Garnish with sweetened whipped cream flavored with vanilla, if you wish, and maraschino cherries for color.

RASPBERRY PUDDING
SERVES 4–6

1 quart raspberries, washed and hulled	2 envelopes unflavored gelatin
1 cup sugar	½ cup cold water
½ cup dry white wine	½ cup boiling water
	2 cups heavy cream, whipped

Note: Reserve some of the whipped cream and raspberries for garnishing.

Press the rest of the fruit through a fine sieve. Add the sugar and wine, stirring, then chill for 30 minutes.

Soften the gelatin in ½ cup cold water, add the boiling water, and stir to dissolve. Let cool, then combine with the fruit and beat with a rotary beater until fluffy. Fold in the whipped cream and turn into a fancy 2-quart mold. Chill for at least 3–4 hours, then unmold and serve garnished with the remaining raspberries and whipped cream.

RIZ À L'AMANDE
SERVES 4–6

2 cups cold cooked rice	½ cup blanched, slivered almonds
2 cups cream, whipped	Cherry Heering (or other liqueur)
¼ cup sugar	

Mix together the rice, cream, sugar, and almonds and chill thoroughly. Pour the Cherry Heering over it at serving time.

MARZIPAN

2–3 DOZEN

1 pound powdered sugar	1 egg white
1 pound almonds, grated	1 tablespoon rum

Cream the above ingredients together thoroughly and knead well. There are many things you can do with marzipan. Try one—or all—of these:

1. Shape the marzipan into cookies and roll them in vanilla powdered sugar (see page 272).

2. Shape the marzipan into cookies and first dip them into egg white and then roll them in powdered sugar.

3. Shape the marzipan into cookies and dip them into Chocolate Icing (see page 321).

4. Cover maraschino cherries, stems left on, in marzipan and then frost with Chocolate Icing.

5. Stuff pitted prunes or dates with marzipan.

6. Form the marzipan into little balls around a filling of nuts, citron, candied ginger, or candied orange rind.

The more imagination you use, the more uses you'll find for marzipan to make pretty little candies and sweets.

ZABAGLIONE

SERVES 6–8

4 egg yolks	1 cup sherry or Marsala
4 tablespoons sugar	cinnamon or nutmeg

Beat the egg yolks with the sugar until very light and lemon colored. Gradually add the wine, beating constantly with a rotary beater. Place over hot water and continue to beat until thick. Pour into dessert glasses and sprinkle with cinnamon or nutmeg.

CHILLED ZABAGLIONE

SERVES 6–8

4 egg yolks	1 cup sherry or Marsala
5 tablespoons sugar	1 teaspoon unflavored gelatin

1 tablespoon cold water
2 tablespoons hot water
3 tablespoons Cointreau

2 tablespoons cognac
1 pint heavy cream, whipped
1 teaspoon vanilla

Beat the egg yolks with 4 tablespoons of the sugar until light and lemon colored, then gradually add the wine. Place in a double boiler and cook, beating constantly with a rotary beater, until thick.

Soften the gelatin with 1 tablespoon cold water, then dissolve in 2 tablespoons hot water and add to the zabaglione. Remove from the heat and let cool, then add the Cointreau and cognac. Flavor the whipped cream with the vanilla and remaining tablespoon sugar and fold lightly into the zabaglione. Chill before serving.

Dessert Sauces

CHOCOLATE SAUCE
SERVES 6–8

3–4 tablespoons sugar
1 teaspoon water
2 tablespoons milk or water

1 cup semisweet chocolate
pieces

Boil the sugar with the 1 teaspoon water to a syrup over a low flame, being careful not to scorch the mixture. Add the 2 tablespoons milk or water to the chocolate and melt over hot water or in the oven. Combine the two mixtures and serve hot, keeping the sauce warm in the top of a double boiler, if necessary, until serving time.

FOAMY EGGNOG SAUCE
SERVES 6–10

2 egg yolks
3 tablespoons sugar
½ cup milk

dash salt
1–2 tablespoons rum or cognac
2 egg whites, stiffly beaten

Combine the egg yolks with 2 tablespoons of the sugar and the milk in the top of a double boiler. Cook over low heat, beating constantly with a rotary beater, until thickened. Add the salt and rum or cognac. Fold in the egg whites, which have been stiffly beaten with the remaining tablespoon sugar, and serve warm.

WINE SAUCE FOR DESSERTS #1 (*Chadeau*)
SERVES 6–8

4 egg yolks
dash flour
4 tablespoons sugar
few drops vanilla

1 cup dry white wine
1 stick cinnamon
1–2 cloves

Beat the egg yolks with the flour, sugar, and vanilla until yellow and smooth, then add the rest of the ingredients and let stand, refrigerated, until cooking time. Strain out the spices and cook in the top of a double boiler over low heat, beating with a rotary beater. Serve hot with cakes, fruits, or in dessert glasses with cookies.

WINE SAUCE FOR DESSERTS #2
SERVES 6–8

2 egg yolks
1 whole egg
3 tablespoons sugar

1 teaspoon flour
few drops vanilla
1 cup dry white wine

Mix the egg yolks and egg with the sugar, flour, and vanilla and beat until thick and yellow. Blend in the white wine and cook in a double boiler until foamy. Serve with some poured over the dessert and the rest in a separate bowl.

17

. . . AND
BE MERRY

Beverages, Alcoholic and Non

Wines

Every country has its fashionable ailments, and in Europe liver (*foie*) trouble is at the top of the list. Every year there, thousands of people head for spas and health resorts, seeking a little rest for the *foie*, which has been greatly burdened by rich and heavy meals. Wine, of course, is not bad for the *foie*; it is good for it, as any European will tell you. But wine enables you to eat so much that, indirectly, wine can be a culprit too!

Wines can add great enjoyment to almost every meal. Much intimidating nonsense has been written about wine by those who would make a snobbish cult of it. However, everyone is agreed upon one very simple rule—serve white wines chilled and red wines at room temperature, uncorking the reds long enough in advance of your meal to let them "breathe" a bit and develop bouquet.

It is generally agreed that it is preferable to serve:

WITH RED MEATS AND ENTRÉES
Claret
Red Bordeaux
Red Burgundy

WITH FISH
White Burgundy
White Bordeaux
Moselle
Riesling

WITH FOWL OR VEAL
Red Burgundy
Claret
Chablis
Any dry white wine

WITH DESSERT OR FRUIT
Sweet dessert wines
Light reds or whites

WITH ALMOST ANYTHING
Champagne

If you happen to like white wines better than reds, or vice versa, drink the wine you enjoy and forget the rules, unless you're serving a formal dinner. And remember that although "great" wines are expensive, good wines are not.

Wine connoisseurship is a very interesting—as well as a sophisticated—hobby to cultivate. The sizes and shapes of the bottles and even the labels themselves—not to mention the contents—are all different and fascinating. If this hobby appeals to you, I would recommend that you keep a wine notebook, listing the wines you buy and what you thought of them. And if you want to make a really interesting book of it, you can soak the labels off your bottles carefully and paste them in, so you can be sure of duplicating your favorites when you go shopping again.

Coffee

Coffee need not be a taken-for-granted beverage. Here are an even dozen recipes to add interest and excitement to the service of coffee. Any one of them could become the specialty that is your trademark as a cook.

Rules for good coffee are simple. Use a very clean pot. Use the best coffee you can find, and make your coffee with fresh, cold water. (Bottled spring water is really ideal.) Be generous with your coffee measurement—and try adding a few grains of salt for extra flavor.

DOUBLE COFFEE
SERVES 4–6

1 cup chocolate-flavored milk
2 teaspoons instant coffee
dash each cinnamon, nutmeg
2 cups cold water

2 ripe bananas, sieved
2 teaspoons vanilla
vanilla flavored whipped cream
shaved semisweet chocolate

Mix all the ingredients together except the whipped cream and shaved chocolate and chill thoroughly. Pour over Frozen Coffee Cubes (see following recipe) and garnish with the whipped cream topped with the shaved or grated chocolate.

FROZEN COFFEE CUBES
SERVES 4–6

2 cups very strong coffee or 2 tablespoons instant coffee plus 2 cups water

Mix the instant coffee with the 2 cups water, or use your own strong brew, and pour into an ice-cube tray. Freeze until solid.

ITALIAN COFFEE
SERVES 4

2 egg yolks
4 tablespoons sugar
3 tablespoons finely ground
   coffee

2 tablespoons brandy or cognac
3 cups water

Mix the egg yolks, sugar, coffee, and brandy in the top of a double boiler and beat with a rotary beater, adding the 3 cups water gradually. Cook over hot water, beating, until light and thick, but do not allow to boil. Serve hot in glasses.

COFFEE ROYALE FRAPPÉ

2 parts coffee
1 part cognac

Half fill a cocktail shaker with shaved ice, add the coffee, which should be very strong, and the cognac. Shake well and serve in champagne glasses.

COFFEE MAZAGRAN

2 parts double-strength coffee sugar to taste
1 part dry red wine 1 stick cinnamon

Mix the coffee with the wine, add sugar to taste and the cinnamon. Heat to blend the flavors and serve either hot, or cold over ice.

COFFEE BRÛLOT #1
SERVES 4-6

2 cloves ¼ cup rum
1 stick cinnamon ¼ cup brandy
1-inch square orange or 3 cups double-strength coffee,
  lemon rind very hot
8 lumps sugar

Combine the spices, rind, sugar, and liquor in a chafing dish. Light with a match and stir to dissolve the sugar, then pour in the hot coffee and serve.

COFFEE BRÛLOT #2
SERVES 4-6

rind of 1 orange and 1 lemon ½ cup Cointreau
6 lumps sugar ½ cup cognac
1 stick cinnamon 3 cups hot, strong coffee
3 whole cloves

This should be done at the table with a certain amount of ceremony. Peel the orange and lemon and place the rinds in a chafing dish. Add the sugar, cinnamon, cloves, and liquors. Heat this mixture and then ignite, ladling it over the sugar cubes to dissolve them. Slowly pour in the coffee and serve at once in demitasse cups.

IRISH COFFEE

1 SERVING

1 teaspoon sugar
fresh, hot coffee

1 jigger Irish whiskey
1 tablespoon whipped cream

Use footed goblets or Irish Coffee glasses for this. Place 1 teaspoon sugar in each glass and add a little hot coffee to warm the glass, then add a jigger of Irish whiskey and fill with hot coffee. Carefully float 1 tablespoon whipped cream on top of the coffee and serve, the coffee to be sipped through the cream. For a second serving, use fresh glasses.

COFFEE ROYALE

1 cup fresh hot coffee
  per serving

sugar lumps
cognac

Fill a cup with fresh hot coffee. Place a lump of sugar in a spoon and saturate with cognac. Allow this to warm above the coffee, then light with a match. Slip the flaming liqueur and sugar into the coffee, stir and serve.

COFFEE CHANTILLY

1 SERVING

cognac
1 cup fresh hot coffee

whipped cream

Add 1–2 tablespoons cognac to the cup of hot coffee and float a tablespoon of whipped cream on top. Serve.

COFFEE À LA RUSSE

SERVES 4–6

1 ounce semisweet chocolate
¼ cup sugar
pinch salt
½ cup water

1 cup half and half
1 teaspoon vanilla
2–3 cups hot fresh coffee
nutmeg (optional)

In the top of a double boiler, melt the chocolate, sugar, salt, and ½ cup water. Cook, stirring, for 5 minutes, then add the cream and reheat, but do not boil. Add the vanilla and then the coffee. If you wish, serve sprinkled with nutmeg.

TURKISH COFFEE

2 teaspoons pulverized Turkish   1 demitasse cup cold water
    coffee per serving   per serving
1–2 teaspoons sugar
    per serving

For each demitasse cup, place 2 teaspoons powdered Turkish coffee and 1–2 teaspoons sugar in a Turkish coffee maker or small pot. Pour in a demitasse cup of cold water for each serving and bring to a boil on low heat. Remove from the heat until the boiling stops. Return to the heat and boil up again, then remove. Boil up three times altogether, then pour and serve.

Cold Beverages

Here are my recipes for "special" cold beverages, some alcoholic and some not, but all delicious. Many of them are fine for children and non-drinkers, and all are ideal for warm weather luncheons, Sunday brunches, buffets, and outdoor festivities.

To serve cold drinks with a little extra flair, frost the rims of the glasses by dipping them in egg white, then in granulated sugar. Chill to harden the frosted rims. This is a simple touch, surely, but it looks very professional!

AMBER ICED TEA

SERVES 6–10

8 tea bags or 3 tablespoons   1 lemon, sliced
    bulk tea   1 lime, sliced

½ cup sugar
2–3 cups fresh cold water

mint sprigs and lemon or lime
for garnish

Bring 2 cups water to a boil in a teakettle, then add the tea and let it brew for 4 minutes. Strain into a pitcher. Add the sliced lemon and lime and the sugar. Let it sit for 20 minutes, then remove the fruit with a slotted spoon. Blend in the fresh cold water and pour into ice-filled glasses. Garnish with mint sprigs and slices of lemon or lime.

SPICY ICED TEA
SERVES 6–10

7 cups water
1 cup sugar
dash salt
⅛ teaspoon nutmeg
2 whole cloves

1 stick cinnamon
8 tea bags or 3 tablespoons
    bulk tea
lemon or lime slices for
    garnish

Combine 1 cup of the water with the sugar, salt, and spices and simmer for 20 minutes. Remove from the heat. Strain, cool, and chill.

Bring 2 more cups of cold water to a boil in a teakettle. Add the tea, stir, and brew for 4–5 minutes. Strain into a pitcher and add 4 cups cold water, then blend in the chilled syrup. Pour into ice-filled glasses and serve garnished with lemon or lime slices.

GINGERADE
SERVES 12–16

1 can frozen orange juice
1 can frozen lemon juice
2 cups pineapple juice

½ cup granulated sugar
2 cups water
1 quart ginger ale

Over ice cubes in a pitcher, pour the frozen juices, the pineapple juice, the sugar, and the water. Stir until dissolved, then pour in the ginger ale. Serve very cold.

LIMEADE
SERVES 8-10

1 cup water
juice of 5 limes
½ cup sugar, at least

1 quart sparkling water
mint sprigs for garnish

Mix the 1 cup water with the lime juice and sugar (add more sugar to taste if the limes are very tart) and the carbonated water. Serve in glasses filled with crushed ice, each decorated with a sprig of mint.

TOMATO JUICE COCKTAIL
SERVES 2-3

1 pint can tomato juice
1 tablespoon lemon juice
1 teaspoon sugar

few drops Tabasco or dash
    cayenne pepper
lemon or lime slices for garnish

Mix all the ingredients together and serve in juice glasses with a slice of lemon or lime for garnish.

SPECIAL MILK SHAKE
SERVES 2

1 banana, mashed
2 tablespoons honey
1 cup milk

1 cup yogurt
nutmeg for garnish

Mash the banana smooth with the honey, then add the milk and yogurt and shake or beat until thoroughly mixed. Serve chilled, topped with a dash of nutmeg. (For a thinner drink, add a little more milk.)

LEMON MILK SHAKE
SERVES 2

2 tablespoons undiluted
    frozen lemonade
1 scoop lemon sherbet
2 scoops vanilla ice cream

1 cup milk
additional sherbet or lemon
    slices for garnish

Mix the lemonade, sherbet, ice cream, and milk in an electric blender until smooth. Pour into tall glasses and serve with an additional scoop of lemon sherbet or a lemon slice.

CLARET COBBLER
SERVES 2

Fill two highball glasses with shaved ice and pour a jigger of claret in each. Decorate with a slice of lime.

RUM COBBLER
SERVES 2

1 jigger light rum	1 jigger pineapple juice
1 jigger dark rum	lemon peel for garnish

Fill two glasses with shaved ice. Mix the rums and pineapple juice in an electric blender, pour into the glasses and serve with a twist of lemon peel on top.

MINT COBBLER
SERVES 2

2 jiggers vodka	½ jigger lemon or lime juice
1 jigger crème de menthe	mint sprigs for garnish

Mix all the ingredients together and pour over shaved ice into a pitcher. Serve in collins glasses containing 3 ice cubes and decorate each with a sprig of mint.

EGGNOG
SERVES 6–8

6 eggs, separated	½ pint cognac or rum
2–3 tablespoons sugar	1 pint heavy cream, whipped
1 pint bourbon	nutmeg for garnish
2 cups milk	

Beat the egg yolks with the sugar, bourbon, milk, and cognac or rum. Beat the egg whites until stiff and fold them in, then fold in the whipped cream. Chill for 2–3 hours and sprinkle with nutmeg before serving.

CREAMY EGGNOG
SERVES 6–8

1 quart eggnog ice cream	½ pint bourbon
2 cups milk	nutmeg for garnish

Combine the ice cream and milk in a bowl. Let the ice cream melt until creamy, then stir in the bourbon, mixing well. Sprinkle with nutmeg before serving.

HOT TODDY
SERVES 1–2

1 teaspoon sugar	dash cinnamon
1 teaspoon water	1 clove
1 jigger rum	1 slice lemon rind
2 jiggers red wine	dash nutmeg for garnish

Dissolve the sugar in the teaspoon water, then add the rum, wine, and spices. Place in a saucepan with the lemon rind and bring to a boil. Serve very hot, topped with a dash of nutmeg.

RELAXING TODDY
SERVES 2

1 pint claret	1 stick cinnamon
2 tablespoons sugar	1 clove
1 slice lemon	

Put the claret into a saucepan and bring to a boil. Add the remaining ingredients and simmer gently. Serve, very hot, in wineglasses.

CHOCOLATE COCKTAIL (*with chocolate*)
1 SERVING

1 egg yolk
¼ jigger Chartreuse
¾ jigger white rum

1 teaspoon crushed semisweet
chocolate

Mix the ingredients, then shake with crushed ice and strain into chilled cocktail glasses.

CHOCOLATE COCKTAIL (*without chocolate*)
SERVES 1–2

1 teaspoon sugar
1 egg

1 jigger maraschino
1 jigger Chartreuse

Shake the ingredients well with cracked ice and strain into chilled cocktail glasses.

MILK PUNCH
SERVES 4

1 quart milk
½ cup cognac
½ cup rum

grated nutmeg for garnish
powdered sugar (optional)

Mix the milk, cognac, and rum and pour over a large piece of ice in a bowl. Serve with grated nutmeg and powdered sugar for those who prefer it sweeter.

PARTY PUNCH
SERVES 16–20

1 quart orange juice
1 quart pineapple juice
1 quart ginger ale

1 pint orange sherbet
1 pint pineapple sherbet

Mix together the juices and ginger ale. Pour into a punch bowl and top with the sherbets in scoops. Chill thoroughly before serving.

PARTY CUP

SERVES 12–14

½ cup Cointreau or curaçao   1 bottle champagne, chilled
½ cup cognac   1 bottle sparkling water, chilled

Combine the Cointreau or curaçao and cognac and chill. Add the champagne and sparkling water just before serving.

FRUIT CHAMPAGNE PUNCH

SERVES 12–14

1 orange, sliced   ½ cup Triple-Sec, Cointreau,
½ fresh pineapple, sliced   or curaçao
2 tablespoons sugar   1 bottle champagne, chilled
½ cup cognac   1 bottle sparkling water, chilled

Put the fresh fruit in a chilled pitcher or bowl and sprinkle with the sugar. Add the cognac and the Triple-Sec, Cointreau, or curaçao and chill well. Add the champagne and sparkling water just before serving.

Note: This punch can be made a little more potent by substituting a bottle of chilled Moselle or chilled champagne for the sparkling water.

CHAMPAGNE COCKTAIL

1 SERVING

½ cube cocktail sugar   champagne
1 drop angostura bitters   twist of lemon peel for
½ ounce cognac   garnish

Put the cocktail sugar in a champagne glass with a drop of bitters on the sugar. Add the cognac and fill the glass with chilled champagne. Garnish with a twist of lemon.

Appendix

THOSE VITAL LITTLE DETAILS

Every experienced cook has stored up little bits of knowledge that are important to his cooking. The following is a list of mine, and I've found it very helpful. I won't say that they are responsible for my reputation as "the cooking producer," but I do know they've added to it.

THE DIFFERENCE BETWEEN BOIL AND SIMMER:

This is like the difference between a laugh and a smile. Simmer is a moderate activity—a smile. Boil is more active—a laugh. So, if I say simmer, then smile—use low heat. If I say boil, then laugh and use high heat.

HERBS:

I use less herbs in hot than in cold dishes, for they should be sensed, not strongly tasted, and heat brings out more flavor. And I am always very careful never to overseason a dish.

HERB BOUQUET:

A Herb Bouquet consists of the following: 1–2 sprigs of parsley, a pinch each of thyme and sweet marjoram, a few peppercorns, and a tiny piece, sometimes, of green ginger. All of these are tied into a little square of cheesecloth, which makes for easy removal after cooking.

PAPRIKA:

I often use paprika by the spoonful to lend a special pungency and flavor to certain dishes. In Hungarian, paprika is called *nemes édes,* which means "noble and sweet." It is always added to the fat of the dish off the heat, so that it retains its rich, red color and its sugar content will not burn and turn bitter. Used properly, this lusty spice imparts a vigor to cookery that no other ingredient can do.

COLD WATER IN PASTRY:

Pastry made with cold water is flaky. Pastry made with hot water is crumbly.

SKEWERS AND TOOTHPICKS:

These handy little objects are often used to fasten foods together. And nothing's worse than biting down on one. Always remove them before you serve your dish.

SWEET BUTTER:

If you use sweet butter in cooking, add a little extra dash of salt to the dish.

EGG WHITES:

Remove your eggs from the refrigerator and let them come to room temperature. Separate them carefully, for the slightest dab of yolk in the whites will keep them from beating to a proper stiffness.

When stiffly beaten egg whites are added to a dish, never, never, never *stir* them in—*fold* them in very carefully. And don't stir or beat after they are incorporated.

WARM WATER:

When a recipe calls for warm or hot water, never take it from the faucet. Heat a little fresh cold water on the stove and use that to avoid the stale and chemical taste hot water from the faucet could have.

SIFTING:

If flour is not presifted, sift before measuring; sift confectioners' sugar if lumpy.

TESTING CAKES:

Insert a toothpick into the center of a cake to see if it has baked long enough. When the toothpick comes out clean, the cake is done.

SPONGE CAKE:

Don't take a sponge cake from its baking pan until it has cooled. If you do, it will collapse.

CRISPING SALAD:

After you have washed your salad greens and shaken the loose water off them, you can put them in a plastic bag or a brown paper bag in the refrigerator to chill and get crisp. If the bag is tightly closed, the greens will stay fresh for several days.

SERVING:

Serve hot food *hot* on *hot* plates and cold things *cold* on *cold* plates.

BASIC STOVESIDE MEASUREMENTS:

1 pinch or dash is slightly less than ⅛ teaspoon.
2 teaspoons equals 1 dessertspoon.
3 teaspoons equals 1 tablespoon.
8 tablespoons equals ½ cup.
16 tablespoons equals 1 cup, or ½ pint, or 8 ounces.
1 tablespoon equals ½ ounce of butter, milk, salt, sugar, and water.

BASIC SERVINGS (FOR EACH PERSON):

½ chicken or 1 tiny spring chicken
¼ goose or duck
½ pound veal, pork or lamb
½ pound beef (except for steak, which is ¾–1 pound per person)
2 veal chops
2–3 lamb chops
½ pound or 1–2 slices liver
½ pound fish

TIME AND TEMPERATURE CHARTS

	(In Fahrenheit degrees)
Very slow oven	250°
Slow oven	300°
Moderate oven	350°
Moderately hot oven	375°
Hot oven	400°
Very hot oven	450°–500°

TIMETABLE FOR MEATS (to roast):

Beef, rare—15 minutes per pound
Beef, medium—18 minutes per pound
Beef, well-done—20 minutes per pound
Fowl—20 minutes per pound average
Lamb—30 minutes per pound average
Pork—30 minutes per pound average
Veal—30 minutes per pound average

DEEP FAT KETTLE COOKING:

Doughnuts and fritters—3 to 5 minutes at 370°
Fish, croquettes, uncooked food in general—
 1–2 minutes at 390°–395°
Chops, cutlets, and breaded foods—5 to 8 minutes at 390°–400°

BAKING CHART:

Cakes, according to recipe	300°, 350°–400°
Cookies, according to recipe	375°–425°
Pastry	450°
Pies, according to recipe	425°
Custard, 30 minutes to 1 hour	325°–350°
Meringues, 15 minutes	300°–350°
Baking powder biscuits, 10–15 minutes	425°–450°
Quick breads and corn bread, 30–40 minutes	400°–425°
Muffins, 20–25 minutes	400°–425°
Strudels, 30 minutes to 1 hour	375°

Index

ABOUT THE AUTHORS

JOSEPH PASTERNAK, celebrating his hundredth motion picture this year (*Made in Paris*), has been producing successful films in Hollywood for almost forty years—and has been cooking for even longer than that. Born in Hungary, he came to America after high school, a penniless immigrant. Seven years later he had become a successful motion picture producer! In 1936 he made his first box-office hit, *Three Smart Girls*, which established Deanna Durbin as a star and Pasternak as a major Hollywood figure. He joined MGM in 1941 and the next year married actress Dorothy Darrell. They have three sons, Michael, Jeffrey and Peter.

Always a believer in romance and the happy ending, he has applied this philosophy to everything he does, whether it be such splendid films as *One Hundred Men and a Girl, Destry Rides Again, Anchors Aweigh, The Great Caruso, Please Don't Eat the Daisies*, or his sumptuous repasts.

MARGO RIEMAN is a writer currently based in Los Angeles, whose specialty is cookbooks. She is the author of *Twelve Company Dinners*.